MASTERS OF
INTERNATIONAL
THOUGHT

MASTERS OF INTERNATIONAL THOUGHT

Major Twentieth-Century Theorists and the World Crisis

Kenneth W. Thompson

Louisiana State University Press

Baton Rouge and London

Copyright © 1980 by
Louisiana State University Press
All rights reserved
Manufactured in the United States of America

Designer: Dwight Agner
Typeface: Garamond
Typesetter: Graphic Composition, Inc.

Second Printing (February, 1982)

LIBRARY OF CONGRESS
CATALOGING IN PUBLICATION DATA

Thompson, Kenneth W   1921–
  Masters of international thought.

  Includes bibliographies and index.
    1. International relations—Addresses, essays,
lectures.   2. World politics—20th century—
Addresses, essays, lectures. I. Title.
JX1391.T5   327   79–20030
ISBN 0–8071–0580–5
ISBN 0–8071–0581–3 pbk.

Contents

viii

Preface

Emerson once wrote: "It is better to watch a big fish jumping, than to catch a string of minnows." This book is about men of large and capacious thought. My discussions of them are ordered within four large categories of international studies: normative thought, European-American concepts of power and politics, Cold War conflict analysis, and world order theory. I have analyzed and discussed their dominant approaches, educational backgrounds, assumptions, presuppositions, concepts, hierarchies of values, stages in their thought, their contributions to public policy and visions of the future, as well as other thinkers who have influenced them. I have drawn on their writings, fugitive essays, criticisms and defenses of their work, interviews, memoirs, letters, and my own personal contacts with some of them. Selected bibliographies and annotations or comments on particular works by each thinker are also included.

My purpose in writing this book is the simple, straight-forward wish to share with others the wisdom and knowledge of leading writers in international relations whose work has illuminated the international scene for me over the past thirty years. Their selection rests on certain assumptions that others may discuss, evaluate, even reject. Their writings, in my judgment, are central to both the understanding of international politics and the forming of a viable and coherent framework of thought. International writings are sometimes described as little more than high-class journalism. Others speak of international studies as glorified current events. The merit of each writer chosen for discussion is the contribution he has made to an organized and systematic approach to the field. His mode of thought can be applied to a succession of issues and problems arising over a broad time frame.

The enduring value of the writings of these thinkers influenced my selection. Their works can be judged by criteria other than the promotional and commercial tests of success employed by many publishers and readers. Few if any of the selected writers have been on best-seller lists. With perhaps one exception, none have won Book-of-the-Month awards. Yet, unlike writers whose status might be described as "made by Madison Avenue," the master thinkers discussed herein are still read by policy makers and scholars, even though some of their books go back fifty years.

I must hasten to add that identifying my choices was obviously both an objective and a subjective venture. It is clearly possible to point to certain ostensibly objective indicators of significance, but evaluators may view these differently. One indicator is the writer's bibliography. Although some are larger than others, each contains a critical mass of serious work. Journalists and scholars refer to the importance of this body of work by quoting and citing the authors with the kind of respect James Reston has often expressed for Sir Herbert Butterfield in his columns, or David Broder for Hans J. Morgenthau. Scholarly reviews and recurrent discussions at professional meetings provide another indicator. Dissertations, journal articles such as Stanley Hoffmann's review of international studies in *Daedalus* (Spring, 1978) and festschrifts that celebrate particular writers afford another index. Important writers often tend to generate controversy, open new sectors of inquiry, contribute "breakthroughs" in thought, have a formative influence, and enjoy successive revivals of interest after the more faddish and transient approaches have passed.

Time has a way of providing its own strict and exacting assessments. A journal may ignore a particular writer, a certain publisher may refuse his work, an anthology of writers on a certain problem may omit him, or leading pedagogues may denounce his work. Yet in literature and philosophy, readers continue to read Shakespeare and Milton, Plato and Aristotle, or Hobbes and Locke long after their time. These master thinkers and their work may not parallel such immortal figures as Shakespeare, but it is noteworthy that they continue to be read among contemporary thinkers. Most of them head the list of international relations writers when the *International Encyclopedia of the Social Sciences* selects thinkers who are deserving of attention in twenty-five- or fifty-year reviews of major figures. Among those who prepare lists of master thinkers for such long-term reviews, their work apparently has lasting value.

One qualification deserves mention. It may still be too early to measure the influence of some of these thinkers; their writings are too recent to have withstood the test of time. The organized study of international politics is a newcomer to academia. Yet for writers like Walter Lippmann and Reinhold Niebuhr, the evidence strongly suggests that their work is destined to occupy a significant place in literature for years to come.

Having said this, I should acknowledge the element of subjectivity in my selections. Not only have I known the writings of these thinkers; in most cases I have also been close to the men themselves. The human element creeps into all scholarly evaluations, and it would be misleading to deny its influence here. Whatever the magnitude of their contributions or the weight of their personal examples and influence, I have not eschewed personal and intellectual criticism. In my opinion most of these men are intellectual giants, but they are human beings, not gods. If I have been overgenerous in my praise, I ask their indulgence; if unfair in my criticisms, I ask their forgiveness. The example of their intellectual integrity has inspired honest analysis, I trust, not a mindless or too worshipful approach to their greatness.

PART I

The Search for a Normative Foundation for Politics

It is not surprising that theoloogians and religious historians are in the forefront of those who search for a normative foundation for politics. It is true that not every religious tradition encourages concern for morality and politics. Some view politics as another of life's heavy burdens, which man escapes only by setting aside the concerns of this world. Buddhists long for the blessed state of Nirvana in which being gives way to nonbeing and human strivings and emotions are ended. Within most Western religious traditions, though, people live in the world and are destined to grapple with life's unending moral and political dilemmas.

Even though Western religions prepare men for living in this world as well as the next, the number of contemporary religious thinkers whose writings are read and reread by students of morality and foreign policy is limited. One reason for this may be the complexity of the international realm, which calls for a mastery of foreign relations that only a handful of ethicists achieve. Another may be the tendency of religionists to be in the vanguard of social reformers

1

caught up in crusades for worthy, though often transient, social and political programs. Religious thinkers concerned with politics often retreat to the high spiritual ground of eternal verities or join the fast-moving stream of those who would transform society, leaving the harsh and morally ambiguous tasks of politics to secular leaders.

Fortunately, the observer who approaches the study of political ethics with an open mind can point to the few who, within the several religious traditions, are exceptions. It has become fashionable for secular political writers and political scientists to speak of religious writers as mere preachers. These judgments throw a shadow as much on those who make them as upon religionists. Having broken the shackles of religious orthodoxy, modern secular thinkers run the risk of blinding themselves to what religious thought has to offer. It is as incumbent on an open intellectual society to draw upon the truths contributed by the giants in the major religious traditions as it is to recognize the wisdom of the best secular thinking. Freedom of thought is imperiled both by religious and secular dogmatism; those who seek a viable political ethic must follow truth wherever it leads them.

Sir Herbert Butterfield towers above religious historians who have written about international ethics. With the publication of *The Whig Interpretation of History*, Butterfield established himself as one of Britain's immortals in traditional historical writing. Soon thereafter, he turned to religious history in such books as *Christianity and History*, *Christianity in European History*, and *Christianity, Diplomacy, and War*. Moreover, Butterfield extended his influence in political ethics through the work of the British Committee on the Theory of International Politics, founded by him at Cambridge University. Especially noteworthy is the contribution Butterfield and his associates have made to an understanding of the ethical dimensions of the Cold War and their discussion of such classical concepts as the balance of power.

Reinhold Niebuhr, who in the words of George F. Kennan is "the father of all of us," wrote about contemporary international politics. It would be difficult to exaggerate the contributions of this remarkable theologian to recent intellectual history. Walter Lippmann assessed Niebuhr's contribution when he asked: "How many generations will it be before we see his equal again?" In a vast outpouring of books and articles, Niebuhr undertook to discover the main elements of what he called "Christian realism" as applied to international politics. Temporarily set aside in the late 1960s and early 1970s by Christian and social activists, his writings have been rediscovered in the late 1970s. No one in search of a coherent and consistent approach to political ethics can afford to ignore his work.

The Reverend John Courtney Murray stands out among recent Roman Catholic writers concerned with ethics and modern warfare. Although Murray subsumed his writings on international ethics in a broader approach to morality and government, he is deserving of attention beyond what is possible in the brief compass of an introduction to his thought. Alone among the writers on morality and foreign policy, Murray rested his thought upon the ancient and respected Roman Catholic tradition of natural law—a tradition in which I lack the grounding to do him full justice.

It is necessary to return to a British writer to complete this review of religious thinkers. Martin Wight's work was cut short by his early death, but his influence has been perpetuated by the legion of students whom he inspired. Both a historian and a student of international politics, his scholarly output, though more restricted than Butterfield's or Niebuhr's, has enduring value. Some of his works have been published posthumously through the devoted efforts of colleagues and students. More than any modern writer, he attempted to reconstruct present-day thought on ethics as it had evolved in the traditions of Western civilization to which he remained committed to the end of his life.

It is impossible in an introduction to the writings of these religious thinkers to summarize their agreements and differences. Butterfield as historian never ventured far from the firm ground and well-established tenets of historical scholarship. Niebuhr and Murray began and concluded their work primarily as theologians, though less as systematic theologians (this was particularly true of Niebuhr) than as theologians concerned with urgent contemporary social and political problems. For Wight, the focus of his concern was alternately European and contemporary history, reflecting his abiding interest in classical thought and present-day international politics.

Niebuhr and Murray confronted each other periodically in debates over the relevance of natural law and its application to the nuclear age. All four of these master thinkers recognized the irrationalism of contemporary relationships among states, but Murray more than the others saw traditional natural law as providing permanent norms for the conduct of state relations. None questioned the ultimate meaning of religion for international politics, though each defined such meaning in his own way.

Obviously, an introduction to the thought of these and other master thinkers is no substitute for a careful reading of their texts. My intention, simply and exclusively, is to introduce my readers to such thinkers—their writings, their underlying assumptions about man and politics, their concepts of the nature of the international system, their views of the normative structure of international politics and of the role and limits of power.

HERBERT BUTTERFIELD (1900–1979)

The Historical Perspective

Herbert Butterfield was born into a devout Methodist family on October 7, 1900, in Oxenhope, an industrial revolution village with two thousand inhabitants, located at the edge of the moors and a few miles from the Lancashire-Yorkshire border. Although Butterfield's father left school at ten to work as a wool sorter in the mill, he educated and trained himself to become a bookkeeper. He carried with him through life his frustrated ambition to have been a Methodist minister; and, without untoward pressure, the senior Butterfield made it clear that he would like to see his son move in that direction. It was partly in the knowledge of the pleasure it would give his father that Herbert, from the age of sixteen, became a lay preacher, a step that provoked the impatience of the man who was his most stimulating teacher at the local grammar school, a man very outspoken in his hostility to Christianity. Later, when Butterfield was at Cambridge University working under the famous historian Harold Temperley, his growing interest in history and his consciousness of being too shy to succeed in pastoral work dissuaded the young Herbert from the ministry. But whereas religious and political thinkers have characteristically rebelled against the tenets of their childhoods, Butterfield has never wavered from a fundamental Augustinian theology that included belief in the infinite worth of human personality, the reality of sin, the sovereignty of God, the limitations of human nature, and the fragmentary character of human existence. He never espoused Marxism as did Reinhold Niebuhr and Paul Tillich, two philosophers and theologians with whom he had some affinity. He studied Marxist thought, however, and extracted from it certain insights on conflict in history and the importance of economic and social factors in history. The focal points of his thought are British history, the relations of Christianity to history, and the theory of international relations.

5

But for the formative influence of his childhood and family life, Butterfield might have remained content with traditional historical scholarship expected of a professor of modern history at Cambridge University and the editor of the *Cambridge Historical Journal*. He was educated at Cambridge, where he earned the degrees of master of arts and doctor of literature. In 1923 he became a fellow of Peterhouse at that university and in 1955 its master. He served as president of the Historical Association of England in the late 1960s and, as a historian, was invited to take up residence at the Institute for Advanced Study at Princeton University. His first publication, *The Historical Novel* (1924),[1] reflected his early concern with the relation between literature and history. He demonstrated the role of literary imagination in furthering the actual rediscovery of the past. It was an anachronism, he believed, to assume that the events from another era could be understood in the context of the present or recent past. Shorter and more concentrated books in which the historian drew on literary if not poetical skills might help recreate the past. This became the standard for almost all of Butterfield's writing. He followed his first book with a detailed study, *The Peace Tactics of Napoleon, 1806–1808* (1929), an analysis of the relation between military and diplomatic tactics of the period, including the 1807 Treaty of Tilsit. Reviewers praised his historical portraiture and observed that he had disproved the claims of German historians that Czar Alexander of Russia had conspired to desert Britain; it was the Prussians who persuaded the czar to meet with Napoleon on a raft in the River Nieman. He edited *Select Documents of European History, 1715–1920* (1931), and he began research on what was to be a lifelong interest in George III, publishing *George III, Lord North, and the People, 1779–80* (1949) and *George III and the Historians* (1957). His intention to write the definitive work on Charles James Fox and George III was sacrificed, however, to a new interest in analytical historical studies that would dominate his research for the next four decades.

The first clear evidence that Butterfield was to go beyond traditional historical research came in 1931 with the publication of *The Whig Inter-*

---

1 This and all works by Sir Herbert Butterfield are listed chronologically, with full publication data, beginning on p. 17, herein.

pretation of History, a critical analysis of the Whig and liberal view of inevitable progress in history. His concern for historiography was clearly demonstrated in this study, which earned for him a reputation as an authentic historical genius. Although the book criticized liberal politics and historical Protestantism, Butterfield questioned in a more fundamental way the failure of historians to do justice to the unique conditions and mentality of former ages. It was evident in this work that Butterfield would follow in the steps of J. E. E. D. Acton (even though he was a chief object of Butterfield's criticism) and Leopold von Ranke, rather than in those of traditional British historians who concentrated on primarily descriptive history. Subsequent works—*Napoleon* (1939), *The Englishman and His History* (1944), and *The Statecraft of Machiavelli* (1940)—carried him even further along the path of the philosopher of history and the political theorist.

In the late 1930s and 1940s, Butterfield, whose eminence as a leading British historian was by then unquestioned, entered a second phase of historical writing that was inspired by the world crisis. In 1939 he lectured at four German universities on the history of historiography, emphasizing developments in the sixteenth and seventeenth centuries. He argued that it was the Whig historians whom he criticized, not the Whig politicians who had fostered freedom and moderation from the later years of Charles II. The lectures enabled him to say that, although he still regarded the Whig interpretation as fallacious, he believed it had helped in the development of liberty in England. It was the Whig historians who had perverted the story, not the politicians who used political compromise and political persuasion rather than coercion and force.

In 1948 he turned to religion and history, delivering a series of seven lectures at the request of the divinity faculty of Cambridge University. He expanded these lectures into six broadcasts aired in April and May, 1949, by the British Broadcasting Corporation. He amplified the major themes of these lectures in a book entitled *Christianity and History* (1949). Butterfield had hesitated to undertake these lectures, because he doubted that a layman was qualified to prepare them and he knew the suspicion such an enterprise could generate among his fellow historians. But it became difficult for him to avoid the invitation when the representatives of the divinity faculty made it clear that they believed the undergraduates might be more ready to listen to a man who had made his name as a historian rather than to a clergyman. Butterfield's turn to philosophical questions was doubtless inspired by the dual crisis confronting the West: the formidable challenge of the Soviet Union with its Marxist creed and the position of the Western countries as "frightened defenders of the status quo, upholding the values of an ancient civilisation against the encroachments of something new."[2] Butterfield warned that the idolatrous worship of some superperson, society, state, or other large-scale organization could so transform man's perspective that he would see his world as comparable to the world of the ants. It is dangerous to bypass history or to imagine that the natural sciences can safely be left to shape human destiny. It is not enough to look for God or man in nature or to conclude, with Adolf Hitler in *Mein Kampf*, that since nature is concerned not with individual human lives but with the development of the species, history inevitably imposes its cruelties, idolatries, and human sacrifices. This attitude Butterfield described as "the facile heresy of the self-educated in a scientific age" and counseled: "Too easily we may think of man as merely the last of the animals and in this way arrive at verdicts which we are tempted to transpose into the world of human relations."[3] *Christianity and History* reasserted the author's profound belief in the central place of human personality in the historical process. He protested against the opposing view of certain behavioral social scientists and naturalists that history is the story of great collectivities to be studied through science and mathematics as no more than another chapter in the great book of biology.

Butterfield elaborated upon and extended this criticism; he restated the Christian perspective in a succession of writings in which he claimed to speak not as a theologian, as had Arnold J. Toynbee, but as a historian. He wrote as an individual scholar, not interacting with other historians and theologians or propounding an elaborate historical scheme as had Toynbee. His aim, as he conceived it, was to challenge Christians and non-Christians alike to renew awareness of the historical place of

2 Herbert Butterfield, *Christianity and History* (London: G. Bell, 1949), 5.
3 *Ibid.*, 6.

the Christian view. He added books on *Christianity in European History* (1951), *History and Human Relations* (1951), and *Christianity, Diplomacy, and War* (1953). Whatever the questions critics have raised about his Christian perspective, Butterfield has resolutely maintained that history seen in its broadest dimensions is consonant with a Christian view of history. He has inveighed against technical history, which falls short, in his view, of a subtle comprehension of the past. For him history at its core is a drama, often tragic in dimension, of human personalities. The tenets of historical scholarship require the historian to practice intellectual humility and flexibility of mind. He must walk alongside the actors in history, placing himself in their position, seeking to recapture their perceptions of events and to understand the problems with which they had to cope.

Another facet of Butterfield's contribution stems from his study of science. Beginning in 1931, he had lectured to Cambridge undergraduates on modern history from 1492, with attention to such larger developments and long-term movements as the Renaissance, the French Revolution, and the interconnections of these movements. His approach, which followed the example of Lord Acton, was a reaction against the overspecialization that had come to dominate the university study of modern history with its use of outlines and dry textbook accounts of the external relations of states. Instead, he focused on the emergence and major developments of the modern world and of modern thought, devoting, for example, approximately six lectures to the rise of modern science. These lectures brought him into contact with prominent Cambridge scientists, such as Joseph Needham and the people at the Cavendish Laboratory who were in search of an ally among historians. Under the influence of these people, a history of science committee was appointed in 1947. This committee, after a considerable conflict, induced Butterfield to deliver in the 1948 Michaelmas term a course of lectures on the subject. The lectures led to the publication of his most successful book, *The Origins of Modern Science* (1949), and to a reawakening of interest in the subject in England and America. It brought trained scientists into contact with serious historical study and helped produce a new generation of historians of science.

In 1953 Butterfield was asked to deliver the Wiles Trust Lectures at

Queens University, Belfast, and he chose to return to the history of historiography in the eighteenth and nineteenth centuries. The subject had been a preoccupation of German and a few American historians; but, despite the efforts of Acton and his disciple G. P. Gooch (who wrote *History and Historians in the Nineteenth Century* [1913]), this subject had not taken root in England. The Wiles lectureship brought Butterfield, speaking on *Man on His Past* (1955), into contact with some ten European and British historians who, as authorities on differing aspects of his subject, criticized and commented on his presentation. When published in 1955, these lectures led to a considerable reawakening of interest in historiography among university undergraduates, research students, and professors. Subsequently, he wondered if enthusiasm for historiography had gone too far and urged that universities limit its study to historians who were equipped by temperament and experience for the task. Although he was pleased that he had been able to advance the work of Acton and Gooch, he believed that for the ordinary research student training in the processing of evidence and the main techniques of research must come first.

Ten years later, in 1965 and 1966, he was asked to deliver the famed Gifford Lectures at the University of Glasgow, a series in which Americans such as William James, John Dewey, and Reinhold Niebuhr had participated. Butterfield chose to address the broad question of how the human race had come to possess a concept of the past and how and why mankind had been interested in its past before historical writing had begun. He speculated that early religion might have had some influence, but wondered if it might not also have been the enemy of genuine history. The historical mentality, he concluded, had gradually emerged from the conflicting desire to reconcile religious and secular history. He believed that conclusions based on recent research in Egyptian, Mesopotamian, and Jewish languages were adaptable to the kind of questions that Western historians characteristically studied. The lectures constituted his boldest historical adventure, for he undertook to survey the entire history of historiography. His effort inspired interest particularly in the United States, but it left him uncertain about whether he had or could ever acquire the universal knowledge necessary to produce a published treatise on the subject. Then, in the mid-1960s, the focus of

Butterfield's interest shifted, and he never returned in a systematic way to the theme of his Gifford Lectures.

In all his historical writings, he has argued that, at one level, historical interpretation calls for painstaking research and the ability to relive "the lost life of yesterday," using the accumulated traces of history "to recapture a bygone age and turn it into something that is at once a picture and a story."[4] In the pursuit of this goal, Butterfield was following the tradition he had absorbed from his teacher, the master historian of diplomacy Harold Temperley, seeking always to write history of a high and complicated texture. At another level, the historian has the obligation to identify with his subject in order neither to praise nor to blame him, but rather to understand the circumstances confronting him. In studying the diplomatic interchanges that accompanied Napoleon's campaigns against the Fourth Coalition, Butterfield felt compelled to consult major archives in London, Paris, and Vienna, the correspondence drawn from the Prussian and Russian archives, and the reports of ambassadors, ministers, and spies to the leading statesmen of that day. His purpose was to mirror the thoughts of the major personages of the time and to uncover "the strange tangle, the hidden undercurrents and the clash of personalities that lay behind a Napoleonic war."[5] Even in the two studies of Napoleon written early in his career, the structure of Butterfield's maturing view of history was visible. The unfolding story was for him unpredictable and wayward, based on the interaction of diverse personalities proceeding not in accordance with predetermined doctrines of a superior people or of inevitable progress, or with consequences clearly linked to their intentions, but as efforts deflected by the mysterious workings of Providence.

Butterfield's essential ideas about historical studies were well defined before he was thirty-one years of age. He had won the LeBas Prize at Cambridge for his first book, *The Historical Novel*; but his third, *The Whig Interpretation of History*, laid the foundations for all of his later works with their underlying theme of "the complexity of human change and the unpredictable character of the ultimate consequences of any

---

4 Herbert Butterfield, *The Historical Novel* (Cambridge: Cambridge University Press, 1924), 8.
5 Herbert Butterfield, *The Peace Tactics of Napoleon, 1806–1808* (Cambridge: Cambridge University Press, 1929), vii.

given act or decision of men."[6] Historical writing must communicate the texture of such complexity. Historical change for Butterfield necessitated reform more than revolution, which inevitably left a legacy of hatred, human suffering, and destruction.

In his early thirties, Butterfield was persuaded that the Christian interpreter more than other political historians is safeguarded against the worst illusions and idolatries, since he is prepared by his faith for accidents and surprises in history. By his worship of God, he is rescued from such distorting influences as a fanatical worship of the state, the idea of progress, or an abstract political ideology. By devotion to the ultimate ends of religion, the historian is able to understand "the web spun out of the play of time and circumstances."[7] Providence holds mankind under judgment, but God is not a tyrannical ruler so much as the source of grace in history. Even the clash of human wills, reflecting man's pride and indestructible egotism, can serve to further God's will and bring good out of evil. For example, the American Revolution led the British to invent a new and more civilized concept of empire. Man's most creative achievements are usually born out of human distress and inner pressures; political systems founded on brigandage, such as those of ancient Rome and the British Empire, may evolve in time in the direction of some tolerable measure of justice and order.

For Butterfield, therefore, historical studies and theology cohere and reinforce each other, for both have their center in a concern for human personalities. His dual emphasis on history and religion, however, has opened him to criticism not leveled at the traditional historian. Some critics see in his religious writings a diversion from the historian's primary task of producing a large corpus of solid historical works, such as might have resulted had he continued his researches on Charles James Fox and George III. His position as scholar-statesman for more than a half-century in the Cambridge University community, culminating in his appointment as vice-chancellor from 1959 to 1961, was certainly dependent to some degree upon his recognized preoccupation with moral values. His positions at Cambridge and his leadership roles in

6 Herbert Butterfield, *The Whig Interpretation of History* (London: G. Bell, 1931), 21.
7 *Ibid.*, 66.

national and international educational bodies drew him away from full-time scholarship, as did the series of endowed lectures, characteristically on religious themes, in Germany, the United States, and the United Kingdom. Pieter Geyl[8] and other historians have questioned his emphasis on the persistence of evil in man's behavior and of human cupidity in society and his low estimate of the capacity of honorable men to effect social change through actions that had predictable consequences. This criticism of his questioning of the consequences of the moral and rational intentions of statesmen overlooks his debate with twentieth-century British historians like Lewis Namier and his disciples, who portrayed politics largely as a struggle for gain and selfish interests. For Butterfield, ideas, attitudes, and rational intentions interact with self-interest in politics, and historians err when they reduce politics for all individuals and every century to the same level. The Namier school, according to Butterfield, in so often assuming that politicans are no more than the repository of self-interest, misinterprets the political movements and political parties, which do not merely advance group interests but also articulate values and ideals.

A more serious and partly legitimate criticism of Butterfield's use of the Christian perspective has been leveled at some of his historical judgments. In *Christianity and History* (1949), he appeared to explain the defeat and destruction of Germany in World War II as divine punishment for the sins of the German people. Yet critics ask: What of the many Germans who at grave personal risk opposed Hitler's regime? And what about the Baltic peoples who had not committed the brutalities of the Nazis, but who suffered as grievously as the Germans? Butterfield has written of the need for thinking historically at two different levels—that of technical history, which deals with the limited and the mundane and takes into account hard and tangible historical evidence, and that of Providence, which is beyond the reach of the technical historian. Critics have maintained that Butterfield, especially when he enters the realm of general history, smuggles into his interpretations the Christian points of emphasis and doctrine that have been excluded from his more technical writings in narrative history, where he is more cau-

8 Pieter Geyl, *Encounters in History* (London: Collins, 1963).

13

tious in his assessments of individual leaders. Worst of all, he sometimes appears to speak *for* Providence. In fairness, those critics who extract from his writings moral valuations, such as his indictment of the entire German people contained in a wider discussion of militarism, will find him going on to say: "If Germany is under judgment so are all of us—the whole of our existing order and the very fabric of our civilisation."[9]

Finally, Butterfield's influence on Western thought is not exhausted in his major contributions to traditional and Christian history. In 1958 he founded the British Committee on the Theory of International Politics and has served for approximately two decades as its chairman and honorary chairman. This group took as its mandate the making of an inquiry "into the nature of the international state-system, the assumptions and ideas of diplomacy, the principles of foreign policy, the ethics of international relations and war." The committee's approach reflected Butterfield's historical and religious perspective. The interests of this group of British thinkers contrasted with those of American colleagues who formed a similar committee. Butterfield's committee expressed greater concern "with the historical than the contemporary, with the normative than the scientific, with the philosophical than the methodological, with principles than with policy."[10] The themes of the group's first major publication mirrored Butterfield's own writings and included such topics as natural law, the new diplomacy and historical diplomacy, society and anarchy in international relations, western values in international relations, and the balance of power. Butterfield's closest associate in the venture, Martin Wight, introduced the volume with a paper entitled: "Why Is There No International Theory?"

The British approach was the antithesis of that flourishing in American and Australian schools, which dealt with international relations theory and systems analysis. Its frame of reference was the conduct of diplomacy, international society, and the nation-state system. Its point of view was historical, empirical, and deductive. Its presuppositions were that historical continuities were more important than innovations in the international system; that statecraft provided a historical deposit

9 Butterfield, *Christianity and History*, 52.
10 Herbert Butterfield and Martin Wight (eds.), *Diplomatic Investigations: Essays in the Theory of International Relations* (London: George Allen & Unwin, 1966), 11, 12.

of accumulated practical wisdom; that the classical writers in politics, diplomacy, and law had not been superseded by recent findings in psychology and sociology; and that the corpus of earlier diplomatic and military experience was worthy of study and reformulation to meet contemporary needs. Sustaining the committee's work was a pervasive moral concern about which Butterfield wrote: "The underlying aim . . . is to clarify the principles of prudence and moral obligation which have held together the international society of states throughout its history, and still hold it together."[11]

The influence of Butterfield and the British committee may prove to be greater in the United States than in Britain. American interest in the group's approach coincided with a mounting awareness in the 1950s and 1960s—at first by a handful of political realists and later by decision makers and journalists—that the struggle between the Soviet Union and the United States was too complex to define as a clash between absolute right and wrong. The conflict involved a profound moral predicament, for even if the two superpowers were approximately equal in strength and virtue, each could justifiably fear the other. Each could be sure of its own good intentions without being able to trust the other. Each could feel that its rival was withholding the one thing that could make it feel secure. Each side in a conflict could pursue its security through displays and threats of power, but overlook the fact that it could fully ensure its own security only by destroying the security of the other. For Butterfield, the security-power dilemma was the most urgent problem of war and peace, and for him the only solution demanded that one or the other great power risk something in the name of peace. The only way out of the worst of deadlocks, he prophesied, was through some kind of marginal experiment; but for such an experiment America would need the tough-minded judgment of a hard-boiled Bismarck, not of sentimentalists for whom giving way was always too easy. Butterfield made his proposal more than a decade before the Nixon-Kissinger policy of detente was proclaimed. Butterfield approved this policy and added that what was needed for accommodation was a leader experienced in power politics and capable of bold and subtle yet hard-

11 *Ibid.*, 13.

15

headed acts of political and military judgment. He doubted that either a conventional moralist or an ordinary intellectual or idealist in the White House or in Whitehall could succeed in formulating and defending a policy of coexistence.

In the United States, the response to Butterfield's ideas came from political realists. Although he can be viewed as a spokesman for realism and practical morality, Butterfield's realism has been tempered by his profession as a historian and by Britain's long foreign policy tradition wherein power politics had come to be viewed as unremarkable. Like Reinhold Niebuhr, Butterfield's influence on more thoughtful leaders in the religious community was considerable. He quoted from the Bible as often as from historical texts, applying its wisdom to the realm of foreign policy. He noted that for young and inexperienced democracies one of the major sources of political error is overanxiety, leading a nation like Weimar Germany to throw itself into the arms of a dictator. One of the Bible's most valuable maxims—"Fret not thyself because of evil-doers"—counsels men not to wait to make peace until all the world's evils are eradicated. For Butterfield, the enduring contribution of Christianity to the requirements of international relations lies not so much in choosing actual policies but in providing a background of ideas or a more civilized spirit with which men can work. Christianity can help clarify ideas on human sin by recognizing that, although extraordinarily evil men do exist, the most difficult problem in international politics is the moderate cupidity of large numbers of men who hope to realize through their nations what society denies them as individuals. Such men exercise vast pressures on governments and make normalized relations among states more difficult. Religion's responsibility is to check the sovereign will of the people who want to achieve their objectives by too great an exercise of power, instead of by consciously cooperating with Providence.

In his appeal to American leaders in statecraft and religion—to recognize their limits and to exercise prudence—Butterfield, writing at the height of the Cold War to a citizenry overanxious about the Soviet threat and imperiled by the risk of a thermonuclear holocaust, may have made his most lasting and valuable contribution.

HERBERT BUTTERFIELD

WORKS BY HERBERT BUTTERFIELD

1924

The Historical Novel. Cambridge: Cambridge University Press.

1929

The Peace Tactics of Napoleon, 1806–1808. Cambridge: Cambridge University Press.

1931

Select Documents of European History, 1715–1920. Edited by Herbert Butterfield. New York: Henry Holt.

The Whig Interpretation of History. London: G. Bell.

1939

Napoleon. New York: Duckworth.

1940

The Statecraft of Machiavelli. London: G. Bell.

1944

The Englishman and His History. Cambridge: Cambridge University Press.

1949

George III, Lord North, and the People, 1779–1780. London: G. Bell.

The Origins of Modern Science. London: G. Bell.

Christianity and History. London: G. Bell.

1951

Christianity in European History. London: Oxford University Press.

History and Human Relations. London: Collins.

The Reconstruction of an Historical Episode: The History of the Enquiry into the Origins of the Seven Years' War. Glasgow: Jackson.

1953

Christianity, Diplomacy, and War. New York: Abingdon-Cokesbury Press.

1955

Man on His Past. Cambridge: Cambridge University Press.

1957

George III and the Historians. London: Collins.

1960

International Conflict in the Twentieth Century: A Christian View. New York: Harper & Row.

1966

Diplomatic Investigations: Essays in the Theory of International Relations. Edited by Herbert Butterfield and Martin Wight. London: George Allen & Unwin.

1970

On Chinese and World History. With Cho Ysu Hsu and William H. McNeil. Hong Kong: Chinese University of Hong Kong.

1972

Sincerity and Insincerity in Charles James Fox. London: Oxford University Press.

1975

Raison D'Etat: The Relations Between Morality and Government. The first Martin Wight Memorial Lecture, University of Sussex, April 23, 1975.

WORKS ABOUT HERBERT BUTTERFIELD

Geyl, Pieter. *Encounters in History.* London: Collins, 1963.

Halperin, S. William, ed. *Some Twentieth Century Historians.* Chicago: University of Chicago Press, 1961.

McIntire, C. T., ed. *God, History and Historians.* New York: Oxford University Press, 1977.

REINHOLD NIEBUHR (1892–1971)

From Theology to Political Prudence

Reinhold (Karl Paul Reinhold) Niebuhr was born on June 21, 1892, in Wright City, Missouri, fifty miles northwest of St. Louis, the third son and fourth child of Gustav and Lydia Niebuhr. Two weeks after his birth, the steelworkers went on strike in Homestead, near Pittsburgh, and eighteen workers were killed and many wounded in a struggle with three hundred Pinkerton guards hired by management. His father was a minister in the German Evangelical Synod, a basically Lutheran church, which in 1934 was to merge with a Calvinist church body to become the Evangelical and Reformed Church. The oldest child, his sister Hulda, became professor of Christian education at McCormick Theological Seminary in Chicago; the second, Walter, chose newspaper publishing; a third died in infancy; and a fourth son, Helmut Richard, two years Reinhold's junior, became a renowned theologian and professor at Yale Divinity School. The father had fled Germany at seventeen in rebellion against a tyrannical father and Metternich's German conservatism, rallying around Carl Schurz and the 1848'ers. In the mid-1890s, the family moved to Saint Charles, Missouri, and then in 1902, the year Henry Ford established the Ford Motor Company, to Lincoln in central Illinois.

Niebuhr's early family life was happy despite his father's meager income of $1,200 a year. Neibuhr remembered his father with pride as the most interesting man in town and as the person who taught him history, Greek, and Thomas Macaulay (who wrote, "Nothing is so useless as a general Maxim"). The son inherited his father's courage in challenging rich, conservative, second-generation German farmers to be more conscious of their neighbors and of God. Because ministers' children received special scholarships at Elmhurst, a small denominational college in Illinois, the father sent both Reinhold and Richard there; but

18

not until years later when Richard became its president was the college accredited to offer the bachelor's degree. After spending four years at Elmhurst and not receiving a degree (a deficiency that was to affect his study at Yale), Reinhold proceeded to Eden Theological Seminary for the next three years where he came under the influence of Dr. Samuel Press, the first full-time resident professor to teach theological courses in English instead of German. (Niebuhr described Press as his Mark Hopkins at the other end of a log.) While he was at Eden, his father died in April, 1913, of diabetes. At twenty-one Niebuhr had to assume responsibility for the financial security of his family, first by conducting Sunday services at his father's church in Lincoln, Illinois, and later by combining a scholarship at Yale with occasional preaching.

Niebuhr gained admission to Yale because the standards of its divinity school were less firmly established than older centers, such as Union Theological Seminary. He was thrilled by its educational and library resources and at the same time anxious and self-conscious about his own penurious state and his midwestern accent. John O'Hara, from a similar background, wrote with undisguised contempt of campus hierarchies of Ivy League youth who dressed with elegant casualness and displayed unfeigned masculine arrogance. Niebuhr, in contrast to O'Hara, saw deprivation as a spur, not a wound, perhaps because of happy family memories, his love and respect for his parents, and his own early successes that buffeting by more privileged students could not shake or affect. At Yale he belonged to not one but several minorities. He was a midwesterner in the East, a poor boy among the rich, a second to fourth generation American among children of the first New England families, a religious student in a primarily secular institution, a graduate student without a college degree, and a German when Germany was seen as America's enemy. Years later, when a powerful Yale alumnus asked Niebuhr's permission to put his name forward for the presidency of Yale, Niebuhr did not oppose him but warned that someone with a background such as his would be an unlikely choice—and he was correct. He remained at Yale for only two years, maintaining an A average (a requirement for pursuing graduate studies without a B.A. degree); reading the works of William E. Hocking, William James, and Josiah Royce; and serving a small church on Sundays in Derby, Connecticut.

He left Yale in part because he was bored by the irrelevance of subjects like epistemology and in part because he was under strong pressure from his church to return to a parish.

He was only twenty-three when he returned to the Midwest and the burgeoning urban center of Detroit. From 1915 to 1928, Detroit increased from half a million to a million and a half people. During these thirteen years, membership in Bethel Evangelical Church, Niebuhr's small parish mission, increased tenfold, and the $8,500 chapel was replaced by a $128,000 edifice. Here he was to publish his first and second books, *Does Civilization Need Religion* (1927)[1] and *Leaves from the Notebook of a Tamed Cynic* (1929); to establish himself fully as a pastor; and to challenge the mighty Henry Ford, who in building lower-priced cars turned men into interchangeable parts within the industrial system and ravaged human beings abandoned without jobs or pensions in the prime of life. Ford in retooling from Model T to Model A production put 60,000 people out of work and turned down repeated appeals that he contribute to the Community Fund. In confronting mighty leaders such as Ford, whose creativity Niebuhr acknowledged as one of society's most prized resources, he sought to deal not theoretically but practically with one of the classic questions of social ethics—the relation of liberty and justice.

Throughout his life, Niebuhr never hesitated to criticize powerful men or counted the cost. The list began with a powerful business leader such as Henry Ford; but it also included statesmen such as John Foster Dulles, the publisher Henry Luce, and evangelist Billy Graham, whom Niebuhr condemned for having become a house religionist for President Richard Nixon. Union Theological Seminary in New York was the refuge from which a prophetic voice could speak out free of reprisal because its successive Presidents Henry Sloane Coffin, Henry Pitt Van Dusen, and John C. Bennett defended Niebuhr's right to be heard. His arrival in New York in 1929 coincided with the collapse of the stock market and the beginning of shattering poverty, breadlines, and drought. Disillusionment swept over the society and seized some of its best minds. Three days before the inauguration of Franklin D. Roose-

---

1 This and all works by Reinhold Niebuhr are listed chronologically, with full publication data, beginning on p. 34 herein.

velt on March 4, 1933, Niebuhr wrote in *World Tomorrow*: "Capitalism is dying . . . and it ought to die." (Later he recanted, saying he had had to eat these words.) Niebuhr, whose thought in the 1920s had followed conventional liberalism, turned in the 1930s to the relevance of Marxism for American society. Thus his early thinking proceeded through liberal and Marxist phases in its evolution.

Niebuhr's theology before 1932 was influenced by liberal Protestantism and to some extent by reformist social ethics. From 1915, when he completed his studies at Yale Divinity School, to 1932, when he published *Moral Man and Immoral Society*, his political philosophy most nearly approximated that of twentieth-century liberalism, especially in its practical consequences. During this period such liberal tenets as support for the League of Nations, racial tolerance, and sympathy for labor unions were representative of Niebuhr's dominant views. More important, he accepted many of the liberal philosophical assumptions, which he was later to question or abandon. Witnessing the harmful effects of the American industrial system on the laboring class of Detroit during his pastorate there, he turned energetically to liberal solutions. He criticized Protestantism for stressing metaphysics at the expense of social ethics at a time when the massive and impersonal scientific world necessitated new visions and approaches to the problems of social injustice and to the conflict between and reconciliation of religion and science.

As early as 1929, however, Niebuhr had expressed doubts on certain basic liberal tenets. *Reflections on the End of an Era* (1934) was the turning point in this thought. In 1936, in the journal *Radical Religion*, which he helped found, he enumerated six articles of the liberal creed that blind it to the real world. He suggested that liberalism fervently espouses the following: (1) injustice is caused by ignorance and will yield to education and greater intelligence; (2) civilization is becoming gradually moral; (3) the character of individuals, not social systems, will guarantee justice; (4) appeals to brotherhood and goodwill are bound to be effective in the end; if they have been ineffective to date, we need only more and better appeals; (5) goodness makes for happiness, and increased knowledge of this belief will overcome human selfishness; (6) war is stupid and will yield to reason. Niebuhr indicated that all six of these articles are open to questions and doubts. The failure of liberalism results from its blindness to "the perennial difference between human

21

actions and aspirations, the perennial source of conflict between life and life, the inevitable tragedy of human existence, the irreducible irrationality of human behavior and the tortuous character of human history."[2]

Liberalism that is steeped in faith in man's capacity to subdue nature, in his essential goodness, and in the advance of human history has taken on all the attributes of a religious creed. This condition constitutes a disease particularly difficult to cure, Niebuhr concluded, because the afflicted are classes who imagine that they are unusually robust and clear-eyed. In other words, liberalism is inapplicable to problems of the day because of its naive picture of man and the political order and because it has become a passionate ideological justification for the selfish interests and pursuits of the dominant middle class. One part of his criticism adumbrated the need for a philosophy that would not be refuted by political experience; the other part suggested that Niebuhr's impatience with liberalism was informed and inspired by Marxist assumptions. He was to grapple with these assumptions for almost a decade before casting them irretrievably aside.

In the late twenties and early thirties, Niebuhr's appetite for social realism had fed on his growing disenchantment with liberalism and the consequent appeal of Marxism. The defects of the one were remedied by the strengths of the other. Liberalism had failed to relate the individual organically to society; Marxism made society the beginning and the end. Liberalism maintained that the individual through maximizing self-interest would miraculously serve the interests of all; Marxism showed that this was in practical terms a middle-class ideology. Liberalism concealed the conflicts of interest that prevailed in all communities; Marxism laid bare the struggles that went on between diverse social and economic classes. Liberalism insisted that justice could be attained through a free economic system; Marxism proclaimed that injustice was inevitable as long as economic inequality prevailed. It was Niebuhr's opinion as late as 1932 that Marxism "made no mistake in stating the rational goal toward which society must move, the goal of equal justice, or in understanding the economic foundations of justice."[3]

2 Reinhold Niebuhr, "The Blindness of Liberalism," *Radical Religion*, I (Autumn, 1936), 4.
3 Reinhold Niebuhr, *Moral Man and Immoral Society* (New York: Charles Scribner's Sons, 1932), 165.

Despite the impact of Marxist insights, Niebuhr from the 1920s was skeptical and uneasy about the most fundamental Marxist assumptions and conclusions. In the first issue of *Radical Religion*, he observed that an appraisal of socialism raised many questions which cried for answers. He questioned issues raised by a materialistic interpretation of history. If the materialistic interpretation is rejected outright, he said, a valuable insight is lost. Marxism has rediscovered a truth at the heart of prophetic religion: namely, that man's cultural, moral, and religious achievements are never absolute but are colored by human finiteness and corrupted by human sin. Yet whoever accepts Marxism unreservedly does violence, among other things, to the dialectic between nature and spirit and between freedom and necessity. Niebuhr warned young American parsons reacting to the sentimentalities of liberalism not to capitulate to Marxist dogma lest they find that their liberal faith of a not very unique Christian quality was being supplanted by a radical faith which was more realistic in its analysis of immediate social issues but even less Christian in its total insights into life.[4]

Marxism proved an ally, but a transient one, in Niebuhr's attack on the liberal approach to the problem of justice in society. Liberalism hopes to solve the great issues by asking people to be more kind and loving; Marxism knows that justice cannot be established without a harsh struggle in which the interests of the victims of injustice are set against the beneficiaries of injustice. For Niebuhr by 1935, however, this Marxist insight represented no more than a partial perspective, weakened by Marxism's utopian faith that such conflicts would end with the destruction of capitalism. He distinguished between capitalistic aggravation of the problem of justice and its perennial nature in all human societies. The struggle for power goes on in some form or other in all societies. The Marxist illusion results from equating class conflict with human rivalry, whereas Niebuhr conceived of the struggle for power endlessly elaborating itself as an expression of human finitude and sin.[5]

It is fair to say of Niebuhr that he at no time accepted the Marxist critique of liberalism indiscriminately or without serious questioning or

---

4 Reinhold Niebuhr, "Radical Religion," *Radical Religion*, I (Autumn, 1935), 3.
5 *Ibid.*

criticism. However, it would serve no point to infer that its influence on him was negligible. Coming at a time when the deep gloom of a major depression cast its heavy shadow over the intellectual world, Marxist estimates and predictions gained credence in ever-widening circles. That captialism was destroying itself and must be replaced by social ownership of the means of production seemed inevitable during America's severest economic crisis. Anything less could not provide the basis for health and justice in a technical age.[6] If Niebuhr altered his viewpoint to fit the changing realities of American economic life more quickly than most social observers, he still misunderstood, precisely for Marxist reasons, the pragmatic character of the social revolution of the New Deal, which refuted the Marxist prophecy. At a time when President Franklin D. Roosevelt was painfully effecting a compromise program based on social aspirations shared by Niebuhr, the political philosopher found Roosevelt the politician hesitant, vacillating, and half-hearted in his convictions. Perhaps no other error in Niebuhr's thinking has influenced so profoundly the development of the last or pragmatic and prudential stage of his philosophy.

Moreover, the genuine peril to the nation arising from the combination of economic and political power was frequently underestimated in this period. In 1932 he referred to a prophecy of Bertrand Russell that some form of oligarchy is inevitable in a technological age and asked whether a communistic or capitalistic oligarchy would be more onerous. Probably in the long run, if Russell's prediction was right, the communistic oligarch would be preferable. For in Niebuhr's view; "His power would be purely political, and no special economic interests would tempt him to pursue economic policies at variance with the national interest."[7] Later he emphatically refuted this point and confessed: "It was not realized that even a democratic socialism might face problems of preserving incentives in a completely collectivist economy and would betray the perils of the concentration of economic and political power in the hands of a bureaucracy even when held in a democratic framework."[8]

6 *Ibid.*, 5.
7 Niebuhr, *Moral Man and Immoral Society*, 90.
8 Reinhold Niebuhr, "Christian Faith and Social Action," in John Hutchinson (ed.), *Christian Faith and Social Action* (New York: Charles Scribner's Sons, 195), 227–28.

From much the same standpoint, Niebuhr's criticism and rejection of Marxism reflected the history of the times. To be sure, it was on grounds of philosophy and not experience that he expressed his first doubts. In the early 1930s, he decried as a pathetic illusion the Marxist conception of the nature of man. For Marxists, man would be transfigured with the withering away of the state. For Niebuhr, the illusion that the classless society would eliminate the finitude of man and the problem of power was as utopian as the sentimentality of liberalism. A second point on which he was critical long before many of his fellow intellectuals was the Russian experiment itself. In 1936 he took exception to the book *Soviet Communism: A New Civilization*, by Beatrice and Sidney Webb. He criticized its confusion of legal structures and precepts with political facts. The Webbs' study resembled a discussion of municipal government in New York City that omitted any reference to Tammany Hall. By 1939 there was no disputing the evidence. Marxism's "notion that evil would disappear once capitalism is destroyed is just as completely negated by the facts in Russia, as the liberal notion that education can lift men completely out of their economic circumstances and prompt them to act as discarnate spirits, filled with goodwill alone, is negated in our society."[9]

Beyond this, Niebuhr's full perception of the demonic character of Marxism as a secular religion came at a later stage in his social criticism. Time and again in the thirties, he intimated that Marx, who had caught a glimpse of the truth, had confused the issue by attributing fundamental problems to special causes. Yet it was not until the forties that he wrote: "The deepest tragedy of our age . . . is that the alternative to capitalism has turned out to be worse than the disease which it was meant to cure."[10] This failure, he found, was a natural consequence of Marxist illusions and not a corruption of Marxism by Stalinism. It resulted from ascribing all human virtue to a single class, the proletariat, and all human evil to a single institution, private property. Not only is each of these assumptions false, but in juxtaposition they are mutually contradictory. The one assumes that the good society will come about purely through an economic change, since man is the inexorable product

9 Reinhold Niebuhr, "Reflections on the Retreat of Democracy," *Radical Religion*, IV (Spring, 1939), 8.
10 Reinhold Niebuhr, "The Battle in Berlin," *Christianity and Society*, XIII (Autumn, 1948), 5.

of natural forces. However, the proletariat, acting independently of economic forces based on the Marxist rationale, has chosen to preside with absolute power during the transition from the old society to the new awe-inspiring classless society. These two illusions constitute the deadliest errors of Marxist apocalyptic thinking, since they give divine sanction, free from popular influence and control, to one technique of social reform, one guaranteed solution of the socio-ethical problem, and one group that alone is untarnished by sin. The messianic character of Soviet communism and its absolute totalitarianism are therefore not accidental but follow inevitably from its premises. A partial truth confused with the whole truth and administered by a class posing as God's surrogate thus becomes a universal creed under which cruelty, injustice, and violence are seen as legitimate instruments of the historical process.

Marxism, therefore, which by its illumination of liberalism's worst illusions caught Niebuhr's imagination, ended by constructing laws and precepts more evil and terrifying by far. It is hardly surprising that Niebuhr, twice disillusioned, should embark in the 1930s on the mission of discovering a viable theory of politics. In this quest he retained certain perennial truths inherent in liberalism and Marxism unencumbered by their worst fantasies. Liberalism, for example, provides certain moral objectives that serve as the gentle civilizers of politics in our society. Together these objectives make up what Niebuhr called the spirit of liberalism, which is older than bourgeois culture. They include a spirit of tolerance and fairness without which life is reduced to an almost consistent inhumanity. Freedom or liberty is another moral and political objective, which the spirit—if not the middle-class application and interpretation—of liberalism bequeaths to Niebuhr's enduring political thought.

In the same way, Marxist philosophy, although rejected more completely and emphatically than liberalism, remained at least a residual element in his approach. The three insights from Marxist thought that, if properly interpreted, appear partially valid to him include its emphasis on the social dimension of life and the collective fate of man's existence, which for Niebuhr meant a responsibility to seek justice not only for the individual but at the national and international levels. He added, however, that these organic forms of life will not yield to the efforts of collectivists or idealists to coerce them into new mechanical or artificial molds. Second, Marxism requires that the political and economic structure of human communities be taken seriously. It rejects the belief that structures are of no importance as long as good men operate these systems and structures. Third, in contrast with the liberal concept of an easy harmony of interests, Marxism postulates the idea of class struggle. Niebuhr found this last idea unacceptable unless it is expanded to embrace all political struggles, which go on unceasingly to right the balance between the victims and the beneficiaries of injustice.

Partly from Marxism but even more from the later romanticists such as Henri Bergson, Niebuhr derived a concept that was to save him from the worst errors of Marxism and from the deep pessimism of some of the leading intellectuals in the 1930s. Community and the nation-state for Niebuhr are social organisms that have developed over time. Their source is not exclusively technics and economics but the basic social instincts of man. Societies can be approached through reason, but reason has its limits. Life forces and human vitalities are as important as economic determinants. In the depression era, this led him to forecast the decline of liberal societies. From thinkers such as Oswald Spengler, Niebuhr in the 1930s temporarily adopted and advanced the theme of a catastrophic or cataclysmic view of history reflected in his *Moral Man and Immoral Society* (1932), which he later suggested should have been entitled *Immoral Man and More Immoral Society*, and even more clearly in *Reflections on the End of an Era* (1934). *The Children of Light and the Children of Darkness* (1944) and *The Self and the Dramas of History* (1955) reiterated this theme of catastrophe. However, personal political experience and his use and modification of Augustinianism saved him from unqualified despair. Man has a choice, however limited, in both the ultimate and the proximate questions of life and human destiny. Niebuhr used the writings of Søren Kierkegaard and of modern existentialists to reformulate Augustinian thought and adapt it to the realm of politics. Throughout the development of his own political philosophy, Niebuhr integrated diverse political and philosophic traditions into his own intellectual schema, making it difficult to trace the specific sources of his thinking. What emerged was a philosophic position that was uniquely and distinctly his own. His anxious concern for man's fate was constant, but so was his unquenchable faith that mankind has a future deriving from the Christian vision and the organic view of society.

World War II brought Niebuhr's thinking to its most advanced and definitive stage. His Gifford Lectures, delivered at the University of Edinburgh in the spring of 1939, represented his most systematic attempt to construct a theory of human nature and politics. He began: "Man has always been his most vexing problem. How shall he think of himself?" Niebuhr then went on in a mode of dialectical thought that was to characterize all his writings on the ethical dimension of politics, saying that any affirmation about man involves conflicts and contradictions. If the observer stresses man's unique and rational qualities, he is betrayed by man's greed, lust for power, and brute nature. If the writer holds that men everywhere are the product of nature, unable to rise above circumstances, he neglects man the creature who dreams of God and of making himself God, and man whose sympathy knows no bounds. If the student of history declares that man is essentially good and attributes all evil to concrete historical and social causes, he merely begs the question; for these causes are the consequences of the evil inherent in man. If he concludes that man is bereft of all virtue, his very capacity for reaching such a judgment refutes his premise. All these perplexing conflicts in human self-knowledge exemplify the difficulty of doing justice at one and the same time to the uniqueness of man and to his affinities with nature. The heart of Niebuhr's criticism is that modern views of man which stress exclusively either his dignity or his misery are fatuous and irrelevant and fail to consider the good and the evil— the essential dualism—in man's nature.

A deeper paradox arises from the fact that man is suspended perilously between freedom and finiteness, spirit and nature, the human and the divine. His ambiguous and contradictory position at the juncture of freedom and finiteness produces in him a condition of anxiety, which is fundamental to understanding political behavior. Man is anxious about the imperialism of others and secretly fearful of his own vulnerability and limitations. Because of the finiteness of his reason, he can never wholly judge his own possibilities. So he endlessly seeks security in the pretense that he has overcome his finiteness and human limitations. Only through extending his power and influence is he safeguarded against the domination of others.

The most important observable political expression of human anxiety is the will to power. Man shares with animals their natural appetites, cravings, and impulse for survival. Yet being both human and divine, deriving his powers from both nature and spirit, man's requirements are qualitatively heightened, raised irretrievably to the level of spirit where they become limitless and insatiable. To overcome social anxiety, man seeks power and control over his fellows, endeavoring to subdue them lest they come to dominate him. The struggle for political power is merely an example of rivalry at every level of human life. It manifests itself in relations between husbands and wives, parents and children, spouses and in-laws, ethnic groups, children and remarried parents, states and the nation, and the executive and legislative branches of government.

In the field of collective behavior, the force of egoistic passion is so strong that the only harmonies possible are those that manage to neutralize a rival force through balances of power, through mutual defenses against its inordinate expression, and through techniques for harnessing its energy to social ends. Social unity is built on the virtuous as well as the selfish side of man's nature; the twin elements of collective strength for a nation become self-sacrificial loyalty and the frustrated aggression of the masses. From this it follows that politics, whether in organized political groups or in large organizations, is the more contentious and ruthless because of the unselfish loyalty and commitments of group members. Niebuhr's conclusion is that within international society even a nation composed of men of the greatest goodwill will be less than loving toward other nations. He observed: "Society . . . merely cumulates the egoism of individuals and transmutes their individual altruism into collective egoism so that egoism of the group has a double force. For this reason no group acts from purely unselfish or even mutual interest, and politics is therefore bound to be a contest of power."[11]

In world politics, nations pursue the quest for power, influence, and prestige heightened by the intensity of collective loyalties compounded by present-day alienations and frustrations. All nations claim to seek security and to follow their national interest. Niebuhr is willing to concede that nations on the whole are not particularly generous and that

---

11 Reinhold Niebuhr, "Human Nature and Social Change," *Christian Century*, L (1963), 363.

a wise self-interest is usually the limit of their moral attainment. However, the demands of self-interest and national self-preservation often lead to acts violating accepted morality. In the early 1950s the decision to build the hydrogen bomb gave offense to many sensitive people, but Niebuhr replied that no nation could afford to overlook its own security however hazardous the route by which it pursued protection against subjugation. Yet he was terrified and appalled by the prospect of nuclear proliferation.

Niebuhr was persuaded that men and states cannot follow their self-interest without claiming to do so in obedience to some general scheme of values. This belief led him to ask, first, whether a consistent and unquestioning emphasis upon the national interest is not as self-defeating in a nation as it is in a person's life. Stated differently, does not a nation exclusively concerned with its own interests define those interests so narrowly that it sacrifices the security which rests on common devotion to principles of justice and established mutualities in the community of nations? American foreign policy overemphasizes its benevolence, thereby heightening the resentments of people already envious of its wealth and power. National interest is imperiled by the hazard of moral cynicism on the one hand and by moral pretension, hypocrisy, and ideological justification on the other. In his earlier writings, Niebuhr strongly denounced moral cynicism, but later he became more concerned with hypocrisy and ideological justification. He concluded that cynicism and pretension are two parts of a single problem—a continuing ambivalence toward the responsibility of nations seen at one moment as having no obligations beyond their own interests and at the next as engaging in a high moral crusade without regard for selfish concerns.

Edmund Burke provided Niebuhr with a concept that became central to the final stages of the great theologian's thinking. Theorists, and more particularly scientists of society, have often believed that the historical realm is analogous to the realm of nature and that the adoption of proper scientific or theoretical techniques will assure men mastery over their historical fate. Most scientific studies, for this reason, have been largely irrelevant to the practice of statecraft where the watchword must be "sufficient unto the day is the evil thereof." For Burke the

Burke

problem of relating theory and practice in politics involves the concept of prudence. Prudence, not justice, is first among political virtues; it is the director and regulator. Metaphysics cannot live without definitions, but prudence is cautious in its definitions, for it has learned to live with everchanging reality. Politics is not a science but an art.

As Niebuhr moved toward an increasingly more pragmatic view of world politics, he sensed the limits of rational as well as traditional normative thinking. In the largely irrational realm of politics, the struggle is usually so intense that the only possible peace becomes an armistice and the only order, a provisional balance among forces. Even the proximate moral norms of politics are seldom realized in practice; statesmen must settle for uncertain compromises. It is as necessary to moderate the moral pretensions of every contestant in the power struggle as it is to make moral distinctions regarding the national interest. In the twenties, Niebuhr was a social reformer and optimist; in the Marxist thirties, he was a radical; but in his later years, he became a Christian realist. When critics warned that he was in danger of being little more than a pragmatist and that pragmatism was endangered by its lack of passion and its moral flatness, he replied that his pragmatism was limited and instrumental, even while acknowledging that through it he risked standing "on the abyss of cynicism." What saved him from this position, he hoped, was his openness to criticism by friend, foe, and God. It was also his ability through religion and, in the American constitutional system, through the higher law to stand outside the world of events "in order to get a fulcrum on it." He paraphrased St. Paul and offered as a guide for living: "Nothing worth doing is completed in our lifetime; therefore we must be saved by hope. . . . Nothing we do, however virtuous, can be accomplished alone; therefore we are saved by love. No virtuous act is quite as virtuous from the standpoint of our friend or foe as from our standpoint. Therefore, we must be saved by the final form of love which is forgiveness."[12]

Neibuhr's influence on other thinkers is not difficult to trace. George F. Kennan has called Niebuhr "the father of us all," implying an intel-

---

12 Reinhold Niebuhr, *The Irony of American History* (New York: Charles Scribner's Sons, 1952), 63. Niebuhr often paraphrased Biblical passages and used them to illuminate the present.

lectual tradition that Kennan and others have continued. If Niebuhr is the father of tradition, his children have chosen to interpret him in many diverse ways. Religious people who take pride in Niebuhr's commitment to what he called "Christian Realism" may prefer to forget his words, "Religion is a good thing for honest people but a bad thing for dishonest people . . . and the church had not been impressive because many of its leaders rationalize."[13] Secular leaders were attracted to Niebuhr perhaps because of his "dialogue with doubt," and a group was formed at Harvard called "atheists for Niebuhr." These doubting followers must have been embarrassed by his affirming John Baillie's words, "No matter how far back I go . . . I cannot get back to an atheistic mentality. As little can I reach a day when I was conscious of myself but not of God as I can reach a day when I was conscious of myself but not of other human beings."[14] This unique combination of a critical and a religious perspective has made Niebuhr both the forerunner of other critically minded thinkers and an irreplaceable figure on the American intellectual scene. At the 1974 meeting of the American Political Science Association, Arthur Schlesinger, Jr., summed up Niebuhr's contribution: "No one has taken his place or the role he performed from the 1930s to the 1960s."

Yet Niebuhr's influence was not exhausted in his direct influence on any particular group. He spoke to those Friedrich Schleiermacher called Christianity's "intellectual despisers." He was a modern circuit rider lecturing and preaching to college and university groups in seminars, large public lectures, and sermons. His words carried certainty because he never concealed his own doubts. On a Sunday morning in the 1940s when he had preached at a small chapel near his summer home in Health, Massachusetts, a friend and neighbor, Supreme Court Justice Felix Frankfurter stopped to say: "I liked what you said, Reinie, and I speak as a believing unbeliever." "I'm glad you did," replied Niebuhr, "for I spoke as an unbelieving believer."

Niebuhr's followers increased with the years. Those who gave their names as sponsors to the professorship of social ethics at Union Seminary

13 Reinhold Niebuhr, Sermon at Union Seminary, New York, May 10, 1960.
14 June Bingham, *Courage to Change: An Introduction to the Life and Thought of Reinhold Niebuhr* (New York: Charles Scribner's Sons, 1961), 12.

honoring Niebuhr included literary figures such as W. H. Auden, Alan Paton, and T. S. Eliot; political leaders Adolph A. Berle, Chester Bowles, Heinrich Bruning, Ralph J. Bunche, Hubert H. Humphrey, Jr., Herbert Lehman, Eleanor Roosevelt, Radha Krishnan, Adlai Stevenson, and Norman Thomas; educators Charles W. Cole, C. H. Dodd, Louis Finklestein, William E. Hocking, Clark Kerr, Grayson L. Kirk, Robert M. Hutchins, and Henry Wriston; businessmen Frank Altschul, Paul G. Hoffman, Henry R. Luce, and J. Irwin Miller; labor leaders David Dubinsky, Joseph L. Rauh, and Walter Reuther; theologians Emil Brunner, Truman Douglass, Angus Dun, Sherwood Eddy, George B. Ford, Harry Emerson Fosdick, Will Herberg, Jacques Maritain, and Paul Tillich; and foreign policy analysts Barbara Ward Jackson, George F. Kennan, Walter Lippmann, Arthur Schlesinger, Jr., Arnold J. Toynbee, and Arnold Wolfers. It would be difficult to find any American thinker with so broad and diverse a following or with such warmth, sensitivity, and skill in enlisting younger men of widely differing approaches to write in the journals he edited, especially *Christianity and Crisis*. A host of post-Niebuhrian writers—liberals, conservatives, blacks, white ethnics, radicals, and diverse interpreters of the Cold War—have claimed him as their own. As the author of seventeen books and more than fifteen hundred magazine articles, he inevitably provided grist for many mills.

Yet throughout his writings, Niebuhr centered on a few fundamental themes: human nature and original sin, the pursuit of truth through the tension of opposing views, the paradox of antinomies and ambiguity, the use of reason without allowing rational coherence to become a Procrustean bed, politics and power, prudence and practical morality, community and the convergence of political interests. On ultimate concerns, he has preferred to defy logic and display the complex relationships within the incongruity of the human situation, the irony and final hope of history: "Whether we live or die, we live or die unto the Lord." In political crises, he never shunned the necessity of moral and political choice. Writing on August 25, 1943, in *Christian News Letter* with regard to World War II, he said: "Political expediency is nothing to be ashamed of when the future peace of the world is at stake." Although master political thinkers such as E. H. Carr and A. J. P. Taylor were hesitant about choosing between the preservation of American democracy and the collective vitality of Hitler's National Socialist party, Niebuhr proclaimed that if moral discrimination were impossible on that issue, it would never be possible on this earth.

Communism challenging Western civilization, he wrote after World War II, was not identical with the threat of Nazism but was not thereby any less dangerous. Yet in *The Structure of Nations and Empires* (1959), he envisioned a lessening of the Communist threat and a possible relaxation of tension as second- and third-generation revolutionaries and technocrats replaced crusading revolutionary leaders in the Soviet Union. He supported American resistance to the Soviet Union in Europe through NATO and the Marshall Plan but questioned massive American intervention in Vietnam to halt a nationalist civil war.

He would have been embarrassed by those who found him always right in his political judgments, but he would have taken pride in the words of his biographer that he had demonstrated the *Courage to Change*. His legacy lies mainly in his insistence on the fundamentals of a political theory, not in his strengths as a political pundit however prodigious the volume of his political observations and commentary.

WORKS BY REINHOLD NIEBUHR

1927

Does Civilization Need Religion: A Study in the Social Resources and Limitations of Religion in Modern Life. New York: Macmillan Co.

1929

Leaves from the Notebook of a Tamed Cynic. New York: Willett, Clark & Colby.

1932

The Contribution of Religion to Social Work. New York: Columbia University Press.

Moral Man and Immoral Society: A Study in Ethics and Politics. New York: Charles Scribner's Sons.

1934

Reflections on the End of an Era. New York: Charles Scribner's Sons.

1935

An Interpretation of Christian Ethics. New York: Harper & Brothers.

1937

Beyond Tragedy: Essays on the Christian Interpretation of History. New York: Charles Scribner's Sons.

1940

Christianity and Power Politics. New York: Charles Scribner's Sons.

1941–1943

The Nature and Destiny of Man: A Christian Interpretation. 2 vols. New York: Charles Scribner's Sons. Published in 1949 as one volume.

1944

The Children of Light and the Children of Darkness: A Vindication of Democracy and a Critique of Its Traditional Defence. New York: Charles Scribner's Sons.

1946

Discerning the Signs of the Times: Sermons for Today and Tomorrow. New York: Charles Scribner's Sons.

1949

Faith and History: A Comparison of Christian and Modern Views of History. New York: Charles Scribner's Sons.

1952

The Irony of American History. New York: Charles Scribner's Sons.

1953

Christian Realism and Political Problems. New York: Charles Scribner's Sons.

1955

The Self and the Dramas of History. New York: Charles Scribner's Sons.

1958

Pious and Secular America. New York: Charles Scribner's Sons.

1959

The Structure of Nations and Empires: A Study of the Recurring Patterns and Problems of the Political Order in Relation to the Unique Problems of the Nuclear Age. New York: Charles Scribner's Sons.

WORKS ABOUT REINHOLD NIEBUHR

Bingham, June. *Courage to Change: An Introduction to the Life and Thought of Reinhold Niebuhr.* New York: Charles Scribner's Sons, 1961.

JOHN COURTNEY MURRAY (1904–1967)

Christianity and War

One of the most important American theorists writing on problems of morality in international relations from within the Roman Catholic tradition was the Reverend John Courtney Murray. Murray, a strongly independent theologian, proclaimed the responsibility of the individual Christian thinker to speak out forcefully on the issues of international politics. He maintained that morality had to govern the use of power. On the nature and problems of power, Murray wrote: "Power can be invested with a sense of direction only by moral principles. It is the function of morality to command the use of power, to forbid it, to limit it, or, more in general, to define the ends for which it may or must be used." The rule of morality is the rule inherent in the tradition of reason, particularly as understood by Catholic natural-law thinkers. He reasserted the importance of the just-war doctrine, the idea of proportionality, and the political virtue of prudence. This notion of morality enabled Murray to evaluate current issues and gave him a standard for judging the moral reasoning of others. For example, he warned of the danger of believing the "simplism of saying that to use power is prideful and therefore bad, and not to use it is irresponsible and therefore worse."[1]

John Courtney Murray was born in New York City on September 12, 1904. His mother was Irish; and his father, a lawyer who died when Murray was twelve, was Scottish. Both parents were Catholics, but his mother exerted the strongest religious influence in the family. Although Murray displayed an early interest in medicine as a profession, his education at a Jesuit high school, St. Francis Xavier, led to his joining the Society of Jesus at sixteen. He attended Weston College in Massachu-

1 John Courtney Murray, *We Hold These Truths* (New York: Sheed & Ward, 1960), 273, 288.

setts and nearby Boston College, earning his B.A. degree in 1926 and his M.A. degree in 1927.

As was customary in the Jesuit order, his study was interrupted by a three-year interval during which he taught Latin and English literature at Ateneo University in Manila, the most respected of several outstanding Catholic institutions of higher learning in the Philippines. Returning to the United States in 1930, he studied theology for four years at Woodstock College in Woodstock, Maryland, a school of theology for Jesuit priests, followed by four years of graduate theology at the Pontifical Gregorian University in Rome, from which he received his doctorate in theology. In 1937 Murray returned to Woodstock as professor of theology, a post he held until his death. He lectured at other institutions including Yale, where he was visiting professor of medieval philosophy and culture. At Woodstock, he specialized in the doctrines of the Trinity and grace and the problem of contemporary atheism. He published *The Problem of God, Yesterday and Today* (1964) and joined with other theologians, such as Gustav Weigel, to make Woodstock one of the strongest centers of theology in the United States.

Murray began publishing in the Jesuit scholarly journal *Thought* in the early 1930s while he was still a theological student. However, he did not emerge as a prominent religious thinker until the 1940s with his landmark articles on the problems of the Catholic church in a democratic age and in a pluralistic state. In 1941 Murray became editor of *Theological Studies*, published at Woodstock College. In that forum and in the *Ecclesiastical Review*, Murray argued untiringly for greater cooperation between Catholics and Protestants within American society. He contended that the Vatican should not only tolerate the pluralistic situation in the United States but recognize it as a new system good in itself, for the position of American Catholics as a minority alongside a non-Catholic majority had given Catholics a more favored status than at any time since the fourth century. The debate that Murray initiated became so lively that his order eventually silenced him with instructions to clear all his future writing on church-state matters with Jesuit headquarters. His essay in *The Catholic Church in World Affairs* (1954) caused such consternation in the church that, according to its editor Waldemar Gurian, there was a move to withhold the church's imprimatur because of Murray's paper.

Murray's views were vindicated, however, by the process of change begun by Pope John XXIII. Opponents hostile to his views of religious liberty managed to deny him participation at the first council meeting of Vatican II, but Pope Paul VI invited him to participate as an expert in the second council meeting. In addition, Murray's ideas formed the basis for the document declaring that every person has the right to freedom of conscience. That document, largely written by Murray, begins: "A sense of the dignity of the human person has been impressing itself more and more deeply on the consciousness of contemporary man. And the demand is increasingly made that men should act on their own judgment, enjoying and making use of a responsible freedom, not driven by coercion but motivated by a sense of duty. The demand is thus made that constitutional limits should be set to the powers of government in order that there may be no encroachment on the rightful freedom of the person and of associations."[2] Hence the American experience of church-state relations ought to serve as the model for the universal Church. As Reinhold Niebuhr once said of Murray: "What makes Murray significant is that he thinks in terms of Catholic theology and the American tradition at the same time. He rejoices in being in the American tradition."[3] The relation between Murray and Niebuhr, their mutual support and their differences, and their famed discussions and debates provide one of the most fruitful dialogues in the history of American religious and political thought. Both were powerful and determined thinkers, and neither tempered his fundamental beliefs and faith simply to be congenial.

Just as Murray believed that the American tradition had value for the Catholic tradition, he also believed that the Catholic tradition had significance for the American experience. In *We Hold These Truths* (1960), Murray wrote: "The question is sometimes raised, whether Catholicism is compatible with American democracy. The question is invalid as well as impertinent; for the manner of its position inverts the order of values. It must, of course, be turned round to read, whether American democracy is compatible with Catholicism."[4] He argued for the primacy of

2 Walter Abbott (ed.), *The Documents of Vatican II* (New York: Guild Press, 1966), 675.
3 Quoted in *Current Biography*, 1961, p. 332.
4 Murray, *We Hold These Truths*, ix–x.

religion in a wide variety of secular and religious journals from the *Annals of the American Academy of Political and Social Science* to *Catholic Mind*. He also became known for his calm, reasoned discourse and for the intellectual clarity and unfailing courtesy that characterized his approach. In the 1960s, Murray became a member of the Center of the Study of Democratic Institutions at the invitation of Robert Maynard Hutchins, joining Reinhold Niebuhr, Henry Pitt Van Dusen, Eleanor Stevenson, A. A. Berle, and Eric Goldman among others. In 1966 Murray became director of the Jesuit-founded John LaFarge Institute, designed to bring together leaders from all sectors of society for off-the-record discussions of religious liberty, racial discrimination, censorship, abortion, business and political ethics, religion and the arts, war and civil disobedience, and the population explosion. As Murray saw it, the purpose of these discussions was not agreement but the kind of understanding that honest disagreement presupposes. Murray believed in a wider consensus through natural law, and Douglas Auchincloss wrote in *Time*, December 12, 1960: "If anyone can help U.S. Catholics and their non-Catholic countrymen toward the disagreement that precedes understanding, John Courtney Murray can." Six feet four inches in height and speaking in a resonant baritone whether declaiming on natural law or ordering a "dreadfully dry martini," Murray cut a striking figure in American intellectual life.

As an American citizen concerned with the preservation of Western civilization, Murray sought to bring Catholic teaching on the just war to bear on life and death issues of the nuclear age. Rather than abandon the teaching as irrelevant, Murray insisted that theories on the just war be recognized as central in policy formulation. "The triple traditional function of just war," he wrote, was "to condemn war as evil, to limit the evils it entails, and to humanize its conduct as far as possible." He criticized the "theorists of desperate alternatives" who force themselves into the extremes of sentimental pacifism or cynical realism. "The basic fallacy is to suppose that *war* and *peace* are two discontinuous and incommensurable worlds of existence and universes of discourse. . . . We live in an intermediate state between peace and war."[5] For Murray,

5 *Ibid.*, 269, 270.

the public debate ought to include limited war, even limited nuclear war. (Such views led some of Murray's critics to call him a moralist of nuclear war.)

For Murray, the basic propositions of just war were still valid in the nuclear age. All wars of aggression fall under the ban of moral proscription. However, the real question is not one of aggression but one of injustice, and no longer may an individual state presume to take the cause of justice into its own hands. (Had Murray lived to witness the attacks of Third World countries on an unjust international order, he might have had some engaging discussions with moral philosophers such as the Indonesian, Soedjatmoko.) On the other hand, a defensive war is morally permissible in principle and in fact. Regarding justice and injustice, the principle of proportion is the moral guide. Consideration must be given to the suffering caused by an unjust order weighed against the damage that a war to end injustice might bring. This comparison involves a moral calculation grounded in the understanding that physical death and destruction are not the gravest evils which might result from war. Further, the use of force ought to be limited to what is necessary and sufficient to uphold the purposes of law and politics. In this regard, such concepts as total war and unconditional surrender violate the rules of proportion and of limitation of power. As the war in Vietnam progressed, Murray, had he lived, might increasingly have applied this standard to the conduct of warfare there.

The natural law standard provided Murray with a framework for addressing other theories of morality. While rejecting the oversimplifications of pacifism and cynical realism, Murray also criticized moral ambiguism. As he saw it, this moral ambiguity had its roots in the voluntarist, subjectivist individualism of Protestantism, with its emphasis, not on what one does, but on why one does it. (In part, he directed this criticism at Niebuhr.) The new morality that superseded this older morality saw the older morality as too simple, so it emphasized instead the ambiguities of moral decisions. For the ambiguists, the final category of moral judgment is not right or wrong but ambiguity: to act is to sin. Murray agreed that moral problems were complex, but he insisted that right or wrong could be identified. Moral ambiguists have offered a powerful critique of existing political relationships, but they contribute little in the way of constructive thought to build new structures and relevant policies. Anticipating the objection that reason has legitimized unjust political arrangements, Murray wrote: "The traditional ethic, which asserts the doctrine of the rule of reason in public affairs, does not expect that man's historical success in installing reason in its rightful role will be much more than marginal. But the margin makes the difference."[6] Murray's call, then, was for a return to natural law as the way to restore America's self-understanding.

The attacks of the Curia on Murray kept him from attending the Second Vatican Council's first session. When asked how he felt about this, he replied, "A man doesn't live long; and if something this big is going on, a man feels that he ought to be there." But the next year he attended, witnessed the triumph of Pope John XXIII's *aggiornamenta*, saw his ideas written into the council's Declaration on Religious Liberty, and concelebrated mass with Pope Paul VI. He could be devastating in his criticisms, as I learned when he challenged a paper I delivered, at the Council on Religion and International Affairs. He was wrong sometimes, as the Catholic writer John Cogley once observed: his political prophecies were sometimes wide of the mark; his conservative bias frequently betrayed him; he occasionally missed the point another thinker was making. But Cogley declared that Murray never said a stupid thing, a sentimental thing, or a consciously cruel thing. His style was classical in origin, aristocratic in nature, disciplined in structure sometimes to the point of rigidity, but courtly in manner. His concern was to point up the rational issues at stake in an argument. His intellectual adversaries were always slightly suspicious that he had something up his clerical sleeve, but what he never concealed was an abiding faith in reason.

He inveighed against three opposing approaches to war: (1) the view of relative Christian pacifism that war has become so destructive that it is now a moral absurdity (yes, but not every war, he replied); (2) that the enemy is completely unprincipled and that opponents must be unprincipled to survive; and (3) that the United Nations can act to make war illegal. Atomic war, he insisted, is not in and of itself morally

6 *Ibid.*, 289.

unjustifiable. There are greater evils than physical death. Moral calculus is required to judge the morality of forceful repression against the overthrow of injustice. War and peace are not two discontinuous and incommensurable worlds of existence. Men live most of their lives in an intermediate state between peace and war. Policy is always the meeting place of the world of power and the world of morality. Pope Pius XII had looked forward to a duly constituted international authority possessing a monopoly of armed forces in international affairs, but the United Nations fell short of this goal.

Murray urged a return to an earlier and older morality which affirmed that the good is good because God commands it. The basic issue is the nature of morality itself. According to natural law, society and the state are rational institutions with relatively autonomous ends or purposes that are predesigned in the social and political nature of man. It is true that the morality proper to the life and action of society and the state is not univocally the morality of personal life. From the point of view of political morality, self-interest as the motive of national action is both legitimate and necessary. Yet the tradition of reason maintains that it is wrong to say that all use of power is prideful; reason calls for a distinction between force and violence. Force is the measure of power necessary and sufficient to uphold the valid purposes of law and politics. (But for states that oppose an unjust international order, who is to say what purposes are valid?) What exceeds this is violence. As an instrument of international politics, force in and of itself is morally neutral.

Murray sought to counter the criticism that natural law is confounded by abstractionism, intentionism, legalism, and immobilism. On the contrary, its major purpose is to make man reasonably human and society essentially civil. The Christian is called to transcend nature, not to escape it. Natural law affords a secure anchorage in the order of reality. It rests on the premises of a realist epistemology (it is possible for man to know), on nature as teleology (history is tending toward some end or purpose), on a natural theology (God is at the summit of the order of being), and on the belief that the order of nature is not an order of necessity to be fulfilled blindly, but an order of reason and therefore freedom. Natural law is an elaboration of common sense and experience. It has changing content and progressive applications. It is conservative of all acquired human values but dynamic in its progress toward fuller human realization.

Murray believed in the educative character of laws and in the supremacy of law as reason, not will. The source of political authority is community reflecting the organic character of the state. The authority of the ruler is limited, and government is based on the contractual nature of the relations between the ruler and the ruled. In holding tenaciously to these classical ideas, Murray provided a counterpoise to opposing views of national and international politics, which he did not reject but sought to transcend. Politics for him was the rational and moral activity of men.

Murray died of a heart attack on August 16, 1967, at the age of sixty-two, having left his mark on the Catholic church and the nation. In his eulogy, Walter Burghardt tried to capture the essence of the man when he said: John Courtney Murray was the embodiment of the Christian humanist, in whom an aristocracy of the mind was wedded to a democracy of love. We have been privileged indeed; we have known and loved the Christian man, the "man who lives with wisdom."[7]

WORKS BY JOHN COURTNEY MURRAY

1958

Foreign Policy and the Free Society. With Walter Millis. New York: Oceana Publications, for the Fund for the Republic.

1959

The Moral Dilemma of Nuclear Weapons. Essays from *Worldview*. Edited by William Clancy. New York: Council on Religion and International Affairs.

Morality and Modern War. New York: Council on Religion and International Affairs.

1960

We Hold These Truths: Catholic Reflections on the American Proposition. New York: Sheed & Ward.

1964

The Problem of God, Yesterday and Today. New Haven, Conn.: Yale University Press.

1965

Freedom and Man. Edited by John Courtney Murray. New York: P. J. Kenedy Publishers.

1965

The Problem of Religious Freedom. Westminster, Md.: Newman Press.

7 Walter Burghardt, "He Lived with Wisdom," *America*, CXVII (September 9, 1967), 249.

MARTIN WIGHT (1913–1972)

The Values of Western Civilization

Martin Wight was preeminently the teacher of international relations, a subject he chose to approach not through the prevailing fashions of social science methodology and systems theory but in the classical language of history, politics, law, and theology. American students studying abroad with the British scholar Charles Manning or his disciples, who claimed to be transforming international studies through the scientific approach, often turned for serious guidance to Wight, who usually became their principal mentor. Wight, in contrast with Manning, saw international studies as an approach rather than a science. No teacher has ever encouraged and nourished his students with more sympathetic understanding and unchanging patience than Wight. His influence, therefore, must be sought as much in the maturing thought of his students as in his own writings.

Wight was born in 1913 in Brighton, where his father was a doctor. Wight was educated at Bradfield and Hertford College, Oxford, where in 1935 he earned a first in modern history (Herbert Butterfield was one of his examiners). Wight's friends remember him as tall, serious, and infinitely courteous, Lincolnesque in stature, with a deep respect for the truth. He early became the complete scholar. He collected manuscripts, artifacts, and statues from Europe's past and displayed a voracious appetite for detail. His friend Adam Watson has noted: "He was a magpie for details."

Wight left Oxford to join the staff of the Royal Institute of International Affairs at Chatham where he continued his research and writing until 1949, interrupted only by World War II and by a year as a columnist at the United Nations. At Chatham House, established by public and private donors and foundations in the United Kingdom and the United States, Wight came under the influence of Arnold J. Toynbee.

The younger man and the world-renowned historian collaborated on successive volumes of the institute's *Survey of International Affairs*, as well as Toynbee's *A Study of History*, and Wight appended what was nearly a small book of comments and notes to Volume VII reflecting his differences with Toynbee on both historical and theological issues. Whatever their differences, Toynbee and Wight shared an enduring religious commitment, a conception of history as universal not parochial, a concern with the interrelationship of secular and sacred history, and a capacity to find parallels between the present and the past. H. A. L. Fisher in reviewing a volume of the *Survey* observed that Toynbee, and by inference Wight, sought to connect the present with broader streams of history and to identify meaningful historical analogies. Toynbee's approach to contemporary problems gave a distinctive quality to the *Surveys*, in contrast with the journalistic reporting of the annual volumes published by the Council on Foreign Relations in New York. Their approach also placed Toynbee and Wight outside the mainstream of academic historiography and of descriptive summaries of the year's events in the *United States in World Affairs* and the annual volumes of foreign relations councils in other nations. As a headmaster, Wight was to speak of history as a prophetic drama or "philosophy teaching by example," an approach that set him apart from the more conventional academic and foreign policy groups.

During the years just preceding and including World War II, Wight held the post of headmaster at Haileybury where, though lacking in experience, he immediately established himself as a brilliant teacher. He inspired students to view history as more than factual knowledge—to see each decision as having its own moral content considered against a Toynbeean background. Wight applied Toynbee's concepts of internal and external proletariats and routs and rallies of civilizations to a wide range of historical eras. He emphasized not only history but the issues of the day, although throughout his career he was seldom an advocate— perhaps reflecting his disillusionment with his advocacy of the League of Nations.

In the years before World War II, Wight was a Christian pacifist and initially a supporter of the League of Nations, profoundly disappointed by its failure to apply collective sanctions against Il Duce Mussolini in the Abyssinian crisis. He had hoped that the League would provide a new structure for peace; if Ethiopia were overrun, he feared for the survival of other states. His pacifism in 1936[1] reflected the influence of Dick Sheppard, who was successively vicar of St. Martin's in the Field, canon of St. Paul's Cathedral, dean of Canterbury, and founder of the Peace Pledge Union. Wight not only embraced Christian pacifism but managed a pacifist bookstore on Ludgate Hill. His pacifism was uncompromising and severe; it bore little resemblance either to the pragmatic pacifism of the American Quakers or to Christian asceticism. In words that anticipated Herbert Butterfield's plea that one or the other superpower in the Cold War must take a substantial risk for peace, Wight saw pacificism as requiring one nation to make some sacrifice of security in the long-range cause of peace.

Wight was a conscientious objector in World War II on the grounds of his Christian faith. The war, he found, was a judgment upon Western civilization for its secularism and materialism, reflecting the spiritual apostasy of the age. World War I was one of the traumatic events of his life, for he saw in it a European civil war that largely destroyed the fabric of European civilization. The evils that wars tried to correct were not as great as the evils that they caused. The tawdriness of postwar Italy, which Mussolini exploited, and the disappearance of "the glory that was Greece" produced in Wight a deep sense of sadness about the future. The Christian recognizing God's judgment had no choice but to refuse to participate in war, seeking instead to prepare the way for a new civilization more in keeping with the tenets of the Kingdom of God. Even at this point in his life, Wight seemingly had not resolved the interplay of two contending convictions that were emerging as the cardinal principles of his world view: he was without illusions about the harsh realities of international politics, and he never believed that pacifism could bring about the defeat of Adolf Hitler. He had unabashed admiration for the wartime speeches of Winston Churchill, and at the same time he expressed open moral revulsion at the necessities of world politics. With the passage of time, his pacifism receded, perhaps because some of his loneliness disappeared when he married somewhat late

1 Martin Wight, "Christian Pacifism," *Theology*, XXXIII (July, 1936).

in life. Only those who were closest to him knew of the depth of his Christian commitment. If he ever resolved the tension between his realism and his pacifism, the resolution took the form of a truce between the two contending forces.

From 1941 to 1946, Wight joined Margery Perham (an authority on Nigeria and a pioneer student of the problems of the developing world) and other researchers at Oxford at work on colonial issues. Out of his experience, Wight published three books: *The Development of the Legislative Council, 1606–1945 (1946), The Gold Coast [Ghana] Legislative Council* (1947), and *British Colonial Constitutions, 1947* (1952).[2] It is worth speculating that Wight turned to the issues of the less-developed and less-privileged countries during World War II partly because of his Christian values. He collaborated with three major scholars—W. Arthur Lewis (who became vice-chancellor of the University of the West Indies), Michael Scott, and Colin Legum—in the publication of *Attitudes to Africa* (1951). If his work in the field of colonial studies represented his most substantial contribution as a traditional or technical historian and if it signaled his break from the Toynbeean framework of universal history, it represented something less than his most abiding intellectual concern. The triumph of the idea of power over the idea of right in World War II channeled Wight's major work from an approach based on pacifism or moralism to a concern with power politics and the balance of power. Butterfield's influence on him and his own persistence in analyzing the logic of events led to this shift in the focus of his writing. He came to recognize the damage caused by following simple moral principles as the sole guide to foreign policy.

Wight entered the third phase of his work in 1946 (universal history being the first and colonial problems the second) with the publication of *Power Politics.* Had Wight written nothing else, this slender volume would have earned him the rank of master thinker. Its contents summarized all the fundamental issues of international politics for the next three decades: great powers, small powers, international anarchy, vital interests and prestige, balance of power, buffer zones, the League of

---

2 These and all works by Martin Wight are listed chronologically, with full publication data, beginning on p. 60 herein.

Nations, the United Nations, and beyond power politics. Future scholars would be hardpressed to add to the agenda of basic issues. The book remains his best-known work. An expanded version was edited from his notes and completed by Hedley Bull, his most brilliant student, and Carsten Holbraad.

In 1949 Wight left Chatham House and his short-term assignment in 1946 as the *Observer*'s United Nations correspondent to join the Department of International Relations at the London School of Economics at the invitation of his intellectual nemesis, Charles Manning. (I marveled at the mutual tolerance the two expressed for one another when I visited them throughout the 1950s and 1960s.) For students who sought exposure to two diametrically opposing viewpoints, the interaction of Manning and Wight must have been comparable to that experienced by University of Chicago students who studied with the realist Hans J. Morgenthau and the idealist Quincy Wright. Manning, the lawyer turned social scientist, probably appealed more to the new science of politics school in the United States (Arnold Wolfers, William T. R. Fox, and Karl Deutsch in the United States saw Manning as the hope of British scholarship); but Wight, whose scholarly apparatus remained that of classical history and politics, cast his spell on almost everyone who sought to grapple with the real issues of contemporary diplomacy. Not only scholars but American journalists such as Howard K. Smith and Sander Vanocur found Wight far more relevant to their dominant concerns, even though he reserved his most passionate words for topics in philosophy and history. My visits with Manning confirmed what others had reported. Manning busied himself with the technicalities of establishing a new school of thought more than with building a corpus of his own writings, and he directed my attention to colleagues whom he felt were partners in his crusade. Wight appeared almost aloof from the architects of the new international studies as he made his way along the well-trodden path of the search for broad designs in the grand sweep of history and politics. He earned an authority verging on reverence from students and colleagues based on the quality and thoroughness of his work.

At the London School of Economics, noted for its radical socialist approach but also a stronghold of conservatism in economics and history, Wight lectured on international institutions, beginning with the Conciliar Movement of 1409–1449 and moving through seventeenth- and eighteenth-century peace plans to the League of Nations, which for him was an application of the ideas of Thomas Hobbes, and to the United Nations, which was Lockean in design. For Wight these novel international institutions were pseudoinstitutions, secondary in importance to alliances and diplomacy. Wight's favorite course of lectures was in international theory, concentrating on three major traditions in Western thought: the realist or Machiavellian, the rationalist or Grotian, and the revolutionist or Kantian. He saw the main issues in international theory crystalized in the debate between the three traditions and developed this idea in a paper entitled "Western Values in International Relations," which became a chapter in the book, *Diplomatic Investigations* (1966).

In 1961 Wight left the London School of Economics to return to Brighton as professor of history and dean of the School of European Studies at the new University of Sussex. To those who viewed London as the intellectual capitol of the world, his move was as surprising as Arnold Wolfers' move from Yale University to the new Center for American Foreign Policy Research at the School for Advanced International Studies in Washington, D.C. It may be that Wight, as well as George F. Kennan, had a streak of the romantic in him or he may have been excited by Lord Fulton's challenge that he join the planning of a new university or he may have chosen to return to European studies because of Europe's overwhelming importance in his design of world politics. The School of European Studies at Sussex was something new on the British intellectual landscape. Wight became absorbed in the study of European civilization from the Greeks to the present and offered tutorials on ancient history, Dante, Jacob Burckhardt, and international relations. He held the enthusiasts among his new colleagues on an even keel and joined firmness with compassion in relationships with individual students. He had his own enthusiasms (religious studies, the history of art, the university library, and the "Year Abroad"), and he flourished as a teacher and an academic planner. Yet he never abandoned his dominant interest in international theory; and the British Committee on the Theory of International Politics provided an outlet for his most original writing (he succeeded Herbert Butterfield as convenor). The most rewarding hours of his life were those spent in trying out his ideas with civilized thinkers on the British committee; the resulting essays became his most enduring scholarly contribution. When the committee was threatened by dissolution, Wight held it together, raised funds, and expanded its membership.

Wight's realism was grounded in William Stubbs's concept that modern history is distinguished from medieval history by the primacy of the idea of power over the idea of right. The great powers, like gas expanding to fill a vacuum, are checked not by laws or the will of God but by other powers. They cease to expand only when they reach their limits imposed by the balance of power and an induced sense of restraint. Hedley Bull has differentiated Wight's realism from that of E. H. Carr (whose *Twenty Years' Crisis* profoundly influenced Wight in the 1940s), Hans J. Morgenthau, and George F. Kennan, who, Bull maintains, were more polemical, systematic, and didactic than Wight. Wight, like other realists, was fundamentally pessimistic (he has been described as a Christian pessimist). He did not agree that the world was moving from power politics to a new and better international order. In his essay "Why Is There No International Theory?" he speculated that Sir Thomas More or Henry IV returning to England or France in 1960 would find the domestic scene closer to their goals but that on the international scene "the stage would have become much wider, the actors fewer [a characterization that had greater relevance in 1960 than in 1980], their weapons more alarming, but the play would be the same old melodrama. International politics is the realm of recurrence and repetition; it is the field in which political action is most necessitous."[3] Wight looked for recurrent patterns: the struggle between the Soviet Union and the United States resembled that between France and the Habsburgs; the ideological clash between the West and Communism suggested the schism of Western and Eastern Christendom; Marxism was a secular perversion of the New Testament Messianic idea; and Nazism's *ubermensch* (superman) was a debasement of the Old Testament

3 Herbert Butterfield and Martin Wight (eds.), *Diplomatic Investigations* (London: George Allen & Unwin, 1966), 26.

concept of a chosen people. In *Power Politics*, Wight wrote: "Powers will continue to seek security without reference to justice, and to pursue their vital interests irrespective of common interests, but in the fraction that they may be deflected lies the difference between the jungle and the traditions of Europe."[4] Bull notes a shift of emphasis after *Power Politics*, written when Wight was thirty-three. In his later writings, Wight directed attention more to common interests and obligations, for example in his plea that Britain join the European Economic Community. To say that he had rejected the precepts of power politics would be carrying the point too far. While recognizing Bull's excellent and penetrating introduction to Wight's posthumous volume, *Systems of States* (1977) (on which much of the foregoing analysis is based), the reader wonders whether the student occasionally introduces ideas of his own into interpretations of the master.

Power Politics remains Wight's major contribution to the definition and conceptualization of international politics, a field that has suffered the curse of a popularized if more elegant discussion of current events. More than is acknowledged, most writers go back to a series of definitions in this great work. "Power politics," he wrote, "means the relations between independent powers. This implies two conditions: independent units which acknowledge no political superior, and continuous and organized relations between them."[5] One is hard pressed to imagine that Wight, whatever the shifts in his thinking, would recast this definition in the 1980s. Yet Wight recognized that the international system he described has not always existed but came into being roughly at the time of the Reformation. He acknowledged that phrases like "Britain's foreign policy" are shorthand for an infinitely complex pattern of policy formulation involving not only foreign offices but the prime minister, the House of Commons, and a multitude of traditions, interests, and generations living and dead. Nor is force or the threat of force the sole ingredient of power politics, but to ignore this dimension, he insisted, is to ignore a perennial if disturbing political reality.

The rank of great power was first recognized in diplomatic practice

---

4 Martin Wight, *Power Politics* (London: Royal Institute of International Affairs, 1946), 68.
5 *Ibid.*, 7.

51

by the Congress of Vienna in 1814. In British diplomacy Viscount Castlereagh invented the concept when he argued that negotiations at the congress should be in the hands of "the six Powers most considerable in population and weight"—Britain, Russia, Austria, Prussia, Spain, and the defeated France. In practice, the four allies managed the congress. This was to be repeated in the Paris Peace Conference of 1919, with decisions being made in advance largely by the United States, Britain, France, Italy, and Japan. "A Power," Wight maintained, "becomes a Great Power by a successful war against another Great Power."[6] Great-power status is lost, as it is won, by violence and war. Great powers first obtained *legal* recognition under the League of Nations through gaining permanent seats on the League Council. Since they have wider interests and greater resources, they have the major responsibility for dealing with international problems. The test of a great power is its potential ability to stand alone. Middle powers, which are given special status in international bodies such as the United Nations, depend on the goodwill of a great power, like Mexico and the United States or Poland and the Soviet Union. However, great powers have tended to decrease in number and to increase in strength, heralding the rise during World War I of so-called world powers. Small powers can defend only limited interests, and some who pursue these interests negatively through policies of neutrality are in effect powers by courtesy. With the technological revolution in modern warfare, the gulf between small powers (who can survive only by association with a great power) and great powers has grown even greater despite concepts of state equality. In a system of power politics, the duty of rulers is to preserve a state's independence and its vital interests (interests that it will wage war to defend) against the competing interests of other peoples. The vital interests of a state are what it thinks them to be, however uncertain and subject to change; they are not what another power says them to be. Prestige is the halo around power or the recognition by other peoples of a nation's strength. Power is based in part on reputation, and reputation, in turn is based on power.

A major source of conflict is the general tendency of all powers to

6 *Ibid.*, 19, 20.

expand—economically, culturally, and politically—summed up in territorial expansion. Not only do the great colonizing and empire-building states such as Britain, Russia, and the United States show these tendencies but so do small powers such as Portugal, Holland, and Belgium, who after World War I acquired colonial empires many times their size. "Every Power tends to expand until it reaches an equilibrium that is the product of two factors: external pressure and internal organization."[7] Conversely, powers in general refuse to suffer territorial loss without a struggle. Britain in particular and the United States are exceptions to the rule; they have been educated by adversity into becoming good neighbors.

The central principle of a power politics system is the balance of power. Objectively, it is an application of the law of self-preservation: "When one Power grows dangerously strong, other Powers combine against it. The Balance of Power comes into play each time that a Dominant Power has tried to gain mastery of the world."[8] Balances of power have been multiple, resembling a chandelier. Such was the case in eighteenth-century Europe when Britain, France, and Spain balanced each other in Western Europe and overseas while Austria, Prussia, Russia, and Turkey balanced each other in Central and Eastern Europe and the two balances interacted as well. A simple balance or pair of scales replaces the chandelier when the great powers are divided into opposite camps. This occurred in Europe in the late nineteenth century when the Franco-Russian Alliance of 1893 balanced the Triple Alliance of Germany, Austria-Hungary, and Italy or in 1936 when the Berlin-Rome Axis aligned against the League powers.

Balance, like national security, may have two meanings—equilibrium or preponderance (as with a balance in the bank). Here the subjective interpretation of the balance of power comes into play. The historian viewing conflicts dispassionately may discover a balance when opposing groups appear roughly equal in power. The statesman maintains there is a balance when his side is somewhat stronger than the other side. Within the United States, each successive public debate on

7 *Ibid.*, 41.
8 *Ibid.*, 44.

national defense has rested on the two competing ideas of balance—equality with the Soviet Union asserted by diplomatists or a preponderance of American power proclaimed by military leaders. In the past, certain powers were the holders of the balance, free to shift their weight to one side or the other. Britain's "splendid isolation" and American isolationism particularly in the nineteenth century were expressions of this concept, but Americans in the twentieth century deluded themselves in believing that such freedom of action was a permanent attribute of American foreign policy.

Wight pointed out that politics is not an exact science and that there are no laws of politics without exceptions. Yet he maintained that "the Balance of Power is as nearly a fundamental law of politics as it is possible to find: it is easy to see from history that it is the way most Powers have pursued self-preservation in most cases."[9] The law of the balance of power is practiced more consistently by states with strength, confidence, and international cohension. Americans who would quarrel with Wight about the permanence of the balance of power have been reminded by statesmen such as Churchill that what peace the world has known since World War II has rested on a bipolar political balance and a technological "balance of terror." No master thinker has defined the working principles of a system of power politics with greater succinctness, cogency, and clarity than Martin Wight. However much he may have expanded or elaborated his thinking in later writings, his early definitions of the core realities of power politics have permanent validity.

To end a discussion of Martin Wight's thought with a review of his unflinching description of power politics would be to do him an immense injustice. There was also a religious dimension to his thought. He was an orthodox Christian and a devout Anglican, strongly influenced by Herbert Butterfield and Reinhold Niebuhr. He joined secular pessimism with theological hope. Religion for him was not a decoration; it lay at the core of his being. He questioned whether, as well-meaning people, we were assured of muddling through: "We are not well-meaning people doing our best; we are miserable sinners, living

9 *Ibid.*, 47.

under judgment. . . . We are doing our best like Caiaphus, for our idolatrous loyalties; we are well-meaning like Pilate, every day crucifying Christ afresh."[10] He spoke mockingly of a welfare-state, United-Nations type of Christianity and emphasized that Christianity applied to world politics is more than the Sermon on the Mount. Wight saw the necessary differentiation between the realm theologians had defined as Caesar's and that which was God's. He doubted that war could be eradicated, since Christianity itself from the seventeenth century had been infected by the idea of progress. Although particular wars might be avoided, as a statistical possiblity, war continues to be inevitable. He wrote in 1946 that a "Third World War is as certain as the return of Halley's Comet." Wight wrote less about his religious views in the final years of his life, but he never wavered in his commitments to traditional Christianity, which brought a fixed point of reference to the main body of his thought. He substituted practical morality and prudence for Christian perfectionism and continued to search for a new theory of international morality based on the wisdom of the past.

Three of Wight's most important essays appeared in the first publication of the British Committee on the Theory of International Politics—*Diplomatic Investigations*, edited by Butterfield and Wight. In the first of his essays entitled "Why Is There No International Theory?" he asked why the phrase *political theory* requires no explanation whereas *international theory* does. The former involves speculation about the state; but the latter, which is often understood as the methodology of the study in international relations or some new conceptual system, meant for Wight speculation about the relations among states. Political science with all its tensions is held together by political theory. In contrast: "In the nineteenth century and earlier, there is no succession of the first-rank books about the state system and diplomacy like the succession of political classics from Boden to Mill."[11] Before the twentieth century, speculation on the society of states was derived from international law and the following sources: (1) writers who foreshadowed the League of

10. Martin Wight, "The Church, Russia and the West," *Ecumenical Review*, I (Autumn, 1948), 35–36.
11 Martin Wight, "Why Is There No International Theory?" in Butterfield and Wight (eds.), *Diplomatic Investigations*, 18.

Nations, such as Erasmus, William Penn, and the Abbé de St. Pierre; (2) Machiavellians or writers on *reason of state*, of whom Friedrich Meinecke is the foremost interpreter; (3) philosophers and historians who at the margin of their activities grappled with basic problems of international politics, as in David Hume's "The Balance of Power," Jean Jacques Rousseau's "Project of Perpetual Peace," Jeremy Bentham's "Plan for an Universal Peace," Edmund Burke's "Thoughts on French Affairs" and "Letters on a Regicide Peace," Leopold von Ranke's essay on the great powers, and J. S. Mill's essay on the law of nations; (4) speeches, dispatches, memoirs, and essays of statesmen and diplomatists, such as George Canning's classic dispatch of 1823 on the doctrine of guarantees, Bismarck's *Gedanken und Erinnerungen*, and Lord Salisbury's early essays on foreign affairs in the *Quarterly Review*. Only Burke among political philosophers turned exclusively from political to international theory, and only Machiavelli appeared to address his precepts as much to relations among states as to politics within states. In the quest for an international theory, the third body of literature on international politics, along with the writings on international law, comprises the most useful source for a future international theory.

Taken together, these sources are fragmentary and scattered. They stand in opposition to a belief in progress and political ideas about the state, the individual, virtue, and the good life. International politics is less susceptible to progressivist interpretations. Efforts to erect progressive theories have about them an air of desperation that places conviction ahead of evidence. Wight observed: "It is surely not a good argument for a theory of international politics that we shall be driven to despair if we do not accept it. But it is an argument that comes naturally to the children of Hegel (and Kant). . . . Communists, as the Germans neared Moscow, the Nazis, as the Russians returned upon Germany, alike cried that defeat was unthinkable because if they were defeated history would be meaningless."[12]

Two other tendencies corrupt most international theory, the most recent being the curiously progressive notion that nuclear weapons have transformed international politics making war impossible. For Wight

12 *Ibid.*, 28.

this idea was comparable to the nineteenth-century view that public opinion made war impossible. Political theory is linked with political reality; international theory, especially in its legal expressions, calls not for understanding but for transformation of diplomacy: "When diplomacy is violent and unscrupulous, international law soars into the regions of natural law; when diplomacy acquires a certain habit of cooperation, international law crawls in the mud of legal positivism."[13] The tension between international theory and diplomatic practicalities lies at the heart of the problem of international theory. The only acknowledged classic in the study of international relations comparable to the great classics in political philosophy is found in the historical writings of Thucydides. To understand American government and the founding fathers, a student reads the Federalist Papers. To understand statecraft, a student should read history in the mold of John Seeley's *Growth of British Policy*, Garrett Mattingly's *Renaissance Diplomacy*, or John Wheeler-Bennett's *Brest-Litovsk* rather than international theory based on the new methodologies.

Wight tried to demonstrate the disharmony between international theory and diplomatic practice caused by the different contexts of international, as compared with domestic, politics: "Political theory and law are maps of experience or systems of action within the realm of normal relationships and calculable results. They are the theory of the good life. International theory is the theory of survival. What for political theory is the extreme case (as revolution or civil war) is for internationalist theory the regular case."[14] The boundaries of international theory encompass Hugo Grotius' noble effort to establish the laws of war to Joseph de Maistre's "occult and terrible law" of violent destruction. The issues of international theory involve national existence and national extinction, including controversies over appeasement, debate about a nuclear deterrent, or questions of security or disarmament. Such issues break through the language of the social sciences in which they are normally considered and limit every form of international theory except that derived from history.

13 *Ibid.*, 29.
14 *Ibid.*, 33.

Thus Wight illuminated the hard issues of international theory even as he helped men understand power politics and the Christian tradition applied to international problems. Two other contributions deserve attention: first, his comparative study of state systems (the modern or Western state system and the classical Greek state system) and, second, Western values in international relations. The former is similar to the work of contemporary social scientists on the nature and limitations of the state system and the emergence of an interdependent world. A state system for Wight involves the relationship of states that recognize no political superior and have permanent or semipermanent relations with one another expressed in messengers, conferences and congresses, and a diplomatic language and trade. Only three systems have all these characteristics: the modern or Western state system, which emerged in the fifteenth century and is now worldwide; the Hellenic-Hellenistic or Greco-Roman system; and the state system of China in the era of the ancient warring states. Wight drew important distinctions concerning such systems, the most important being the norms and values that animate the system and the institutions through which they are expressed. A state system presupposes a common culture, whether limited to a common morality and code leading to rules of coexistence or extending to deeper religious and ideological assumptions. He asked but did not answer the question: Do all such codes represent common practices of the human race in men's search for a natural law? Fractures of cultural unity have recurred in religious wars and in the French Revolution, and systems tend to seek cultural differentiation from outside forces. Wight questioned whether cultural unity still exists with the expansion of the modern state system beyond the confines of Europe. Finally, he analyzed the uncertain boundaries in today's world between what is and is not a state system and thereby prepared the way for others to consider more fully the role of transnational groupings, mutinational corporations, and world revolutionary movements.

Wight's concern with ethical and religious questions was a recurrent theme throughout his writings. In one of his last papers, he explored the place of Western values in international relations. By values, Wight meant a coherent pattern of ideas at the center of what he described as the Whig or "constitutional tradition" in diplomacy, exemplified in different ways by Hugo Grotius, Edmund Burke, Alexis de Tocqueville, Abraham Lincoln, Guglielmo Ferrero, J. L. Brierly, Harold Nicolson, Winston Churchill, and Paul A. Spaak. He identified four dominant themes. First is the international society, which involves "the habitual intercourse of independent communities, beginning in the Christendom of Western Europe and gradually extending throughout the world . . . [and] manifest in the diplomatic system; in the conscious maintenance of the balance of power to preserve the independence of the member communities; in the regular operations of international law, whose binding force is accepted over a wide though politically unimportant range of subjects, in economic, social and technical interdependence and the functional international institutions." Second, the maintenance of order involves an even distribution or balance of power but also a core of common standards, such as the principle of resisting aggression and balancing order with justice. The third is the doctrine of intervention, reflecting the interdependence of states and the fact that events which take place in any one of them must be of interest and concern to all the rest. Intervention for Wight can be justified as an occasional and unfortunate necessity because of the permanent instability of the balance of power and the permanent inequality of the moral development of its members. On a moral scale, maintaining the balance of power is a better reason for intervening than upholding civilized standards, but upholding civilized standards is a better reason for intervening than maintaining existing governments. Finally, international morality introduces the place of individual conscience in international politics and the notion of ethical limits to political action. Wight observed: "Political expedience itself has to consult the moral sense of those it will affect . . . [and] is softened into prudence, which is a moral virtue."[15] That Wight, who began as a conscientious objector, should end as a justifier of prudence and practical morality testifies to the inherent relationship of core Western values to the stubborn realities of power politics. Wight had hoped that power politics might yield to new structures, such as the League of Nations, but in the end he had to return to principles enshrined in international history.

15 Martin Wight, "Western Values in International Relations," in Butterfield and Wight (eds.), *Diplomatic Investigations*, 96–97, 128.

Like Herbert Butterfield, who was his teacher, and Reinhold Niebuhr, who inspired his thinking, Martin Wight devoted much of his scholarly energies to the search for a normative foundation of politics. These three master thinkers represent the three giants among Protestant historians and theologians who have written about morality and foreign policy. That all three concluded after a lifetime of thought that practical morality and prudence represent the highest and most viable approach to political morality is instructive to those who would continue their work. The Reverend John Courtney Murray, writing from within the Roman Catholic tradition, held to the historic natural law viewpoint. Yet on issues of war and peace, and especially on the principle of proportionality in the ethics of war and foreign policy, Murray's thinking was not radically different. It would be difficult to find other thinkers in any culture who struggled more valiantly and with greater moral courage to establish a viable normative foundation for politics.

WORKS BY MARTIN WIGHT

Books

1946

The Development of the Legislative Council, 1606–1945. London: Faber & Faber.

Power Politics. London: Royal Institute of International Affairs.

1947

The Gold Coast Legislative Council. London: Faber & Faber.

1951

Attitudes to Africa. With W. Arthur Lewis, Michael Scott and Colin Legum. New York: Penguin Books.

1952

British Colonial Constitutions, 1947. Oxford: Clarendon Press.

1977

Systems of States. Edited with an introduction by Hedley Bull. Leicester: Leicester University Press.

1978

Power Politics. Edited by Hedley Bull and Carsten Holbraad. New York: Holmes & Meier Publishers.

Journal Articles

"Christian Pacifism." *Theology*, XXXIII (July, 1936).

"The Tanaka Memorial." *History*, XXVIII (March, 1943).

"The Church, Russia and the West." *Ecumenical Review*, I (Autumn, 1948).

"History and Judgement: Butterfield, Niebuhr and the Technical Historian." *Frontier*, I (August, 1950).

"What Makes a Good Historian?" *Listener*, No. 17 (February, 1953).

"War and International Politics." *Listener*, No. 13 (October, 1953).

"The Power Struggle Within the United Nations." *Proceedings of the Institute of World Affairs, 33rd Session, 1956.*

"Why Is There No International Theory?" *International Relations*, II (April, 1960).

"Brutus in Foreign Policy: The Memoirs of Sir Anthony Eden." *International Affairs*, XXXVI (July, 1960).

"The Place of Classics in a New University." *Didaskalos*, no. 1 (1963).

"International Legitimacy," *International Relations*, IV, (May, 1972).

Essays in Books

"Spain and Portugal," "Switzerland, the Low Countries and Scandinavia," "Eastern Europe," "Germany," "The Balance of Power." In Arnold Toynbee, ed. *The World in March, 1939.* London: Oxford University Press, 1952.

"European Studies." In David Daiches, ed. *The Idea of a New University: An Experiment in Sussex.* London: Andre Deutsch, 1964.

"Why Is There No International Theory?" "Western Values in International Relations," and "The Balance of Power." In Herbert Butterfield and Martin Wight, eds. *Diplomatic Investigations.* London: George Allen & Unwin, 1966.

"The Balance of Power and International Order." In A. M. James, ed. *The Bases of International Order: Essays in Honour of C. A. W. Manning.* Oxford: Oxford University Press, 1973.

PART II

Power and Politics

Immigrants in search of freedom and security have come to the United States, as have intellectuals of widely differing national origins. Among successive waves of migration, one of considerable importance for international thought occurred in the 1930s and 1940s during the flight of intellectuals from Hitler's Germany. Some were to find their way into positions of government and others into science and business. Especially noteworthy is the contribution of refugee scientists to the Manhattan Project carried out under Stagg Field at the University of Chicago, which lead to the discovery of the atomic bomb. In the humanities and social sciences, Alvin Johnson, who founded the graduate school of the New School for Social Research in New York, provided an academic home to some of the best minds of Europe, including Leo Strauss, Hans Spier, Arnold Brecht, Kurt Riessler, Hans Jonas, and Erich Hula. Many of the most original thinkers in the social sciences in postwar America were refugees from Hitler, and today they are esteemed for their contributions to American social thought.

No field profited more from

this migration than international studies, and it is difficult to list all the premier thinkers. Some made their contributions primarily in the classroom; and others turned to philosophy (Leo Strauss, Hannah Arendt, Hans Jonas, and Eric Voegelin), comparative government (Carl Joachim Friedrich, Franz and Sigmund Neumann, Otto Kirchheimer, Chancellor Bruning, and Waldemar Gurian), or international law (Leo Gross and Hans Kelsen). Younger men, such as Secretary of State Henry Kissinger and national security advisor Zbigniew K. Brzezinski who came to the United States as students, constitute second-generation thinkers who excelled in statecraft. Others remained in England (George Schwarzenberger and Hersh Lauterpacht), still others chose countries such as Switzerland and Spain. Finally, history, sociology, economics, and literature claimed other leading European thinkers, such as Jacob Viner, Frederich von Hayek, Karl Mannheim, and Joseph A. Schumpeter. It would be difficult to discover a comparable migration of human talent in all of intellectual history. Fortunately, American university life was receptive to influences from British and European scholars.

In international studies in particular, European-American and British scholars introduced an approach that emphasized the fundamental importance of power in politics. Americans had been shielded from the facts of power politics because of the nation's geographic isolation from Europe and the surrogate role of the British navy in protecting American interests, particularly over the seaways of the Atlantic. Over a period of three centuries, Britain and Europe had come to accept the reality of power politics. Power was seen as an inescapable factor in government and politics, unlikely to disappear with the emergence of a new international order. Americans, following the inspiring leadership of President Woodrow Wilson, were more optimistic about international law and international organization. Wilsonians predicted that old practices, such as alliances and the balance of power, were being replaced by new structures reflecting the common interests of mankind.

The years between World War I and World War II supported the British and European view of power. Hitler stated openly that the Allies' disparagement of power enabled him to conquer much of Europe.

The small group of European-American scholars who migrated to the United States testified to the risks of powerlessness, which had destroyed Weimar Germany, and to the need for an organized concert of power to resist Nazi expansionism. Novel international institutions would be only as strong as the will of their member states.

The first writer to call for realism in international relations was not a European-American in the United States but an Englishman in the United Kingdom—E. H. Carr, diplomat, journalist, and historian. In *The Twenty Years' Crisis*, written on the eve of World War II, Carr attributed the crisis less to defections from Wilsonian internationalism (including that of the United States) and more to the failure of the Allies to organize power effectively to resist aggression. Never had the gulf between words and deeds or between declarations and policies been greater than on the part of the Western nations. Utopianism, which is always the first stage of any system of social thought, had to give way to realism if the West was to survive.

Hans J. Morgenthau followed Carr, and his views were if anything more uncompromising and outspoken on the need for political realism. Whatever the ultimate ends of policy might be, power in the present international system was inescapably the means to such ends; and power in defense of the nation had to be organized and defined in terms of the national interest. The community of scholars in the United States took offense at Morgenthau's earliest writings, especially *Scientific Man vs. Power Politics*, *Politics Among Nations*, and *In Defense of the National Interest*; but as the struggle between America and the Soviet Union intensified, his views became more acceptable. The breadth of his thought and the comprehensive character of his political realism, especially his views on the limitations of power, were not appreciated until he applied them to the crisis in Asia and Vietnam.

Arnold Wolfers and John H. Herz were also European-American interpreters of power politics. However, they sought to reconcile realism and idealism, which made them more acceptable to the American tradition of political idealism. Wolfers' *Britain and France Between Two Wars* was the best-documented study of the tragic failure of the two leading Western powers to join together to resist German expansionism. Wolfers demonstrated that the foreign policies of the

65

democratic nations, more than the rhetoric of statesmen at the League of Nations, determined the quest for peace. In their later writings, both Wolfers and Herz sought to identify points of consensus between competing schools of thought in the United States.

The scientific method was another uniquely American perspective on world politics. Karl Deutsch, a European-American scholar, mastered communications theory, cybernetics, demography, and quantitative analysis and unified them in a thorough scientific view of international politics, which asserted the importance of power. To the extent that American scholars of international relations developed a scientific perspective, Deutsch's influence was far-reaching, although he never abandoned his European outlook.

Younger European-American writers, such as Stanley Hoffmann and George Liska, have modified these earlier approaches, but they have been the first to acknowledge the formative influence of the earlier writers. The time was ripe for a strong injection of realism when Carr and Morgenthau wrote. America had been catapulted overnight into a position of world leadership without much attention to the corresponding political and military requirements. Because these early writers were single-minded and uncompromising in maintaining that power was essential to leadership, their views gained authority especially in the postwar era.

E. H.
CARR
(1892–)

The Immanence
of Power
as the Standard

Edward Hallett Carr was born on June 28, 1892, in north London, the son of a small manufacturer whom Carr described as belonging to "the middle middle class." He was educated at the Merchants Taylors' School and in 1911 matriculated on scholarship to Trinity College, Cambridge University. His contacts with Trinity's most celebrated dons, such as Alfred North Whitehead, A. E. Housman, James Frazer, and Bertrand Russell, were limited; but he earned a first in the classics tripos and university prizes in Latin epigrams, Latin poems, and Greek translation.

Had World War I not intervened, Carr might have become a classics don at Cambridge, but instead he spent twenty years as a diplomat. The contingencies of history were to shape his intellectual journey for more than sixty years. One year after joining the Foreign Office, he was, in his own words, "shifted onto the Russian Revolution." By accident he was present at the 1919 Paris Peace Conference and later served as assistant adviser on League of Nations affairs in the Foreign Office. In *The Twenty Years' Crisis*,[1] he tried to unravel the tangled web of international politics that he had experienced. During World War II he was assistant editor of the *Times* and exercised quiet influence in supporting a Labor government in 1945. (The *Times* in this period was referred to as the *"Thrupenny" Daily Worker*, and conservative critics identified Carr as a member of a band of *etatist* radicals.) The two world wars, especially the first, led to the erosion of his faith in the established values of liberal England and to his search for a world other than the conventional one of his childhood. He followed not the route common to intellectuals in the 1930s of flirtation with Leninism but one that led to a discovery of

1 This and all works by E. H. Carr are listed chronologically, with full publication data, beginning on p. 79 herein.

the intellectual world of nineteenth-century Russia and the writings of
Feodor Dostoevski and Mikhail Bakunin. Twice he returned to university life. In 1936 he became Wilson Professor of International Politics
at the University College of Wales at Aberystwyth, leaving the Foreign
Office (and acknowledging that he had stayed too long) to have greater
freedom to write about the Russian Revolution. In 1953 he returned to
Cambridge to begin a quarter-century of research on the history of Soviet Russia, culminating in fourteen books published in ten volumes.
His return to Cambridge University came not because he was asked to
leave the *Times* but because, at fifty-two, he was determined to return
to the writing of his history of Soviet Russia with its dual fascination of
"other worldness" and capacity for planned social change. As a journalist, he had been denounced in the House of Lords as "an active danger,"
and in 1946 Sir Randolph Churchill had charged that Carr "had been
mainly responsible for *The Times* becoming, apart from the Communist
Daily Worker, the main British apologist for policies of the Kremlin."[2]
He had influenced the *Times* to support the Beveridge Report and postwar planning in Britain that resembled experiments in Soviet Russia.
Having been part of "the Riga School" (he was second secretary in Riga,
Latvia, from 1925 to 1929)—a school identified in the United States
with hard-line policies toward the Soviet Union—he was charged by
his critics as having led the *Times* to soft-line policies. (Carr has said
that this criticism was prevalent only in his last year at the *Times* as the
Cold War set in.)

Yet Carr's intellectual contribution ultimately will be judged less by
his journalism or his diplomacy than by his theoretical writings in international relations and his *History of Soviet Russia*. The latter, while
representing prodigious scholarship, is the more difficult to assess. Carr
as historian on Russia represents no clearly identifiable school of
thought. Reviewers note that he has written contemporary history on a
highly volatile subject, which is not yet sufficiently removed in time to
allow dispassionate scholarship. He has emphasized the broad economic,
social, and political aspects of the Russian Revolution without attempt-

2 Peter Scott, "Revolution Without the Passion: Peter Scott Talks to E. H. Carr Whose Epic
History of Soviet Russia Will be Completed This Autumn," *Times Education Supplement*, July 7,
1978, pp. 7–8.

ing much historical judgment of its more brutal and controversial aspects. His volumes, published over twenty-eight years, reflect the rise and fall of British attitudes toward the Soviet Union. (Carr acknowledged that he would approach the first volume differently if he were writing in 1980, putting less stress on constitutional arrangements and more on the social and economic environment in which the new Soviet state operated.) Thus his *History*, written from three to six decades after the revolution, stands as an ambiguous historical classic, marred by its lack of passion and historical imagination, too cautious in its moral judgments for some of his critics and too sympathetic toward collectivist social change for others, but accepted by all for its persistent scholarship on the first ten years of Soviet rule and for Carr's single-mindedness in exploring the actions of Soviet decision makers. More than any other historian, he sought to discover the forces that motivated Soviet leaders.

During his career Carr combined the professions of political scientist and historian with those of journalist and man of action. He joined the Foreign Office as temporary clerk in 1916. More than two decades later, while serving as assistant editor of the *Times*, he wrote anonymous editorials on the need for a better understanding of Russia and its role in the postwar world. Although frequently at odds with the prevailing approach of the British foreign policy establishment, he served on various study commissions; held diplomatic posts in Paris and Riga, Latvia; was assistant adviser on League of Nations affairs and first secretary to the Foreign Office; and served as director of foreign publicity in the British Ministry of Information. He wrote extensively on intellectual and diplomatic history of the nineteenth and twentieth centuries and on the philosophy of history. He contributed biographical studies of Mikhail Bakunin, Aleksandr Herzen, Feodor Dostoevski, and Georges Sorel; theoretical works on international politics; and the monumental ten-volume history of Soviet Russia, comparable to Theodor Mommsen's history of Rome.

Carr's major theoretical contribution to international studies has been to lay the foundations for political realism. His *Twenty Years' Crisis, 1919–1939* was published in 1940 as the rise of Hitler and the outbreak of World War II shattered the illusions of the interwar period. Expressing the euphoria of their era, statesmen such as Woodrow Wilson and William Howard Taft in the United States and Lord Robert Cecil in Great Britain had heralded the rise of new forms of international relationships that were modifying the ancient and destructive patterns of national rivalries and power politics. Intellectuals and scholars had dedicated themselves as much to the reform as to the study of the existing international system. This prompted Carr to assert that international studies were becoming encumbered by utopianism, half-truth, and ignorance. Foreign policies were judged by categories of good and evil; there were good nations and bad nations, good internationalism and bad nationalism. Labeled a heretic and a renegade by the prevailing establishment, Carr, as the editor of the *Ambassadors at Large* series, wrote in the introduction to the volume on France: "In international politics, few of us have got beyond the stage of the small child which says, 'you are naughty,' to anyone who does something it doesn't like; for the temptation to impute moral terpitude to policies which do not suit our interests is almost irresistible."[3]

Carr explained that *The Twenty Years' Crisis* was written "with the deliberate aim of counteracting the glaring and dangerous defect of nearly all thinking, both academic and popular, about international politics in English-speaking countries from 1919 to 1939—the almost total neglect of the factor of power."[4] In explaining such neglect, he concluded that the science of international politics was still in its infancy. Every science, Carr explained, passes first through a utopian phase in which purpose gives to analysis its initial impulse and direction. In the biological sciences, the desire for improved health led to the emergence of medical science; the need for roads and bridges ushered in the science of engineering. In this first phase, the element of wish or purpose is overwhelmingly strong and that of analysis of facts is weak or even nonexistent. For political science, the impulse in studying war comes from a desire to cure a profound illness of the body politic. Whereas the laboratory scientist is often several steps removed from the eradication of a disease and his emotions are irrelevant to his research, the political scientist is never far from the urgent social need that his

3 Wassily Comte d' Ormesson, *France*, introduction by E. H. Carr (London: Longmans, Green, 1939), iv.
4 E. H. Carr. *The Twenty Years' Crisis*, 1919–1939 (London: Macmillan, 1946), vii.

inquiry is intended to serve. Indeed, the ends of social research themselves become determining factors; for example, economists who seek to preserve or defend capitalism or Marxists, however "scientific," whose analysis of capitalism becomes inseparably joined with the goal of overthrowing it. The social position and the moral and political purpose of the observer inevitably shape and affect his research and give both meaning and direction to his analysis and interpretation.

In the second phase, realism in the social and political sciences succeeds utopianism. What *is* comes to be distinguished from what *should be*. Realism demands both the acceptance of facts and a search for their causes and consequences. By 1932 Winston S. Churchill had observed that never had the gap been so great between what statesmen said and what was actually happening. Carr undertook to diagnose and criticize utopianism. He found that its weakness lay in its proponents' attempts to carry over the principles of nineteenth-century liberal rationalist thought from homogeneous national societies to the current heterogeneous and half-anarchic international order. The League of Nations and other experiments in collective security were efforts to translate principles and institutions that had achieved relative success within particular nation-states into universal principles for the world of international affairs. Underlying these enterprises was the belief in a natural harmony of interest among nations, derived from the doctrines of laissez-faire economics in the nineteenth century. The passionate desire to eliminate war determined the first phase of international studies, and criticism of the means proposed to achieve it was branded mischievous or destructive. "The advocate of 'collective security,'" wrote Carr, "replied to the critic . . . by a statement that it must be made to work . . . or by a demand for some alternative nostrum."[5] The concept of a natural harmony of interests, fundamental to the idea of a community among nations, conflicts with the division of the world into satisfied and unsatisfied or "have" and "have-not" nations and the need for hard bargaining on conflicting interests. Both power and interest remain centered in independent sovereign nation-states. Conflicts result not only from a failure of understanding among national leaders but also from the clash

5 *Ibid.*, 8.

of incompatible goals and aspirations, which can be accommodated not by a priori rational principles but only by compromise and diplomacy. International politics lacks objective and disinterested moral or legal standards for resolving conflicts.

Thoroughgoing realist though he appeared to be, Carr recognized that realism was not enough. He declared: "Consistent realism excludes four things which appear to be essential ingredients of all political thinking: a finite goal, an emotional appeal, a right of moral judgment, and a ground for action."[6] Utopian and realist thinking are both needed throughout history. They exist in dialectical relationship with one another, although the need for one or the other will be greater in a particular era. Having demolished the cornerstone of the utopianism of the interwar period, Carr acknowledged the necessity of a new international vision for the future. Such a vision must be free of illusions; he warned a young assistant lecturer: "I hope you will . . . steer clear of SUNDFED, ECOSOC and all those other horrors which have no substance in them."[7] Carr's vision for the period between the wars called for greater stress on the need for peaceful change among the defenders and foes of the status quo based on what was just and reasonable and reflecting shifts in international power relationships. Those who are the major beneficiaries of a particular status quo (France and England between the wars) must prepare themselves for sacrifice to the less-satisfied powers. A successful foreign policy, therefore, must oscillate between the poles of force and appeasement. The Munich Settlement of 1938 represented changes in both the distribution of power within the European balance of power and justice expressed in the principle of national self-determination. Critics noted that Carr's general principle which called for relating power and morality was unobjectionable but that its application to the Munich Settlement showed him surrendering to "the immanence of power." Carr had himself fallen victim to a relativistic conception of morality because of his concept that values are conditioned by the power and status of the nations espousing them.

Carr followed his major theoretical work, *The Twenty Years' Crisis*,

---

6 *Ibid.*, 89.
7 C. Abramsky, *Essays in Honour of E. H. Carr* (London: Macmillan, 1974), 179.

with a more topical analysis of the international crisis, *Conditions of Peace* (1942). In it he again warned that the democracies were endeavoring to meet the world crisis with nineteenth-century ideas and institutions. The book was already in press when the attack on Pearl Harbor brought the United States into World War II. Germany and Japan were at the height of their power as Carr prepared the manuscript, and on its publication he added an explanatory note apologizing for the tentative nature of his policy conclusions. He had argued that Soviet Russia and Nazi Germany held the key to the future because they had virtually eliminated unemployment by instituting planned economies. The privileged status quo powers, with the possible exception of the United States, idealized the past while minimizing the advantages of a collectivist approach to economic problems. They suffered from a preoccupation with security and privilege and clung to laissez-faire capitalism and national self-determination, whereas the Germans and the Russians were striving to build a world of larger units under centralized planning and control. Hitler, whom Carr depicted as a twentieth-century Napoleon, "consummated the work, which Marx and Lenin had begun of overthrowing the nineteenth century capitalist system." Carr prophesied that, even if Hitler were overthrown, nineteenth-century German capitalism could not be restored any more than feudalism after the downfall of Napoleon. The idealists of the English-speaking world courted disaster by placing themselves "in opposition to the new world revolution which first broke through the crust of the existing order in the Bolshevik Revolution of 1917."[8]

When the peace settlement of 1919 increased the number of weak and struggling states in the name of national self-determination and left the economic order of Central and Eastern Europe in an enfeebled state, the victorious Allies in effect had lost the peace. It was beside the point to argue that the Versailles Treaty was too vindictive or not vindictive enough. Soviet Russia and Nazi Germany won the peace because their leaders understood the contemporary revolution and made giant strides toward recovery through economic planning; the victors remained helpless spectators and prisoners to nineteenth-century thinking. Political

8 E. H. Carr, *Conditions of Peace* (New York: Macmillan, 1942), 9, 10.

parties in the democratic countries represented powerful established interests; the will of the unorganized majority remained impotent against the might of organized economic power. Democracy's survival depended on the redefinition and reinterpretation of the majority's rights and the discovery of a common moral purpose powerful enough to generate self-sacrifice by the strong in the interests of the weak. Communism, much as had Christianity, discovered its ground for action and its finite goal in a higher purpose: "The cooperation between the Western peoples and Soviet Russia in the war should help to resolve the antithesis, incidental rather than fundamental, between the secular ideals of Christianity and those of Communism."[9] Carr hoped that the democracies might profit from the lessons of communism's moral and economic successes.

In *Nationalism and After* (1945), Carr examined the far-reaching changes between nineteenth- and twentieth-century nationalism, principally the extension of political participation within nations to include new social groups, the visible reunion of economic and political power, and the beginnings of a vast proliferation ultimately quadrupling the number of nation-states following the war. He warned of the bankruptcy of nationalism resulting from the carnage of two world wars and the coming obsolescence of the nation-state no longer able autonomously to provide military security or economic well-being to its citizens. A new international order was necessary to transcend the destructive consequences of rampant national self-determination, but it could not be established by constitutional design. It must rest instead on some new enterprise or common effort such as the worldwide quest for social justice, which meant for Carr equality of opportunity, freedom from want, and full employment. Although acknowledging the unlikelihood of worldwide cooperation, he found that the best means of achieving these goals lay in large multinational and regional groupings and joint planning on programs of full employment or assistance to developing areas. In the aftermath of the age of nationalism, European cooperation for social justice, with British participation, might offer an alternative, Carr suggested, to the Soviet ideology of state monopoly and the American ideology of unrestricted cooperation.

9 *Ibid.*, 121.

In *The Soviet Impact on the Western World* (1947) and *A History of Soviet Russia* (1950–1978), Carr studied explicitly the Soviet challenge to the West. In his biography of Karl Marx, he described his subject as "the protagonist and the forerunner of the whole twentieth century revolution of thought." Reflecting certain continuing Marxist presuppositions, he declared in *The Soviet Impact on the Western World*: "The missionary role which had been filled in the First World War by American democracy and Woodrow Wilson had passed in the Second World War to Soviet democracy and Marshal Stalin." Soviet democracy was an outgrowth of Western democracy. Just as the Cromwellian and Jacobin dictatorships had given birth to political democracy, the Soviet dictatorship of Nikolai Lenin and Joseph Stalin and the Russian proletariat had created social democracy. The first impact of Soviet democracy on the West was to stimulate concern for "the common man"—a challenge "western democrats will be well-advised to ponder." The achievements of the Soviet planned economy helped prepare the ground for Keynesian economics in the West. In foreign policy, the Soviets openly acknowledged the power factor as the determinant of policy, freed of the ideological disguises of League of Nations statesmen. They also perfected the use of propaganda as a normal instrument of foreign policy. However, Carr looked elsewhere for the impact of the Soviet challenge: "The gravamen of the Marxist revolution is . . . that it has called in question the moral authority of the ideals and principles of western democracy by declaring them to be a reflexion of a privileged class." The age of individualism from 1500 to 1900 is drawing to a close, representing little more than an oasis between the totalitarianism of the medieval church and empire and the modern collectivist societies. Two world wars, revolutions around the globe, and far-reaching social and economic upheavals have altered the moral climate and convinced "all but the blind and the incurable that the forces of individualism have somehow lost their potency and their relevance in the contemporary world." The nature of the Soviet threat, therefore, is predominantly moral, not military. "Security is and will remain" the primary factor in the Soviet policy toward Europe. "Nothing in the Russian tradition supports a policy of military action in Europe beyond the eastern zone," which is "for the Soviet Union today what the Monroe Doctrine is for the United States, the

Low Countries for Great Britain, or the Rhine frontier for France." A far more important and likely threat is the penetration of the West by ideas from the East: "The danger for the English-speaking world lies . . . in its relative lack of flexibility and in its tendency to rest on the laurels of past achievements" rather than in its searching "for new forms of social and economic action in which what is valid in individualist and democratic tradition can be applied to the problems of mass civilization."[10]

The question now remains: What will be the enduring value of Carr's contribution? Any answer must be tentative at this stage. By demolishing utopian beliefs in the natural harmony of interests of states, Carr was among the first to restructure the study of international politics in the name of political realism. Making use of the intellectual tools of the sociology of knowledge, he demonstrated the connection between national values and ideals and the interests and power of states. His claim has remained valid that the resolution of international disputes is more likely through hard bargaining that recognizes conflicting national interests than through international processes analogous to national judicial or legislative actions. (Carr's analogy of great power negotiations with collective bargaining in industry is more debatable, given the absence of moral consensus in international relations.) The defects of his contribution to these issues arise more from polemical overstatements than from untruth. His critical analysis of the limitations of Western political thought continues to have value. His history of the Bolshevik Revolution helps explain the actions and motives of Soviet leaders and the wellsprings of Soviet policy.

The following question remains, however: How could Carr have gone so grievously astray in his practical judgments in the interwar and postwar periods. For he found in Neville Chamberlain the exemplar of the moral realist and in the Munich Settlement the paradigm of a political agreement based on principle and power. He linked Hitler and Mussolini as leaders in the revolt against liberal democracy uncritically with Mustapha Kemal, Jozef Pilsudski, and Antonio Salazar. He was not hesitant to make moral distinctions between Wilson and Stalin or be-

10 E. H. Carr, *Karl Marx: A Study in Fanaticism* (London: J. M. Dent, 1934), 302; E. H. Carr, *The Soviet Impact on the Western World* (New York: Macmillan, 1947), 3, 19, 94, 107, 108, 111, 113.

tween American democracy and what he called "Soviet democracy." He could write: "There is . . . no essential incompatibility between democracy and dictatorship."[11] These errors in judgment appear not accidental but rooted in a more fundamental weakness in his political philosophy.

Four explanations are possible for the shortcomings of Carr's philosophy, and all four have roots in the apparent philosophical weakness of his approach. First, his Marxist orientation drove him in the spirit of Georg Hegel and Karl Marx to search for values within and not outside the historical process (he once remarked that he was more truly Marxian than those uncritical and dogmatic Marxists who asked no questions of their ideology). He lacked an objective basis for practical moral judgments. Second, and related to the first explanation, he appears repeatedly to have equated superior morality with superior power. Moral reasoning became for him, not a weighing of good and evil or of competing goods, but exclusively the means for "an escape from the logical consequences of realism."[12] With this weakness in mind, critics have questioned whether he lacks an understanding of the essential nature of morality. Third, Carr, who relied on the inspiration of Reinhold Niebuhr in other respects, has little to say about proximate morality and provides few examples of prudential judgments of contending political movements. (Niebuhr, in contrast with Carr, wrote in the early 1940s that if men could not make discriminate moral judgments between democracy and Nazism, then moral evaluation of any type was in practice impossible.) Fourth, although Carr affirmed the need for a standard of judgment in politics, he developed no transcendent point of view from which to appraise the phenomenon of power. In *What Is History?* he searched for a philosophy of history to supply such a viewpoint but concluded that there is no possibility of discovering an objective standard outside history. The closest approximation for him is to state:

> The absolute in history is not something in the past from which we start; it is not something in the present since all present thinking is necessarily relative. It is still incomplete and in process of becoming—something in the future toward which we move, which begins to take shape only as we

11 Carr, *The Soviet Impact on the Western World*, 11.
12 E. H. Carr, *The Moral Foundations for World Order* (Denver, Colo.: University of Denver Press, 1948), 118.

move towards it, and in the light of which, as we move forward, we gradually shape our interpretation of the past.[13]

If Carr intends to offer this definition as his clearest formulation of an objective standard, he must clarify whether he means that the only basis for judging history is history itself and therefore what survives in history is *ipso facto* good. It is a question by which earlier historians have been judged and found wanting. One critic of Carr concludes: "It is a dangerous thing to be a Machiavelli. It is a disastrous thing to be a Machiavelli without *virtù*."[14]

To this Carr has responded that certain moral absolutes do exist: liberty and equality, justice and democracy. However, as broad categories of thought, they are almost devoid of meaning and impossible to apply unless given specific content. They are blank checks, valueless without a designation of the amount of liberty and its recipients or an indication of who are recognized as equals. History records how a people fill in such checks. These values as defined in the nineteenth century were undermined in World War I. After that war, which revealed the bankruptcy of liberalism, Carr has argued that only one of two responses was possible: the establishment of socialism or the establishment of conservatism. He opted for socialism, in part because he is a man of the left and in part because socialism represented the optimism of change; and he has staunchly arrayed himself against those who find change menacing and the source of doubt, gloom, and fear. At eighty-six years of age, he declared:

> When Sir Lewis Namier warns me to eschew programmes and ideals, and Professor Oakeshott tells me that we are going nowhere in particular, and Professor Popper wants to keep the dear old Model T on the road by dint of a little piecemeal engineering, and Professor Trevor-Roper knocks screaming radicals on the nose, I shall look out on a world in tumult and a world in travail, and shall answer in the well-worn words of a great scientist: "And yet—it moves."[15]

13 E. H. Carr, *What is History?* (New York: Alfred Knopf, 1961), 161.
14 Hans J. Morgenthau, *Politics in the Twentieth Century: Vol. III, The Restoration of American Politics* (Chicago: University of Chicago Press, 1962), 43.
15 Scott, "Revolution Without the Passion," 7–8.

E. H. CARR

WORKS BY E. H. CARR

1931

Dostoevsky. Boston: Houghton Mifflin.

1933

The Romantic Exiles. Boston: Beacon Press.

1934

Karl Marx: A Study in Fanaticism. London: J. M. Dent.

1937

International Relations Since the Peace Treaties. London: Macmillan.

Michael Bakunin. London: Macmillan.

1939

The Twenty Years' Crisis, 1919–1939. London: Macmillan. 2nd ed., 1946.

1942

Conditions of Peace. New York: Macmillan.

1945

Nationalism and After. New York: Macmillan.

1947

The Soviet Impact on the Western World. New York: Macmillan.

1948

The Moral Foundations for World Order. Denver, Colo.: University of Denver Press.

1950–1978

A History of Soviet Russia. 10 vols. London: Macmillan.

1950

Studies in Revolution. London: Macmillan.

1951

The New Society. London: Macmillan.

1961

What Is History? New York: Alfred Knopf.

WORKS ABOUT E. H. CARR

Abramsky, C., ed. *Essays in Honour of E. H. Carr.* London: Macmillan, 1974.

Bull, Hedley. "The Twenty Years' Crisis Thirty Years On." *International Journal,* XXIV (Autumn, 1969), 625–38.

Deutscher, Isaac. *Heretics and Renegades.* London: Hamish Hamilton, 1955.

Johnston, Whittle. "E. H. Carr's Theory of International Relations: A Critique." *Journal of Politics,* XXIV (November, 1967), 861–84.

Morgenthau, Hans J. *Politics in the Twentieth Century: Vol. III, The Restoration of American Politics.* Chicago: University of Chicago Press, 1962.

Ormesson, Wassily Comte d'. *France.* Introduction by E. H. Carr. Ambassador at Large Series, edited by E. H. Carr. London: Longmans, Green, 1939.

Scott, Peter. "Revolution Without the Passion: Peter Scott Talks to E. H. Carr Whose Epic History of Soviet Russia Will Be Completed This Autumn." *Times Education Supplement,* July 7, 1978, pp. 7–8.

HANS J. MORGENTHAU (1904–)

Principles of Political Realism

Hans J. Morgenthau was born in Coburg, a small town in central Germany, now part of northern Bavaria. The ruler of the duchy was a grandson of Queen Victoria known for his public display of German nationalism and later for his support of Hitler's anti-Semitism. As a schoolboy during World War I and its aftermath, Morgenthau witnessed the defeat of a powerful and confident German army, the flight of the leaders of the imperial government, and their replacement by a Weimar regime, which lacked a sense of power and a broad political base and was supported primarily by the working class and the bourgeoisie.

Because the war ended with no foreign troops on German soil, the enemies of Weimar claimed that Germany had been defeated by a "stab in the back." First the former ruling class (the most influential group in a community like Coburg) and then the Nazis alleged that Germany had not actually lost the war but had been undermined by traitors from within, such as the trade unions, socialists, Jews, Catholics, liberals, and Freemasons. The Nazi party, founded in 1919, turned this legend into a powerful propaganda instrument. For the young Morgenthau, the Weimar era taught him the importance of political power and its interplay with swiftly moving currents of violence and irrationalism in politics. The German people needed a scapegoat to account for military defeat and rampant inflation; they found this in the Jews. Morgenthau remembered his mother (whom he adored) going to the market with a basketful of paper money and his physician father preferring to accept butter, eggs, chickens, or textiles rather than worthless money in return for his services. He learned early that a government must be able to govern, which includes the ability to maintain economic stability.

As an only child, Morgenthau suffered from profound loneliness and frequent illness caused or aggravated by family circumstances. His father was tyrannical and authoritarian, his mother warm and highly intelligent. The father discouraged his son's attendance at the premier University of Berlin, saying: "You are out of your mind. You'll never get in. Go to a lesser school instead." The father's influence helped to create in the son an inferiority complex, a fear of being rejected, and an undisguised shyness that he has carried with him throughout his life. His students were later to observe that no professor was more actively involved in advancing their future but that, paradoxically, none appeared more reserved, indifferent, and detached.

Morgenthau's commitment to the creation of a homeland for the Jews and in particular the opinions expressed in his later writings strongly supporting Israel's quest for security also go back to his formative years. He remembered having been spit upon while marching in the German equivalent of the American Boy Scouts, being denied admission to an upper-class fraternity in a classical gymnasium, and being ridiculed and ostracized when he graduated first in his class and spoke at a founders' day ceremony celebrating the crowning of the duke of Coburg. On this day, as he marched to the ceremony, people shook their fists and shouted imprecations and anti-Semitic insults. When he made his presentation, the duke and the other nobility held their noses, signifying that all Jews smelled bad. For the young boy, this was the worst day in his life.

Morgenthau began advanced studies in 1923 at the University of Frankfurt, where he remained only briefly before transferring to the University of Munich. His professors at both institutions included learned men but not internationally recognized scholars. At first philosophy and literature dominated his intellectual interests. (His interest in literature, discouraged by his father, was a harbinger of his lifelong preference for the concrete in history.) His aspirations were to become a writer, perhaps a professor, and possibly a poet. In September, 1923, he wrote as a senior gymnasium student: "My hopes for the future move in two directions. I hope for the lifting of the pressure to which I am exposed by the social environment, and I hope to find a direction and purpose for my future activities. The latter cannot be realized before the former is fulfilled." In this essay he went on to observe that his relationship to the environment was determined by three facts: he was a German, he was a Jew, and he had matured following World War I. He resolved not to play the role of suffering martyr but to oppose the pressures of anti-Semitism, which, he asserted, shattered all foundations of morality: "The stronger the pressure from outside becomes, the more violent and one-sided will be my reaction to this movement." He saw himself as approaching a choice between two activities—either amassing riches or serving a higher cause. As a guide to the choice he must make, he quoted a passage from Johann von Goethe's autobiography, *Poetry and Truth*: "Our desires are presentiments of the abilities that lie within ourselves. . . . We feel a longing for what we already possess in silence. . . . If such a direction is decisively presented by our nature, every step in our development fulfills a part of the original desire."[1]

His early studies in philosophy were a disappointment except for the writings of Benedetto Croce. The young student was repulsed by the pedantry of minute epistemological distinctions, which included even the dissection of individual sentences in philosophical writings. So he moved to the University of Munich and the study of law and came under the influence of two outstanding teachers: Heinrich Wölfflin, an art historian who had founded a school of aesthetics, and Hermann Oncken, a diplomatic historian who discussed the relationships between history and personalities and lectured on Bismarck and nineteenth-century foreign and military policy. Looking back, Morgenthau wrote in *Fragment of an Intellectual Autobiography,* 1904–1932: "For the first time, I felt the impact of a coherent system of thought, primarily a distillation of Bismarck's *Realpolitik*, that . . . [supported] my isolated and impressionistic judgments on contemporary issues of foreign policy." He was also introduced at Munich to Max Weber's political and social philosophy by Professor Karl Rothenbücher and later wrote: "Weber was everything most of his colleagues pretended to be but were not . . . a passionate observer [as a citizen] of the political scene and a frustrated participant in it, as a scholar . . . [viewing] politics without passion . . . [or] political purpose beyond the intellectual one of understand-

1 Kenneth W. Thompson and Robert J. Myers (eds.), *Truth and Tragedy: A Tribute to Hans Morgenthau* (Washington, D. C.: New Republic Book Co., 1977), 1, 2, 3–4.

ing."[2] Weber became for Morgenthau the model of the political scientist.

Two other schools of thought had largely negative influences on Morgenthau—Marxism and psychoanalysis. Marxism had attracted many younger intellectuals as an instrument for hastening the disintegration of an unjust postwar society and rebuilding it on more equitable foundations. Its focal point in Germany was the Institut für Sozialforschung at the University of Frankfurt. Although Morgenthau acknowledged a limited indebtedness to Marxian sociology, he was repelled, as the Nazi enemy stood at the gate, by Marxian hairsplitting and the pedantry of the frequent searches for the true meaning of phrases, clauses, and sentences. Listening to Karl Mannheim appealing for "free-floating intelligence" against the Nazis, Morgenthau understood Marx's declaration to his son-in-law: "Moi, je ne suis pas Marxiste." As for psychoanalysis, he had no doubt that Sigmund Freud, like Karl Marx, had opened new vistas of human understanding. At one time Morgenthau even tried to construct a theoretical system of politics based on Freudian concepts and insights. He abandoned the effort, however, and never published the results: "What defeats a psychoanalytical theory of politics is what has defeated a Marxist theory of politics: the impossibility of accounting for complexities of political experience with the simplicities of a reductionist theory, economic or psychological."[3]

Morgenthau pursued postgraduate work at the Graduate Institute of International Studies in Geneva, was admitted to the bar, and served as acting president of the labor law court in Frankfurt. From 1932 to 1935, he taught public law at the University of Geneva. Due to Hitler's rise in 1933, he did not return to Germany but taught in Madrid from 1935 to 1936. He came to the United States the following year, without friends or sponsors. Through his persistence and intellectual vitality, he obtained successive faculty appointments at Brooklyn College (1937–1939), the University of Kansas City (1939–1943), the University of Chicago (1943–1971), the City College of New York (1968–1975), and the New School for Social Research in New York (1975–).

2 *Ibid.*, 6, 7.
3 *Ibid.*, 4.

Morgenthau's influence on the study of international politics derives from his dual emphasis on philosophy and politics. His first major work, *Scientific Man vs. Power Politics* (1946), is an original and forceful criticism of the social, political, and moral philosophy of modern Western thought and its consequences for political life. Refering to the rise and fall of the Roman Empire, he traced the crises of the first half of the twentieth century and the general decay in political thought reflected in "the belief in the power of science to solve all problems and, more particularly, all political problems." Although pessimistic about the future and especially about the failures of liberalism and influenced by Reinhold Niebuhr, Morgenthau called for a renewal of faith in "those intellectual and moral faculties of man to which alone the problems of the social world will yield."[4] The study also challenged the scientific approach to politics, prevalent in the United States since *New Aspects of Politics* (1924) by Charles E. Merriam. When Professor Leonard White, a supporter of Merriam and Morgenthau's chairman at the University of Chicago, read *Scientific Man vs. Power Politics*, he suggested that Morgenthau teach a course in administrative law to put *him* back on the right track. At Chicago, Morgenthau contended with an intellectual atmosphere in political science that was hostile to philosophy (the dominant interest of the Chicago department was public administration and international law). His main encouragement came from the university's top leadership, particularly Robert M. Hutchins; a few of his younger colleagues; and most of all from his students, who entered his classes with skepticism and generally left with enduring respect for his approach. The empiricists and behaviorists saw in him a threat to their generously endowed research, and the severest critics of President Hutchins (whose own neo-Thomism and world government crusade later caused a breach with Morgenthau) opposed Morgenthau's devotion to philosophy.

By 1948, with the publication of his epoch-making text, *Politics Among Nations*, criticism of his work was redirected at his definition and concept of politics. The subtitle described his purpose as an inquiry into

---

4 Hans J. Morgenthau, *Scientific Man vs. Power Politics* (Chicago: University of Chicago Press, 1946), vi.

The Struggle for Power and Peace, and in it he wrote: "Whatever the ultimate aims of international politics, power is always the immediate aim. The struggle for power is universal in time and space and is an undeniable fact of experience."[5] It would be difficult today to imagine the concern and alarm triggered by this formulation. Power politics at the time was a questionable and controversial phrase at the University of Chicago. It epitomized the evil that world government and public administration were to eradicate so that people could live in a civilized world. American political theorists condemned Morgenthau's "Germanic way of looking at things." Practical politicians, whose popularity depended on their apparent support of less ignoble ends than power, were quick to dissociate themselves, publicly at least, from his definition of politics.

Ironically, critics overlooked Morgenthau's early emphasis on the limitations and proper use of power, its integral relation to national purpose and the constraints of national interest. They also overlooked his extended analysis of international morality and the role of ethics, mores, and laws. He wrote, "From the Bible to the ethics and constitutional arrangements of modern democracy, the main functions of these normative systems has been to keep aspirations for power within socially tolerable bounds." In his first comprehensive treatise on American foreign policy, *In Defense of the National Interest* (1951), he identified as a fundamental error the view that moral principles and the national interest were opposing forces. He insisted: "The choice is not between moral principles and the national interest, devoid of moral dignity, but between one set of moral principles divorced from political reality, and another set of moral principles derived from political reality."[6] He called on Americans to relearn the principles of statecraft and political morality that had guided the founding fathers and had continued, often in moralistic disguise, through the first century of the republic's existence.

Writing prolifically on American foreign policy, Morgenthau continued to examine, test, and apply his central principles of power, interest, and morality. In *The Purpose of American Politics* (1960), he wrote: "In

---

5 Hans J. Morgenthau, *Politics Among Nations* (1st ed.; New York: Alfred Knopf, 1948), 13, 17.
6 *Ibid.*, 169; Hans J. Morgenthau, *In Defense of the National Interest* (New York: Alfred Knopf, 1951), 33.

order to be worthy of our lasting sympathy, a nation must pursue its interests for the sake of a transcendent purpose that gives meaning to the day-to-day operations of its foreign policy."[7] Such moral principles must be applied in the international environment with realism, prudence, and full regard to their political consequences. Military and economic power were not to be employed to serve diverse, universal, humanitarian missions but must be measured against the imperatives of the national interest. He warned against letting fear of communism too strongly influence foreign policy and maintained that indiscriminate anticommunism could not provide the basis for sound policies. In writing about specific foreign-policy problems, including *Vietnam and the United States* (1965), *A New Foreign Policy for the United States* (1969), and *Truth and Power* (1970),[8] he criticized a crusading foreign policy based on moral abstractions and the transfer to Asia and the Third World of those American policies employed with relative success in Europe.

By the mid-1960s he had become America's main critic of the Vietnam War. He based his criticism on a principle enunciated in *Politics Among Nations*: countries should never put themselves in a position from which they cannot retreat without a loss of face and from which they cannot advance without undue risk. He engaged in public debates with such American officials as national security advisors McGeorge Bundy and Zbigniew Brzezinski. He entered the public arena reluctantly, for he tended to agree with J. Robert Oppenheimer's warning: if in politics a man tries at the same time to be both actor and observer, he will fail in both respects. Whatever Morgenthau may himself have written about the limitations of the philosopher in politics, he undertook to defy it in practice. An extraordinarily successful classroom teacher, he sought to make the Congress, successive administrations, and every available public an extended classroom. In his worldwide travels, he was as unsparing of himself as the ancient prophets and as unyielding in denouncing what he considered false teachings and prevailing nostrums.

It is difficult to measure Morgenthau's influence. Writers such as

---

7 Hans J. Morgenthau, *The Purpose of American Politics* (New York: Alfred Knopf, 1960), 8.
8 These and all works by Hans J. Morgenthau are listed chronologically, with full publication data, beginning on p. 90 herein.

Raymond Aron have pointed to his tragic failure in reshaping American foreign policy. His impact has been greatest in influencing foreign policy principles, rather than tactics or day-to-day decisions. By the 1970s, however, no responsible leader in American public life dared to speak scornfully of the need to consider the national interest in formulating American foreign policy. No secretary of state could pretend that the world was rid of international rivalries or power politics. No liberal journalist could ignore the counterforces of nationalism and internationalism. It would be an exaggeration to claim that Morgenthau was alone in his teachings, but it is difficult to conceive of realist principles being as powerfully communicated without his clear and fearless voice. In two respects, at least, he has realized his mission. First, he successfully discovered a cause that would survive him and justify his moral and intellectual journey—a search that he began as an eighteen-year-old. Second, he held firm to a goal he himself has best described:

> Our aspirations, molding our expectations, take account of what we would like the empirical world to look like rather than what it actually is. Thus endlessly, empirical reality denies the validity of our aspirations and expectations. . . . We expect the oracle to give us a clearcut answer. What we get is an enigma compounding the riddle. What remains is a searching mind, conscious of itself and of the world, seeing, hearing, feeling, thinking, and speaking—seeking ultimate reality beyond illusion.[9]

The focus of Morgenthau's search is the relation between power or national interest and morality. His aim has been to interpret to Americans an ancient tradition. He brought to the United States an understanding of the classic problems of power and foreign policy derived from the European experience. From Frederick the Great, who on his first Sunday as king of Prussia appealed for toleration of the Jews and Huguenots, Morgenthau gained a cosmopolitan perspective, as well as an understanding of the realities of power. From German and Greek thought, he learned that the first duty of a state was to defend itself and that only then was it possible to talk of law (Plato). Diplomacy had to be linked with power if international stability and harmony were to be achieved (Frederick the Great). The resulting principle was what came

9 Thompson and Myers, *Truth and Tragedy*, 16–17.

to be called the primacy of foreign policy, associated by Bismarck with the tradition of political restraint. Frederick the Great was the symbol of an aristocratic internationalism in which statesmen viewed the world through the spectacles of supranational culture. Bismarck inherited the controlling views of this tradition but saw that Prussia's state interests lay in being a moderate state with policies of restraint and tolerance, dictated both by moral principle and political necessity.

These traditions were part of Morgenthau's philosophy of international relations, which he brought to the United States. He discovered that Americans were ignoring the ideas of national interest and the primacy of foreign policy. Insulated from great power struggles in Europe by a fortuitous geographic position and the shield of the British navy, Americans had been able to think of international law and morality freed from the constraints of power politics. This favored position was changing, however, and Morgenthau arrived just as the United States entered an era of world leadership in which it could no longer escape the pressures of international politics. Americans were beginning to recognize that they were living in a world in which they were subject to the power and influence of others, whom they in turn could influence. Power was not only the basis for a successful American foreign policy but the means of international stability and harmony. Not only were interests a criterion of foreign policy, but in international relations national interests conflicted or converged. Only through diplomacy could they be compromised and accommodated. When conflicts arose, policy makers were required to go beyond the immediate problem to create a new framework in which adjustments could be made or interests reformulated.

Morgenthau contributed a new set of ideas about foreign policy, attuned to the changing scene. He translated certain traditional European ideas to fit the American experience and formulated them in useful terms. He continued to rethink and restate these ideas to accord with the realities of American democracy, which he accepted and praised, particularly in his later writings. His achievement was the more remarkable because he celebrated the uniqueness of American ideas and institutions at the same time that he defended without compromise what he called the iron law of international politics.

Throughout his writings, he continued to express another principle drawn from Greco-Roman and Judeo-Christian thought, namely that all human actions are limited by moral judgment. He explored the changing role of moral limitations on action and the effectiveness of rules that expressed a belief in the sanctity of human life in war and peace. He pointed to moral improvements and moral decline. The Hague Conventions had distinguished between combatants and non-combatants in war; but obliteration bombing in World War II, first by the Germans over Coventry and Warsaw and thereafter by all belligerents, invalidated this distinction. The relationship between morality and international politics, Morgenthau asserted, is influenced by technological factors but also by time and culture. Moral principles for nation-states are filtered through cultural and social circumstances leading to different applications of apparently universal moral principles.

This approach to morality and foreign policy has most recently focused on the question of human rights. Morgenthau has posed two questions regarding human rights: To what extent is a nation entitled and obligated to impose its principles on other nations? To what extent is it morally justifiable and intellectually tenable to apply certain concepts of human rights to others? He has called attention to the unique and extraordinary protection of human rights in the United States and to the relative absence of such safeguards on the continent of Africa, for example. He has also questioned America's current demand that the rest of mankind accept the American abstract political and moral tradition. The public campaign for human rights by the Carter administration, Morgenthau has argued, is not in the earlier American tradition, which offered our experience to the rest of the world as an example. Woodrow Wilson broke from this earlier tradition by calling on nation-states and the rest of the world to accept American democracy.

Morgenthau's objection to the Wilsonian version of morality and foreign policy and to President Jimmy Carter's campaign for universal human rights is twofold: (1) a universal acceptance of human rights will prove impossible to enforce, and (2) the United States as a great power with manifold interests throughout the world (some more important than human rights) will be unable consistently to pursue a human rights policy. We can and should tell the Soviet Union that its treatment of minorities is contrary to the Declaration of Human Rights, but private channels are more likely to prove effective. It is inconceivable to Morganthau that leaders of the Soviet Union will not consider persistent public pressure by its principal moral and political adversary as a threat to the survival of its present political system.

Human rights represents for Morgenthau, not an atypical situation, but a general example of the connection between morality and foreign policy. All people are moral and social because they are human beings, and all try in varying ways to realize moral principles. In so doing, they face contradictions and logical and moral difficulties. In every great political and moral contest, each party claims to speak and act for God, but God cannot be for and against the same thing. The sole test for statesmen seeking what is morally and politically right is Lincoln's test: to study the plain physical facts of a problem, to ascertain what is possible, and to seek to learn what is wise and just.

In citing Lincoln's test as a guide to statecraft, Morgenthau offered what he has followed throughout his personal life. I have known no one more determined to do what is right and just, no one who has struggled as fearlessly and unendingly to ascertain the right course of conduct. Throughout his life, he has confronted the world essentially alone, yet he never grew bitter. He challenged the established approaches and overthrew the cherished idolatries of American intellectual life and persisted in his search for truth. He was unbelievably generous to his friends and magnanimous to his intellectual and personal adversaries. I can say with Walter Lippmann, he was indeed the most moral man I ever knew.

WORKS BY HANS J. MORGENTHAU

1946

Scientific Man vs. Power Politics. Chicago: University of Chicago Press.

1948

Politics Among Nations. New York: Alfred Knopf. 5th ed., 1978.

1951

In Defense of the National Interest. New York: Alfred Knopf.

Principles and Problems of International Politics. With Kenneth W. Thompson. New York: Alfred Knopf.

1958

Dilemmas of Politics. Chicago: University of Chicago Press.

1960

The Purpose of American Politics. New York: Alfred Knopf.

1962

Politics in the Twentieth Century. 3 vols. Chicago: University of Chicago Press.

1965

Vietnam and the United States. Washington, D. C.: Public Affairs Press.

1969

A New Foreign Policy for the United States. New York: F. A. Praeger, for the Council on Foreign Relations.

1970

Truth and Power. New York: F. A. Praeger.

1972

Science: Servant or Master? New York: New American Library.

1977

Truth and Tragedy: A Tribute to Hans Morgenthau. Edited by Kenneth W. Thompson and Robert J. Myers. Washington, D. C.: New Republic Book Co.

NICHOLAS J. SPYKMAN (1893–1943)

Geography and Power

Nicholas J. Spykman was born in Amsterdam, Holland, on October 13, 1893. He came to the United States in 1920 as a student and earned a bachelor's degree (1921), master's degree (1921), and a doctorate (1923) from the University of California. He had been a young journalist in the Near East from 1913 to 1916, in the Middle East from 1916 to 1919, and in the Far East from 1919 to 1920. He was an instructor in political science and sociology at the University of California from 1923 to 1925 before going to Yale in 1925. In 1935 he became chairman of Yale's Department of International Relations and director of the Yale Institute of International Studies, positions he held until 1940. His early publications were concentrated in the field of sociology and included *The Social Theory of George Simmel*, but his later works fell broadly under geopolitics and international theory. Few scholars in international relations have had a greater impact on their students. In the brief space of forty-nine years (he died on June 26, 1943), he elaborated a view of power politics and national interest that has profoundly affected American thinking.

Spykman did as much as any scholar of his generation to ground international thought in political realities. He called his approach geopolitics: "The fact that certain writers have distorted the meaning of the term geopolitics is no valid reason for condemning its method and material. It is, actually, an appropriate name for a type of analysis and a body of data which are indispensable to the process of reaching intelligent decisions on certain aspects of foreign policy."[1] He dissociated himself from Karl Haushofer and his adherents since the advocacy of policy

---

1 Nicholas J. Spykman, *The Geography of the Peace*, edited by Helen R. Nicholl (New York: Harcourt, Brace, 1944), 7.

is not a scientific endeavor. It was on this point that the German school was led astray: Hitler used geopolitics to justify his policies.

Spykman saw geography as the prime conditioning factor in foreign policy, but he warned that not everything—from the fourth symphony to the fourth dimension—could be explained in geographic terms. The position a state occupied in the world and its relationship to other centers of power defined its problem of security. To assure its position, a nation had to make the preservation and improvement of its security a primary objective. For his candor Spykman was attacked as being excessively cynical and obsessed with *realpolitik*. He replied: "Power has a bad name and the use of power is often condemned. . . . There is a tendency, especially among certain liberals and many who call themselves idealists, to believe that the subject of power in the international world should not be spoken of except in terms of moral disapproval." But, he concluded: "Political ideals and visions unsupported by force appear to have little survival value."[2]

Spykman's major work was *America's Strategy in World Politics* (1942). Perhaps nowhere in the literature on international politics are the arguments about isolationism and internationalism traced more rigorously and systematically. Spykman perceived that the ingredients of these two policies were more constant and persistent than had been generally assumed, especially by those who maintained that the American people could rather easily be educated to an internationalist point of view. For example, he showed that isolationism had both its emotional as well as its strategic aspects. Emotionally, it appealed to immigrants and their families who had turned their backs on Europe and wanted to forget the Old World. Now that the wars and conflicts of the rest of the world had reached their new homeland, they sought refuge in the comforting doctrine that they need not bother about Europe. Moreover, they had inherited a foreign-policy perspective that was nearly two centuries old. When in the early part of the nineteenth century England asked the New World to intervene to redress the balance of power in Europe, when America was asked to participate in the two Moroccan and the Berlin conferences, and when senators debated membership in the

2 *Ibid.*, 3.

League of Nations, the controversy was whether the order and equilibrium of Europe and Asia constituted a vital American interest. Isolationists were prepared to expand their concept of an adequate zone of defense from the national domain to the Caribbean littoral or even to the whole Western Hemisphere. But Spykman found, even in the 1940s, the vestigial remains of the psychology of Fortress America reflected in certain attitudes to the European crisis.

The virtue and the detachment of Spykman's approach resulted from his understanding that the intellectual foundations of much of internationalist thought were no more adequate than those of isolationist thought. He argued that in successive crises the staunchest internationalists "have been those who were inspired by idealistic considerations. Some asked participation [in successive world crises] because they were pro-British; others because they believed that, in a period of ideological warfare, we had a moral obligation to support the people whose social and political structure most closely resembled our own."[3] But few were explicit that the first line of defense for the United States lies in preserving a balance of power in Europe and Asia, albeit the second line falls in the Western Hemisphere.

Spykman moved with rapier thrusts against a whole host of popular doctrines. In 1942 he announced: "Basically, the new order will not differ from the old, and international society will continue to operate with the same fundamental power patterns. It will be a world of power politics." To a nation seeking escape from the anguish of foreign policy, he gave this warning: "An equilibrium of forces inherently unstable, always shifting, always changing, is certainly not an ideal power pattern for international society. But while we can deplore its shortcomings, we shall do well to remember that it is an indispensable element for an international order based on independent states." In discussing collective security, which normally focuses on the definition of aggression, a world police force, and perhaps world government, he stated a more fundamental principle: "Whenever . . . pressures become unequal, boundaries will move. The problem of collective security is the problem

3 Nicholas J. Spykman, *America's Strategy in World Politics* (New York: Harcourt, Brace, 1942), 3–4.

of equalizing these pressures; and as long as that problem remains unsolved, the phenomenon of expansion as such will continue to appear." Despite all the talk of a brave new world, he warned: "History testifies to the constant reappearance of these expansion forms and the ever-recurring conflict patterns that result, and there seems to be no reason to assume or expect that these behavior patterns of states will suddenly change or disappear." This hardly meant, however, that American foreign policy should be enslaved by the past. "Not conformity with the past but workability in the present is the criterion of a sound policy. Not specifically selected instances in the history of the United States, but the general experience of states should be made the guide for a program of action."[4]

All this is worth mentioning for at least two reasons. First, the new approach to international relations, based on the general experiences of states, is today rather widely accepted in the study of international politics. More important, it appears that Spykman used his understanding of existing situations to anticipate the future. For example, in the 1940s, in the era of good feeling toward the Russians, he wrote: "A Russian state from the Urals to the North Sea can be no great improvement over a German state from the North Sea to the Urals." Even more daring, perhaps, was his statement during World War II: "Twice in one generation we have come to the aid of Great Britain in order that the small offshore island might not have to face a single gigantic state in control of the opposite coast of the mainland. If the balance of power in the Far East is to be preserved in the future . . . the United States will have to adopt a similar protective policy toward Japan." During an era of friendly Sino-American relations, he saw in a modern, vitalized, and militarized China of 450 million people "a threat, not only to Japan, but also to the position of the Western Powers." Nor did he comfort those who desired the total destruction of German power. In a statement labeled by one critic the most astonishing conclusion that could be imagined, Spykman insisted: "The present war effort is undoubtedly directed against the destruction of Hitler and the National Socialist Party, but this does not necessarily imply that it is directed at

4 *Ibid.*, 7.

the destruction of Germany as a military power."[5] He placed these predictions in a consistently rational context by adding that the charm of power politics is that one need never grow weary of one's friends. Thus there is in Spykman at least a touch of the quality of political prophecy associated with the wisest philosophers in Western civilization, who saw the future in the light of a more general conception of man and politics. His approach to political realities had a solid European base, and he used his European background to help Americans understand their national responsibility.

WORKS BY NICHOLAS J. SPYKMAN

1919

Hindia Zelfbestwir, bahasa Belanda dan Melajoe. Batavia: G. Kolff.

1925

The Social Theory of George Simmel. Chicago: University of Chicago Press.

1942

America's Strategy in World Politics. New York: Harcourt, Brace.

1944

The Geography of the Peace. Edited posthumously by Helen R. Nicholl. New York: Harcourt, Brace.

5 *Ibid.*, 460.

ARNOLD WOLFERS (1892–1968)

Conceptualizing and Consensus

Arnold Wolfers was born in Gallen, Switzerland, on June 14, 1892, the son of Otto and Clara Wolfers. His educational background included studies in law at universities in Zurich, Lausanne, Munich, and Berlin and studies in economics and political science at Zurich and Berlin. He was admitted to the bar in Switzerland in 1917, practiced law in St. Gallen from 1917 to 1919, was a lecturer in political science at the Hochschule für Politik in Berlin from 1924 to 1930, and was its director from 1930 to 1933. He fulfilled the military service requirement in Switzerland as a first lieutenant from 1917 to 1919. His early publications in Europe were *Die Verwaltungsorgane der Aktiengesellschaft* (1917), *Amerikanische und Deutsche Loehne* (1930), and *Das Kartellproblem* (1931). His career was to span four momentous decades and two continents; his contributions to international thought reflected the breadth of his experience and the depth of his commitments to European and American cultures.

Wolfers received a doctor of law degree from the University of Zurich in 1917 graduating *summa cum laude*, a doctorate from the University of Giessen in 1924, and honorary degrees from Mt. Holyoke College and the University of Rochester. When he died on July 16, 1968, he was buried in his native Switzerland in Sils Baseglia in Engadin. During his lifetime, he often visited Switzerland and Germany and retained close ties with prominent governmental and university leaders in both countries.

Wolfers migrated to the United States in 1933 and almost immediately took an academic post as visiting professor (1933–1935) and professor (1935–1957) at Yale University, where he remained for twenty-four years. He served the government, primarily in an advisory capacity, in wartime and the early Cold War years. During World War II, he

97

was a consultant to the Office of the Provost Marshal General and the Office of Strategic Services and later to the National War College, the Institute of Defense Analysis, the Department of the Army, and the Department of State. He made his mark as a political historian. However, with his aristocratic manners tempered by social concerns, he held a succession of advisory posts that brought him close to the centers of power in Washington.

An assessment of Wolfers' thought is more difficult than that of writers such as Herbert Butterfield, E. H. Carr, or Hans Morgenthau because his theories were less clear-cut and unambiguous, more eclectic and many-sided. He commended himself to a wide diversity of scholars. He dedicated *Discord and Collaboration* to the memory of Professor Spykman, "admired friend and colleague." As Sterling Professor of International Relations, he continued Spykman's pioneering work in international politics, although he supported the understanding of power politics in less forceful and emphatic language than had Spykman. He let it be known that he could not accept Spykman's assertion that the "statesman can concern himself with values of justice, fairness and tolerance only to the extent that they contribute to or do not interfere with the power objective."[1] Although President Whitney Griswold, himself a historian, was outspokenly critical of the newfangled approach to international studies of Frederick S. Dunn and Klaus Knorr in the Yale Institute of International Studies, he found Wolfers more acceptable because of his historical orientation. Yet behaviorally oriented writers, such as Lucian W. Pye, Harold K. Jacobson, Roger Hilsman, and David S. McLellan, contributed essays to a festschrift honoring Wolfers at the end of his career. He was more sympathetic to scientific studies than were the uncompromising critics of political behaviorism, and he encouraged students to read such behaviorists as Robert Dahl and Karl Deutsch. He was supportive of game theory, simulation, and quantitative political science research. It is noteworthy that the move to orient the Yale department to behaviorism began when Wolfers was Sterling Professor.

1 Roger Hilsman and Robert C. Good (eds.), *Foreign Policy in the Sixties: The Issues and the Instruments* (Baltimore: Johns Hopkins University Press, 1965), xii.

Wolfers appeared to Reinhold Niebuhr more as a political philosopher than a political scientist. Niebuhr wrote: "He is a 'philosopher' in that he scrutinizes and weighs the validity of various theories, concepts and presuppositions and discusses the larger patterns of international relations. But as any good philosopher, he is also a scientist in the sense that empirically ascertained facts serve him as the final criteria for the adequacy of general concepts or for the validity of general suppositions." Beyond history and philosophy, Wolfers was also concerned with policy. As Niebuhr put it: "The issues discussed by Dr. Wolfers are by no means 'academic.' They go to the heart of many of the burning problems of contemporary foreign relations."[2] He devoted the last eleven years of his life to organizing and directing the Washington Center of Foreign Policy Research, an affiliate of the School for Advanced International Studies of Johns Hopkins University, in cooperation with Paul H. Nitze, the former director of the policy planning staff of the Department of State. His former students summarized his contribution in this way: "Arnold Wolfers has excelled in making theory relevant to policy and in making the analysis of policy yield insights that further refine theory."[3] He combined the theoretical genius of Europe with the pragmatic genius of America and managed to hold fast to both.

Wolfers' first and quite possibly his most important book was *Britain and France Between Two Wars* (1940). Its subtitle described its content: *Conflicting Strategies of Peace from Versailles to World War II*. In his acknowledgments, Wolfers wrote: "To my friend, Mr. Nicholas J. Spykman, I owe a debt of warm gratitude for his penetrating and careful criticism . . . his unfailing advice, and valuable suggestions." Spykman's influence on Wolfers was more apparent in this classic study than in any of Wolfers' subsequent writings. In *Britain and France Between Two Wars*, he offered a diagnosis of the interwar period that was sharply at variance with most other American writings, which had used the failures of the League of Nations and of America's rejection of the League to explain the disastrous events leading to World War II. Wolfers counteracted these views by analyzing conflicting national policies:

2 Arnold Wolfers, *Discord and Collaboration: Essays on International Politics* (Baltimore: Johns Hopkins University Press, 1962), viii.
3 Hilsman and Good, *Foreign Policy in the Sixties*, xi.

"There is no great power inside or outside of Europe that did not add to the troubles. . . . The Soviet Union by its efforts to undermine the social order of Western Europe, Japan by starting a new era of imperialistic expansion, the United States by a sudden reversal of policy from active participation . . . to political isolation and finally each of the European states in countless fashions. . . . [Yet] when the post-war settlements collapsed and Europe was again plunged into war it was British and French policies, more than any others, that went down to defeat."[4]

The two countries most directly concerned had agreed on the ultimate goals of preserving the peace and resisting the revolt of the dissatisfied powers but had disagreed on how to achieve these goals. France saw the answer in a policy of *securité* and a buildup of power against Germany. The British strategy called for a removal of the causes of revolt and continuous adjustments in the terms of the peace settlement. Complicating the picture was a third approach, the Wilsonian strategy dedicated to collective security and the establishment of democratic regimes in Central Europe. Together with Britain, France, and the United States, these Central European countries were to form a league of democratic states to bring security and justice to all. A triangular dispute over means to preserve the peace resulted. Although Wolfers did not ignore the role of the United States, he chose to focus on the two divergent peace strategies of Britain and France, which worked at cross-purposes and in the end canceled out rather than reinforced one another. Reflecting Spykman's influence, Wolfers attributed their differences primarily to their unique geographical positions and their proximity to Germany. France was preoccupied, if not obsessed, with the German threat to its security if German power exceeded the limits prescribed by the Versailles Treaty. Britain, which was more remote, was prepared to see Germany strengthen itself to improve the balance of power in Europe and to prevent a political explosion of the have-not nations. Germany made Anglo-French unity more difficult by challenging the territorial status quo by expansionist policies in the East, rather than in the West. France viewed the independence of Austria and the

4 Arnold Wolfers, *Britain and France Between Two Wars* (New York: Harcourt, Brace, 1940), 3, 4.

territorial integrity of Poland and Czechoslovakia as a vital national interest, but for Britain the East was the ideal location for making concessions to Germany. Only the advocates of collective security in Britain agreed with the French about Poland and Czechoslovakia, but their approach was in Wolfers' view "of purely academical interest. That any nation would risk sacrificing for the sake of the League what it believed to be necessary in its national interest was hardly probable."[5]

The basic question in the interwar period (Wolfers prophesied that it would also be the basic question after World War II) was how to hold Germany's power—its territory, armaments, and economic influence—below the maximum level that would make it a threat to other European countries but above the minimum level necessary to prevent German resentment and revolt, which would threaten the stability of Europe.

> Only if France, Britain, and Germany can agree on a level for German power somewhere between these two limits is there any chance of a lasting settlement. . . . Experience suggests one and only one way to do this. It bears the name of "balance of power." The difference between the old balance . . . and that of the future lies only in the fact that instead of balancing the others all of Britain's weight must now be put into the scales. . . . Some people may be disappointed to think that Europe may have to go on with the dangerous game of balancing power. But such critics, if they are free of illusions, should find every other solution even more distasteful. As long as there are many great sovereign powers in Europe, a balance of power is the only available alternative to the domination of one nation or of one group of nations over the others.[6]

After World War II, Wolfers continued his writings on foreign policy and the quest for peace. In April, 1945, he published an essay, "Conflict and Compromise at San Francisco," in the Memorandum Series of the Yale Institute. He divided the participants at the United Nations Conference on International Organization into the Big Three, France, and the lesser powers and warned: "The careful work of reaching a compromise between the big powers, started at Dumbarton Oaks and completed at Yalta, may have to be undone if the lesser powers, new-

5 *Ibid.*, 384–85.
6 *Ibid.*, 389–90.

comers to the negotiations, are to obtain any satisfaction of their demands."[7] He analyzed the bargaining power of the participants and outlined the controversial issues, including the permanent membership in the United Nations Security Council for the great powers, peaceful change versus the sanctity of territorial settlements (which had proved so fateful after Versailles), and the relation of regionalism and alliances to the new international security organization. On all these issues, Wolfers insisted that Britain and the United States should play the role of honest broker at San Francisco. The United States in its bargaining should not give the impression that it would be willing to pay any price to avoid the failure of the conference. In Wolfers' essay on the founding of the United Nations, his policy recommendations appear less important than his orientation and perspective. Wolfers viewed the emerging United Nations in the light of the foreign policies of its prospective member states, just as he had discussed the League of Nations in the classic *Britain and France Between Two Wars*. In both instances, the Yale professor was ahead of his time; the majority of his contemporaries preferred to consider the United Nations in institutional and structural terms and neglected the analysis of foreign policies and their effect on peace. Wolfers' singular contribution must be attributed at least in part to the European tradition that had shaped his thought.

In 1950 the Yale Institute published another memorandum by Arnold Wolfers, "West Germany—Protectorate or Ally?" The memorandum was based on a study mission, in which he had enjoyed the cooperation of both high-ranking American and German authorities. During this time, the threat of a resurgent Germany, which at first had appeared remote, was increased by the strong rivalry between East and West. The Soviet Union was likely to attempt someday to draw all of Germany into its sphere. Wolfers argued that American policy should not aim at the elimination of German power but at making Germany a trustworthy partner of the Western world. He compared the prospects of the Bonn Republic in the 1950s after World War II with those of the Weimar Republic in the 1920s after World War I and found the situation of the

---

7 Arnold Wolfers, "Conflict and Compromise at San Francisco," Memorandum number 16 (New Haven, Conn.: Yale Institute of International Studies, April 24, 1945), 1.

Bonn Republic more favorable. He praised the Konrad Adenauer regime and refuted the criticisms of the postwar German government by American journalists. He questioned the success of denazification and argued that "the time has come to put an end to any effort at democratization which we would not be willing and able to apply in any country at present politically associated with us." On the question of disarmament versus the rearmament of Germany, he favored the latter: "German rearmament within the limits set for all European countries may have become a matter of timing—with the chances being that not much time can be wasted." Wolfers was proposing a transformation of the present American protectorate over West Germany into a full-fledged alliance: "She would be permitted to arm to the limits set by a common strategic plan to which she had agreed." The present High Commission would continue "until an Allied-German partnership for common defense has been established under the North Atlantic Pact."[8] The need to reinforce European defenses, which Wolfers found pitifully inadequate, required that Germany's military strength be thrown into the balance.

Whatever the reasons for Wolfers' position in 1950, the record makes clear that he had altered his views. In 1947 he had argued: "The creation of a single Germany, united politically as well as economically, is a *sine qua non* of any Allied agreement. . . . Despite the risks involved in such unification . . . the establishment of a united Germany represents the lesser of two evils. . . . Prohibition of German armaments, military and economic, coupled with an international control of the Ruhr industries offers the greatest chance of success."[9] Nevertheless, it seems clear that he favored German rearmament in 1950 and opposed the delays and the uncertainty that would have followed any attempt (which in the end might have failed) to bring about a reduction of Allied and Soviet forces in West and East Germany as part of an overall political settlement.

In his 1950 memorandum on West Germany, Wolfers clearly asso-

8 Arnold Wolfers, "West Germany—Protectorate or Ally?" Memorandum number 35 (New Haven, Conn.: Yale Institute of International Studies, August 30, 1950), 39, 40, 49.
9 Arnold Wolfers, "United States Policy Toward Germany," Memorandum number 20 (New Haven, Conn.: Yale Institute of International Studies, February 21, 1947), 28.

ciated himself with the American political and military establishment and signaled his fundamental disagreement with political realists like Walter Lippmann, George F. Kennan, and Hans J. Morgenthau and with his predecessor, Nicholas Spykman. The political realists prided themselves on maintaining almost complete independence from the foreign policy elite, which often limited their influence on policy. Wolfers by comparison appeared to have had an insatiable yearning for the corridors of power. (I observed this firsthand when he visited me—a junior officer at the Rockefeller Foundation—and, as we concluded our talks, asked each time to see the president, Dean Rusk.) If Morgenthau and Kennan were too independent of power holders, Wolfers may have sought their presence too often.

In 1956 he coedited with his student Laurence W. Martin a book of readings on *The Anglo-American Tradition in Foreign Affairs*. In 1959 he and members of the research staff of the Washington Center of Foreign Policy Research edited and wrote the center's first major study, *Alliance Policy in the Cold War*. He described alliance policy as "all efforts to prevent other countries from siding with the camp of the Soviet opponent." The book was a Cold War treatise. In the spirit of the times, he pointed to the threat inherent in the growth of Sino-Soviet power (he gave no evidence of anticipating the rift between the two Communist powers). He described American responsibility as located at the hub of a wheel with spokes leading to friends and allies spread out along the rim, each occupying the end of a spoke. Danger to any ally at the end of a spoke would be communicated to the United States at the hub, but its strong defensive reactions were unlikely to be matched by countries located on opposite spokes or remote sections of the rim. Asian allies of the West feared too much concentration of American effort on the Europe section of the rim, and vice versa. This was the persistent problem of America's alliance system. Americans are sometimes chided for their hysteria to the Soviet threat, but Wolfers observed that "Turkey is closer to the United States than to Denmark, Taiwan closer to the United States than to Pakistan."[10] America at the center of the wheel, alone

---

10 Arnold Wolfers *et al.*, *Alliance Policy in the Cold War* (Baltimore: Johns Hopkins University Press, 1959), 2, 8.

among the powers, had responsibility for conflicts that might arise on the periphery and move to the center. That the United States might be cast in the role of world policeman to the neglect of its vital interests based on this concept seemingly did not occur to Wolfers and his colleagues at the Washington center. In addition, the difficulties and complexities of Vietnam and Korea were not foreshadowed in the book.

In 1962 Wolfers published a collection of his essays in *Discord and Collaboration*, an important treatise on international theory, beginning with "The Actors in International Politics" and including an essay on "Political Theory and International Relations." (The student who wishes to compare Wolfers' outlook with Martin Wight's should read this latter essay alongside Wight's "Why Is There No International Theory?") This work provides a panoramic view of international theorizing from decision making to reason of state. No other book illustrates more specifically Wolfers' determination to synthesize European and American thought. Thus he wrote:

> A comprehensive theory does not call for a division of international politics into two compartments, one comprising the realm of the state as the actor in power politics [the European perspective], the other the realm of the human actors, the masses of common men with their psychological traits and their pursuit of human purposes [the American way]. Instead, all events occurring in the international arena must be conceived of and understood from two angles simultaneously: one calling for concentration on the behavior of states as organized bodies of men, the other calling for concentration on human beings upon whose psychological reactions the behavior credited to states ultimately rests.[11]

Other writers who brought the European tradition and perspective to the study of American foreign policy undertook, as we have seen, to translate and adapt it to fit the American scene. Wolfers sought to synthesize the two traditions.

Wolfers' effort made his work more congenial to an important segment of the American intellectual community; but it gave to the main body of his theoretical writings a more tentative, somewhat uncertain, and less definitive quality than that of other writers. In his later writ-

11 Wolfers, *Discord and Collaboration*, 9.

ings, Wolfers appears to be engaged in a continuing debate with himself and with the two traditions he sought to reconcile. Thus in an essay published two years before his death he wrote: "There is no serious quarrel about the principle that national governments shall be guided in their policies by the national interest." But he continued: "What is controversial and frequently disputed is what constitutes the national interest or the national interests of a given nation at a given time." To satisfy the criteria of the two traditions, Wolfers both asserted the reality of the national interest (a characteristic of European writings) and questioned its identification with interest and power, citing the book by Thomas Cook and Malcolm Moos, *Power Through Purpose*, which had criticized the European perspective. Having reviewed the two viewpoints, Wolfers concluded in language not too dissimilar from traditional national interest thought: "That the protection against military attack of the American homeland, or more properly of the North American continent, should figure among these vital interests, presumably topping the list, has only rarely been questioned."[12] It is difficult to recognize the differences between such a conclusion and those of the political realists whom Wolfers periodically took pains to criticize.

Whatever the ultimate judgment may be of Arnold Wolfers and his work, he provides an alternative approach to that of other European-American writers. For his students, he "was an early realist . . . and the discomforter of those well-intentioned but idealistic writers who did so much to shape (and distort) the study of international relations in the years following World War I." At the same time, he was "always too close to the real world of statecraft to become a dogmatist—was never a Realpolitiker." Wolfers in this light, "while acutely aware of the statesman's responsibility to the nation's interest, has rightly been impressed with how ambiguous are the definitions of the content of interest and has correctly discerned that the policies of state in fact run the spectrum from the pole of power acquisition to the pole of relative power indifference." He rejected the distinctions that others made between individual and international morality and affirmed "that the na-

---

12 Arnold Wolfers, "Disarmament, Peacekeeping and the National Interest," in *The United States in a Disarmed World* (Baltimore: Johns Hopkins University Press, 1966), 3, 19; Thomas Cook and Malcolm Moos, *Power Through Purpose* (Baltimore: Johns Hopkins University Press, 1962).

ture of man's moral response to critical problems is determined more by the context of amity and enmity in which the problem presents itself than whether the individual acts as an individual or as a custodian for the welfare of his state."[13]

At the end of his career, Wolfers left behind a group of devoted students who were the equal of those of any other professor of international relations—men such as Robert C. Good, Roger Hilsman, Harold Jacobson, Laurence W. Martin, David S. McLellan, Lucian Pye, Richard Sterling, and W. Howard Wriggins. No one can doubt that his lifelong struggle to bring about a synthesis of European and American thought stimulated and inspired this impressive group of younger scholars. Each was to set out on his own independent intellectual journey, but all have paid tribute to the professor who introduced them to the institutions, instruments, and ideas of world politics. If Wolfers paid a price by assimilating his views with the more dominant American tradition, he would no doubt justify his course by the quality of younger thinkers whose uniquely American perspective he nurtured and fostered. By adjusting his European perspective, he had a more direct impact on actual American foreign policy than any other European-American thinker.

WORKS BY ARNOLD WOLFERS

1940

Britain and France Between Two Wars: Conflicting Strategies of Peace from Versailles to World War II. New York: Harcourt, Brace.

1943

The Small Powers and the Enforcement of Peace. New Haven, Conn.: Yale Institute of International Studies.

1945

"Conflict and Compromise at San Francisco." Memorandum number 16. New Haven, Conn.: Yale Institute of International Studies.

1947

"United States Policy Toward Germany." Memorandum number 20. New Haven, Conn.: Yale Institute of International Studies.

1950

"West Germany—Protectorate or Ally?" Memorandum number 35. New Haven, Conn.: Yale Institute of International Studies.

1956

The Anglo-American Tradition in Foreign Affairs: Readings from Thomas More to Woodrow

13 Hilsman and Good, *Foreign Policy in the Sixties*, xi, xii.

Wilson. Edited by Arnold Wolfers and Laurence W. Martin. New Haven, Conn.: Yale University Press.

1959

Alliance Policy in the Cold War. Baltimore: Johns Hopkins University Press.

1962

Discord and Collaboration: Essays on International Politics. Baltimore: Johns Hopkins University Press.

1965

Foreign Policy in the Sixties: The Issues and the Instruments. Essays in honor of Arnold Wolfers. Edited by Roger Hilsman and Robert C. Good. Baltimore: Johns Hopkins University Press.

1966

The United States in a Disarmed World: A Study of the United States Outline for General and Complete Disarmament. Baltimore: Johns Hopkins University Press.

JOHN H. HERZ (1908–)

Reconciling Realism and Idealism

John H. Herz was born in Dusseldorf, Germany, in 1908 and was educated at the University of Cologne where he earned his doctorate in public law. Like other distinguished German scholars who fled Nazism—some stopping to study or teach at educational centers in neutral Switzerland or in Spain—Herz migrated to the United States via Switzerland before World War II. He was a wartime member of the staff of the Office of Strategic Services and the State Department, joining other German refugees who were to become authoritative scholars on Germany and German politics after the war. He taught first at Howard University and subsequently at Columbia, the New School for Social Research, and the Fletcher School of Law and Diplomacy. His permanent academic position was to be as professor of political science at the City College of New York with responsibility for the doctoral program at the graduate center of the City University of New York. Throughout his career, he has maintained close ties with German universities through research and teaching at the University of Marburg and the Free University of Berlin. His publications on Germany and Europe include *Major Foreign Powers* (1952), *The Government of Germany* (1972), and *Government and Politics in the Twentieth Century* (3rd ed., 1973,).[1] He also conducted research for certain government-financed research centers and held a Fulbright professorship in Germany. In pursuing his research and writing, he collaborated with Gwendolen M. Carter, a pioneering political scientist in the area of African governments and politics.

Long before it became fashionable to connect domestic or national and international politics, Herz was writing in this vein. His collabo-

---

1 This and all works by John H. Herz are listed chronologically, with full publication information, beginning on p. 113 herein.

rative texts in comparative politics were better known to undergraduate students than his more general writings on international politics. The eclectic character of his approach made him acceptable to scholarly journals with widely divergent methodological and philosophical positions (for example, Herz is one of the very few self-acknowledged political realists who has been invited to contribute to *World Politics*). By reconciling such apparently incompatible political theories as political realism and political idealism, he has tempered the sharp divisions between traditionally opposing intellectual positions.

At the same time, Herz must be included among the small group of European-American scholars who have played a decisive role in the emerging study of international politics in the United States. His importance is less easily defined than that of Hans J. Morgenthau, Karl Deutsch, and Arnold Wolfers (with whom he associates himself in a lengthy autobiographical introduction to *The Nation-State and the Crisis of World Politics*). Because of the breadth of his interests, he is often counted as a scholar of comparative government, rather than as a writer on international politics (his writings on international politics are more limited than those of Morgenthau or Deutsch).

If Herz had devoted himself unreservedly to international politics, his stature as a major figure almost certainly would have been proportionately greater. However, more than half of his writings fall within the field of comparative politics, and he is coeditor of the journal *Comparative Politics*. His formative educational background in Germany and at the Geneva Graduate Institute of International Studies was in law not politics, and his mentor was Hans Kelsen, founder of the "pure theory of law." The rise of Hitler was a brutal awakening for the young Herz to the role of power in international affairs. His first book on *The National Socialist Doctrine of International Law* (published under a pseudonym in 1938) warned of the deception of National Socialist party writings in obscuring the warlike intentions of early Nazism. Herz's disillusionment with the world had its origins in the failure of collective security, the destruction of socialism in Russia on the anvil of Stalinism, and the triumph in Germany of Nazi totalitarianism.

Yet Herz's disappointments failed to obliterate the inborn idealism and indestructible romanticism that have characterized all his subsequent writings. In the first essay of *The Nation-State and the Crisis of World Politics*, entitled "Power Politics and World Organization," he delineated the "in-between system," which mediated between the anarchy of power and an unrealizable world government. His continuing blend of realism and idealism was expressed in the seminal work *Political Realism and Political Idealism: A Study in Theories and Realities* (1951), written in the interwar period. Its significance lies more in the value of certain original political concepts (for example, the security-power dilemma) than in his political prescience (he acknowledged his failure to foresee the emergence of a bipolar world or the creation of nuclear weapons). His second classic work, *International Politics in the Atomic Age* (1959), not only remedied the deficiencies of the first book in describing postwar realities but added new concepts; for example, the "impenetrability" of the territorial state and in the Cold War the postwar blocs of "client" and "satellite" states. He also described the strategies of nuclear deterrence used to avert the threat of nuclear annihilation. Taken together these two books of the 1950s brought Herz prominence as a master thinker in international politics.

Yet Herz's lasting influence as a theorist has been somewhat marred by three limiting factors. First, he represents, as he has said, the lonely individual scholar at work in his private intellectual laboratory, seldom if ever interacting with other theorists including those who share his commitments and to whom he may even be indebted. Second, the evolution of his thought reflects this tendency to embrace utopian liberal attitudes (he once described himself as a liberal realist), not self-critically or dialectically as did Reinhold Niebuhr but with his own brand of romantic enthusiasm. Third, Herz's capacity to adjust his thinking to new realities is both a strength and a limitation.

Herz spent the first part of his career studying collective security and problems of the nuclear age as they affect the rise and demise of the territorial state. His later works discuss science and technology and the acceleration of developments in all fields of international relations. Not only has his attention shifted to the problems of food and population, environmental and resource depletion, and "survival ethics" (rather consistently overlooked by most political realists), but he brings the power of a *kulturkritik* and humanist to these vital areas. He postulates that a "minimum ethic of survival" must supersede past reflections on individual or group ethical standards from historic international politics. Yet he despairs over the malfunctioning of the nation-state system and the obstacles to implementing survival ethics in most foreign policy decisions, especially in the United States. America's survival is threatened by its internal division into two societies—the active society and the inactive society (the latter comprising an underclass substantially on welfare)—and by wasteful consumerism and selfish domination by the establishment. The haunting specter of democracy losing out to "benign authoritarianism" or to a "friendly fascism" sweeps over him in the post-Vietnam era. He is concerned with the "power surplus" of the great powers, their shortsighted compromises with popular demands for nuclear and industrial supremacy, and mankind's unwillingness to contemplate without wincing the possibility of the end of civilization (he calls for reflection on the "ethics of a decent demise" or preparing for an exit from survival).

Herz's intellectual journey is a chronicle of the liberal realist responding to successive crises. His path starts with his search for a logical system of norms, progresses to his insights on the nature of states (their impermeability and currently their penetrability) and the complexities of nuclear foreign policies, and leads to his study of the accelerating rush of mankind through a multitude of threats to survival. Although he began as a determined legal idealist, he ends as a despairing and anguished romanticist desperately clinging to René Dubois' axiom, "Trend is not Destiny." If Herz's radical transformation of norms, attitudes, and policies is impossible, mankind may indeed have no future. It may also be true that he has increased the demands he places on foreign policy and has broadened the agenda of political realism in his later writings. The respectful critic cannot help but ask if Herz's despair, as his lofty visions fail one by one, is the result of his having abandoned the essence of political realism. Or does his latter-day worldview, with its stress on worldwide forces of decay, foretell the probable end of civilization? It may be fair to suggest that if Herz were to give his planetary humanism more concreteness and as a liberal realist design a steady incremental path for men and nations to follow in feeding themselves, holding down population growth, and keeping environmental deterioration in check he might even at this late hour help people understand more clearly how to move from where they are to where he would have them go.

Yet no one can doubt that Herz has made a lasting contribution through his independent thought and his unique version of a European-American perspective. More than some of the scholars who have migrated to the United States from Europe, Herz has been willing to shift the focus of his research in response to changing world problems. He has expanded or revised the dominant themes of his study as new and unforeseen problems have appeared. Although he has modified his views on the importance of power or national interest as he has perceived changes in the international political system, he has resisted the attraction of new methodologies for approaching international politics and has retained the time-honored traditions of political history and political and legal theory.

The test of Herz's importance may be that he has exercised a significant influence on international thought despite his position as a solitary individual thinker. He founded no school of thought, attracted no devoted followers, and taught for a considerable period in an institution less famous for its graduate program. Yet scholars have taken Herz's theories seriously and have praised the quality and originality of his writing.

WORKS BY JOHN H. HERZ

1938

Die volkerrechtslehere des national sozialismus. Zurich: Europa-verlag. Pseudonym, Edward Bristler.

1951

Political Realism and Political Idealism: A Study in Theories and Realities. Chicago: University of Chicago Press.

1952

Major Foreign Powers: The Governments of Great Britain, France, the Soviet Union and Germany. With Gwendolyn Carter and John C. Ranney. New York: Harcourt, Brace.

1959

International Politics in the Atomic Age. New York: Columbia University Press.

1961

Government and Politics in the Twentieth Century. With Gwendolyn Carter. London: Thames & Hudson. 3rd ed., 1973.

1972

The Government of Germany. New York: Harcourt, Brace.

1976

The Nation-State and the Crisis of World Politics: Essays on International Politics in the 20th Century. New York: David McKay.

KARL WOLFGANG DEUTSCH (1912–)

Scientific Approaches to Politics

Karl Deutsch was born on July 21, 1912, in Prague, Czechoslovakia, the son of Martin and Maria Deutsch. He was educated at the German University of Prague, from which he received the J.U.C. degree in 1934. He pursued his advanced studies at Charles University in Prague and was awarded the J.U.D. degree in 1938 before fleeing Czechoslovakia to escape Hitler's imperialism. Arriving in the United States, he entered Harvard University's government department, from which he earned the master's degree in 1941 and the doctorate in 1951. Concurrent with his doctoral studies at Harvard, he began his distinguished teaching career at Massachusetts Institute of Technology, first as an instructor from 1942 to 1952 and then as professor of political science from 1952 to 1958. Both at Harvard and at MIT, he impressed colleagues and students with his wide-ranging interests and intellectual versatility in all the social sciences. From 1952 to 1967, he was professor of political science at Yale University. He became professor of government at Harvard in 1967 and Stanfield Professor of International Peace in 1971. He lectured extensively at the several American war staff colleges and was visiting professor at the University of Heidelberg in 1960; at Nuffield College, Oxford, in 1962; at Goethe University in Frankfurt, Germany, in 1968; at the University of Geneva in 1970–1971 and 1971–1972; at the University of Mannheim in 1971; and at the University of Paris in 1973. He was a fellow at the Center for Advanced Study in the Behavioral Sciences in 1956–1957.

Although Deutsch has made his most lasting contribution as one of the founders of the scientific study of American politics and of international politics, he has refused to accept the role of the cloistered scholar. Few political scientists have been more active in the national and international communities of scholars. From 1965 to 1966, he was president

114

of the New England Political Science Association. In 1969 he was elected president of the American Political Science Association; and in 1970, vice-president and thereafter president of the International Political Science Association. He was a member of the National Research Council and the National Academy of Sciences from 1969 to 1970. Few American political scientists have gained greater recognition in the wider scientific community. His knowledge of the several branches of the natural sciences is encyclopedic. Whenever the leading professional associations in the physical sciences have undertaken to collaborate with social scientists, they have turned to Deutsch. He has been a tireless spokesman for the cause of the behavioral social sciences and has demonstrated singular ability to work at the junctures of social and natural sciences. At the same time, Deutsch has been on call for assignments by the Department of State as an American specialist in India in 1962, Germany in 1964 and 1967, and Czechoslovakia and Poland in 1967. To all these tasks he has brought prodigious intellectual energy and physical stamina, whether in Cambridge, Washington, Tokyo, or Rio de Janeiro.

The graduate of a rather traditional government department at Harvard, at home in the historic political science literature, Deutsch has mastered the corpus of knowledge in fields far removed from conventional political science. His pioneering study of *Nationalism and Social Communication* (1953) was a bold new inquiry into the foundations of nationality.[1] Deutsch posed the question of "why nationalist ideas met with wide response at certain times and places, and with almost no response at others." He asked why economic growth sometimes led to national unification but at other times to national diversity. Long before the topic attracted widespread concern, Deutsch examined the impact of ethnic nationality on governments and reviewed the efforts of leading social scientists to account for the structure and development of nationalism, the resources of the various social sciences for such studies, and their implications for the understanding of political power and the dependence of political power on social communications. "Have the events

---

1 This and all works by Karl W. Deutsch are listed chronologically, with full publication data, beginning on p. 123 herein.

of the last few decades tended to unify the world, or have they split it more deeply than before?" he asked.[2] Have internationalism or nationalism, constitutionalism or revolution, tolerance or repression, peace or war been the dominant forces in the first half of the twentieth century? Deutsch's response was that no simple or single answer is possible to these questions but that the social sciences are capable of providing better answers than are yet available. Historians of nationalism and political philosophers have provided the theorists with a wealth of empirical data and techniques for understanding the qualitative dimensions of nationalism. What have been lacking are quantitative measurements and predictive statements.

The subject of nationalism has fallen between the boundaries of the independent social sciences—between linguists who write about national languages, geographers about national settlements, and economists about economic nationalism. New concepts are needed. Deutsch wrote: "If we can find a set of structural concepts in each specialized social science that has a bearing on nationalism and nationality, then we may consider whether these structural concepts from each special field fit together, in accordance with the structure of the single social reality with which all these disciplines are dealing." From sociology, Deutsch appropriated concepts of society, caste, and class; from geography, nuclear and modal areas; from linguistics, speech communities and densities of speech traffic; and from economics, markets and wealth as the aggregate of goods available for reallocation. He proposed that such concepts be joined in the study of concrete situations. To understand the prospects for national unity in a country such as Nigeria, he suggested a map of overlapping clusters representing settlement and traffic patterns, areas of language concentration, market areas for major commodities and services, and predominance of important classes or castes. He acknowledged that such a framework could not account for the successes or failures of particular leaders or political movements in building national unity, but it would give "a background of conditions and a measure of the difficulties under which such movements would have to labor."[3]

2 Karl W. Deutsch, *Nationalism and Social Communication* (Cambridge: Technology Press of the Massachusetts Institute of Technology; and New York: John Wiley, 1953), v, 1.
3 *Ibid.*, 3, 45.

In *Nationalism and Social Communication*, Deutsch drew on communications theory to define political power as "the capacity to preserve negative entropy in a limited positive entropy elsewhere." Power involves the ability to preserve some pattern or arrangement or to achieve a new arrangement of relative order. It preserves the inner structure of one of the systems in a clash at the price of causing large modifications in the conflicting systems: "Politics . . . consists in such production, use, and distribution of power as will prove compatible with social inclusiveness and growth beyond the narrow power field alone."[4] Deutsch found the hard-boiled definition of power too narrow and only partly true, for it ignores the factors that legitimize power.

Why has power thus far remained limited to ethnic, regional, or national units? The answer for Deutsch lies in the fact that power over men requires two things: "first, an assembly of an effective inner structure, an effective past, within the individual or group; and second, the assembly of means to carry into effect the implications of this inner structure, to impose them on institutions in the outside world." The inner source of political power in society depends on facilities for social communications—facilities for storing and disseminating memories and values. These facilities help to constitute a people as a community of social communications. Quantitative concepts can be applied to social, educational, and economic statistics to predict national assimilation and differentiation. A decisive factor is the process of social mobilization, which accompanies the growth of markets, industries, and towns and eventually the growth of literacy and mass communications. Nationalism, which has been strengthened by the Industrial Revolution, has tended to separate people; but at the same time it has prepared them for a more thoroughgoing, worldwide unity than any known in human history. A major barrier to such unity is the unevenness in social communications and national wealth. Deutsch concludes his study with this statement: "Not before the bottom of the barrel of the world's large peoples has been reached, not before inequality and insecurity will have become less extreme; not before the vast poverty of Asia and Africa will have been reduced substantially by industrialization, and by gains in living standards and in education—not before then will the age

---

4 *Ibid.*, 47, 48.

of nationalism and national diversity see the beginning of the end."[5]

In *Nationalism and Social Communication*, Deutsch foreshadowed what was to be a lifelong interest in political integration: *Political Community and the North Atlantic Area* (1957), *Nationalism and Its Alternatives* (1969), *Nationalism and National Development: An Interdisciplinary Bibliography* (1970), and *The Relevance of International Law* (1968). The main explorations in his intellectual journey have been the empirical, sociological, and communications routes for transcending present-day nationalism.

In *Political Community and the North Atlantic Area*, Deutsch and his collaborators looked at the historical experience of Germany, the Habsburg Empire, Norway and Sweden, the United Kingdom, and the United States for perspectives on the building of wider political communities. The work was sponsored by the Center for Research on World Political Institutions at Princeton, founded in 1950. In addition to separate monographs such as Robert A. Kann's *The Habsburg Empire: A Study in Integration and Disintegration*, the center, and especially Deutsch, has established comparative generalizations about political community. With Deutsch as the principal theoretician, the project was aimed at contributing to the elimination of war through the growth and expansion of political communities, especially in the North Atlantic area. Deutsch pointed out that war had been eliminated for all practical purposes over large areas, which he described as political communities— "social groups with a process of political communication, some machinery for enforcement, and some public habits of compliance." Not every political community has permanently eliminated war (even the United States suffered a tragic Civil War), but some have succeeded in achieving political integration through security-communities. Deutsch prophesied: "If the entire world were integrated as a security-community, wars would automatically be eliminated." He distinguished between communities in which amalgamation had occurred with the formal merger of two or more previously independent units into unitary or federal common governments (for example, the United States) and pluralistic security-communities in which separate governments retained

5 *Ibid.*, 49, 165.

their legal independence (for example, Canada and in terms of states' rights the United States). Knowledge of the process by which security-communities came into being should be helpful to planners and existing international organizations. "By integration we mean the attainment within a territory, of a sense of 'community' and of institutions and practices strong enough and widespread enough to assure for a 'long' time, dependable expectations of 'peaceful change' among its popula-tion."[6]

Deutsch chose to study the North Atlantic area to determine whether it constituted a community. He limited the area to countries geographi-cally situated on the North Atlantic Ocean or the North Sea or in the immediate hinterland. He examined certain widely held concepts of political integration, including beliefs that modern life with rapid trans-portation and mass communications make integration more likely. He noted: "Neither the study of our cases, nor a survey of more limited data from a large number of countries, has yielded any clearcut evidence to support this view." Deutsch found fewer cases of successful amalga-mation of two or more sovereign states as he approached modern times, and he questioned whether fear of anarchy or warfare had been a prin-cipal motive for political integration. Although he questioned certain popular views about political integration, he asserted that both amal-gamated security-communities and pluralistic security-communities had historically been pathways to integration. Pluralism (Canada and the United States) is of the two the more promising approach to inte-gration, since it is at least as effective in maintaining the peace as amal-gamated communities. The North Atlantic nations show less mutual responsiveness than needed for political integration, but Deutsch argued that social learning (more information and more contact) would speed the process. He also called for a greater range of mutual transactions, such as trade agreements, greater mobility of persons, and stronger links of social communications. On eight of the fourteen prerequisites for integration, the North Atlantic countries, except for Spain and Portu-gal, had forged bonds of unity. More functional experiments, such as

6 Karl W. Deutsch *et al.*, *Political Community and the North Atlantic Area* (Princeton, N.J.: Prince-ton University Press, 1957), 5.

the European Coal and Steel Community, would improve the prospects of integration. How would men know if the trends toward political integration were moving in positive directions? Deutsch undertook what he confessed was a rather crude quantitative analysis of the inter-country flow of various social transactions, such as trade and mail. On trade, he discovered that "Continental Western Europe . . . did not seem to form any obvious economic unit in terms of the flow of trade in 1952. . . . Rather, many of the main trade flows of its major countries continue to lead to the English-speaking world." With the flow of mail within the North Atlantic area, "the main ties are not among the large countries of continental Western Europe, but rather between these and the English-speaking world."[7] However, in the period studied, the links of postal correspondence among the Europeans were relatively stronger than were those of trade. The data, he acknowledged, were too frag-mentary to be decisive; but from his study he maintained that the den-sity of the web of transactions was greater in the North Atlantic area as a whole than in Western Europe. This suggests that the former was more integrated as a community than the latter.

Nationalism and Its Alternatives (1969) was written by Deutsch for the general reader rather than the social scientist. His analysis of nationalism began with the experience of Western Europe but extended to Eastern Europe and the Communist world, the developing countries, and re-gional federations. In each world area, the development of nationalism had been remarkably similar. That development, he explained, could be summed up as the process of relatively successful political integra-tion: "When several population clusters are united—through interven-ing settlements or through more roads, more communication, and more economic activity—then people begin to think of themselves as a coun-try." A country for Deutsch is an area of markedly high interdepend-ence. Land prices, wages, and the cost of many goods and services are all interconnected; the people in a country feel that their fates are linked together. Language is consolidated, a dominant social elite becomes a model of reference, the feeling of kinship expands from tribal to national groupings, people develop interlocking habits of communications, and

7 *Ibid.*, 22, 206.

separate administrative districts are integrated politically. He explained that "a nation-state is a state that has become largely identified with one people."[8] Social mobilization occurs as people receive a growing exposure to modernity. The mass media create national audiences; monetization takes hold; literacy expands, as do nonagricultural occupations and urbanization; the number of wage earners and internal migration increase. Nationalism has its paradoxes, however, such as the heightened power of the state and the loss of judgment on both local and worldwide problems. In Eastern Europe and the developing countries, linguistic and national assimilation, especially of persistent minorities, has never quite worked. Nation building is incomplete, yet demands for national self-determination go back to Serbia in the 1900s triggering World War I. In some ways, the rise of nationalism in Eastern Europe, disdainfully called the Balkanization of the Ottoman Empire, has been pathetic. Yet Deutsch quoted John Dickinson, who observed that a fool might put on his own shirt better for himself than ten wise men could do it for him.

Nationalism in such areas as Eastern Europe has not been the only alternative. In the interwar period, it "became a creed of monopoly and privilege for the few, and it was embellished with a fantastic fear of the poor." East European resentment against social injustice and desire for self-determination found an outlet in Communist movements. Nationalism and communism reinforced one another, yet communism has not abolished the nation-state. Across the boundary zones of East-West conflict, the Communist and non-Communist worlds face one another, struggling to resolve two persistent and worldwide problems—the conquest of poverty and ignorance and the rise of nation-states with consequent alienation, fear, and suspicion and imminent danger of war. Because neither problem is well understood, Deutsch offers the moving plea that both East and West recognize their failures "to sober us into avoiding a suicidal conflict between different and equally ignorant ideologies." In Asia and Africa the alternative to communism too often has been local dictators backed by foreign governments and dependent on foreign aid. "There is danger that the forces of nationalism and com-

8 Karl W. Deutsch, *Nationalism and Its Alternatives* (New York: Alfred A. Knopf, 1969), 6, 19.

munism will merge into a torrent of popular hatred against the West—
a torrent of hostility that would very seriously strain our limited manpower and resources and that might involve us in a chain of conflicts
with a forseeable end."[9] It is noteworthy that Deutsch, the European,
in his lectures to Americans uses democracy as a model that will outlast
all other alternative forms of government if those living in democracies
remain free and open and continue to innovate and learn.

Thus Deutsch's most lasting contribution to scholars and policy makers is twofold. First, he has consistently championed democracy as the
best hope of mankind, whether in his writings on nationalism, in such
analytical works as *The Nerves of Government* (1963) and *Politics and Government: How People Decide Their Fate* (1970) or in such policy studies as
Arms Control and the Atlantic Alliance (1967). Second, he has drawn on
the behavioral sciences for new conceptual frameworks of analysis and
thought. To a greater or lesser degree, a host of younger scholars—
Bruce M. Russett, Hayward R. Alker, Jr., and less directly David
Singer—go back to Deutsch's works as the inspiration for their scholarship. There is a pervasive strain of humanism in Deutsch's highly
theoretical work, derived no doubt from traditional European thought,
and a deep and abiding concern for the fate of mankind. Like many of
his followers, Deutsch is preeminently the technical social scientist, but
he is far more than a technician. More than any living scholar, Deutsch
has sought to marry the novel techniques of modern social science with
the traditional concerns of political philosophy and international theory.
In this sense, he wholly deserves the characterization of master thinker.

9 *Ibid.*, 52, 65, 91.

KARL WOLFGANG DEUTSCH

WORKS BY KARL W. DEUTSCH

1953

Nationalism and Social Communication. Cambridge: Technology Press of the Massachusetts Institute of Technology; and New York: John Wiley.

1957

Political Community and the North Atlantic Area. By Karl W. Deutsch and others. Princeton, N.J.: Princeton University Press.

1959

Germany Rejoins the Powers. With Lewis J. Edinger. Stanford, Calif.: Stanford University Press.

1963

The Nerves of Government. New York: Free Press.

1964

World Handbook of Political and Social Indicators. New Haven, Conn.: Yale University Press.

1967

Arms Control and the Atlantic Alliance: Europe Faces Coming Policy Decisions. New York: John Wiley.

France, Germany and the Western Alliance: A Study of Elite Attitudes on European Integration and World Politics. By Karl W. Deutsch and others. New York: Charles Scribner's Sons.

1968

The Analysis of International Relations. Englewood Cliffs, N.J.: Prentice-Hall.

The Relevance of International Law. Edited by Karl W. Deutsch and Stanley Hoffmann. Garden City, N.Y.: Anchor Books.

1969

Nationalism and Its Alternatives. New York: Alfred A. Knopf.

1970

Politics and Government: How People Decide Their Fate. Boston: Houghton Mifflin.

Nationalism and National Development: An Interdisciplinary Bibliography. Cambridge: Massachusetts Institute of Technology Press.

PART III

Conflict and the Present Crisis

Modern man has prepared himself to live in utopia, but the real world is one of unending conflict and crisis. No conflict is more intense and no crisis deeper than the Cold War, the great drama of the twentieth century. Today's conflict is filled with deep pathos and inner contradictions, reflecting insoluble problems and conflicting values. Men who have been schooled to think of victory and defeat are having to learn to live with adversity. The requirements of the Cold War are not the same as war, in which a nation in arms unites for a common purpose. The Cold War is much closer to the trials of the human condition, in which the struggle for identity, security, and recognition is endless. In world politics, common purposes are limited; misunderstandings and misconceptions divide men and nations. Wars, like athletic contests, are charted and measured by victory and defeat. Politics and the Cold War are closer to the struggle described by Walt Whitman: "It is provided in the very essence of things that from any fruition of success, no matter what, shall come forth something to make a greater struggle necessary."

Several master thinkers, each with a different approach, have attempted to define more clearly the nature of the present struggle between East and West. Whatever their differences, they have shared certain basic assumptions and world outlooks. All have maintained that statesmen must work in a world which in no way resembles utopia. Instead, it is a world of sovereign nation-states half-organized internationally and threatened since 1946 by a cloud of danger. Nations are caught in a terrible predicament. To safeguard their security, they must prepare for war knowing that such a war might destroy all prospect of human survival. The four writers in this section have insisted on the importance of diplomacy, the need to keep power and commitments in balance, the wisdom of the ancient injunction "sufficient unto the day is the evil thereof," and the central place of leadership in mankind's survival.

Walter Lippmann has been called "the most influential journalist of the twentieth century." The cogency and clarity of his works are unmatched in diplomatic writing. Beginning his career as an internationalist, a Wilsonian, and a socialist, he moved through successive stages in his thought. He became a critic of Wilsonian policies (which ignored the specific territorial and political requirements of peace), a conservative where tradition and economic practices were concerned, an advocate of a political settlement between the Soviet Union and the United States, and a latter-day proponent of natural law and political reason.

George F. Kennan has combined a career in the foreign service with writing prize-winning political history. No less a literary craftsman than Lippmann, his advocacy of certain policies and his activist posture have been more open and direct. His advice has more often been heeded by his countrymen to the distortion of his real intent; for example, President Harry S. Truman's formulation of his containment policy in universalistic rather than prudential terms. Yet no writer has urged moderation and restraint in foreign policy with greater consistency and force.

Louis Halle, who began his career as a naturalist, entered the foreign service and served as a member of the policy-planning staff. His *The Cold War as History* is grounded in political realism, and his monumental *Out of Chaos* is an adventure in universal history like the world histories by Arnold J. Toynbee and Oswald Spengler. No observer in America or Europe has defended with greater intellectual force the need to view the crisis in the light of its historical antecedents.

Raymond Aron has been called "the French Walter Lippmann," and his newspaper columns have a distinct historical and sociological orientation. Elected professor at the University of Paris in the Sorbonne, he has written a monumental work on *Peace and War*. With characteristic French clarity, he has provided a well-structured analytical framework within which the present crisis could be studied and understood, without neglecting the normative elements of international politics.

Taken together, these four leading interpreters provide a coherent basis for grasping the permanent aspects of the present crisis.

WALTER LIPPMANN (1889–1974)

Rationalism and Political Reason

Walter Lippmann was born in New York City on September 23, 1889, and died on December 14, 1974, at the age of eighty-four. His ancestors had immigrated from Germany a half-century before the migration of East European Jews, whom they felt were inferior. Perhaps this foreshadowed Lippmann's alleged indifference to the Jewish problem. His parents, Jacob and Daisy Lippmann, placed the highest value on education, enrolled him in Dr. Julius Sach's Collegiate Academy in Manhattan, took him to Europe, and encouraged an early interest in art and literary criticism. In 1909 he graduated from Harvard College, where he attracted the attention of George Santayana and William James. He continued for another year as a graduate student in philosophy and thereafter maintained a lifelong association with Harvard, serving on its Board of Overseers from 1933 to 1939.

From his earliest years, Lippmann was recognized in America as a force in journalism and politics. In Europe he was associated with such intellectuals as H. G. Wells, George Bernard Shaw, John Maynard Keynes, Bernard Berenson, and Harold Nicolson. The historian and social critic Lincoln Steffens found in the young Lippmann "the ablest mind that could express itself in writing. . . . He understood the meaning of all he learned."[1] Liberal and socialist thinkers looked to him as a bright and shining new light. He became a card-carrying member of the Fabian Society and, at age twenty-four, joined the *New Republic* at the invitation of Herbert Croly. He had published an edition of *The Poems of Paul Mariett* (1913), *A Preface to Politics* (1913)—a book described by Ernest Jones, Freud's biographer, as the first Freudian treatment of politics—*Drift and Mastery* (1914), and numerous articles and

---

1 Walter Lippmann, *Early Writings* (New York: Liveright, 1970), vii.

notes in the *New Republic,* including the article "Force and Ideas" in the first issue.[2]

Nor was Lippmann's early career confined to his literary achievements. His political activism, although concealed, remained a lifelong character trait. Although he warned fellow journalists to keep their distance from men of power, he lobbied furiously in 1916 for Senate confirmation of Louis D. Brandeis to the Supreme Court, helped convert Arthur Vandenberg to internationalism, and favored McGeorge Bundy for secretary of state under John F. Kennedy. He had been active at Harvard, and in 1912 he went to Schenectady, New York, to work for a Socialist mayor, the Reverend George R. Lund. When asked what he loved most, he replied: "The living world." During World War I, he served his country as a captain in military intelligence, joined Colonel Edward M. House and Isaiah Bowman as an aide to draw up American peace terms (he wrote eight of the fourteen points), and subsequently attended the Paris Peace Conference. His tenure as associate editor at the *New Republic* continued through 1921, a period of uninterrupted intellectual growth in which his thinking underwent various transformations. Arthur Schlesinger, Jr., has written of these years: "Born in the Victorian tranquilities of 1889, he was stirred by the ferment of the Progressive era and became a socialist before he left Harvard in 1910. His socialism soon evaporated in any dogmatic form, but it left behind a residue in the shape of a belief in the necessity of rational planning and purpose to master the incipient chaos of modern society." He was conscious of the fact, before it became a byword, that men were living in revolutionary and unstable times in which the value system itself was undergoing far-reaching change. He was to declare in *A Preface to Morals* (1929) that the "acids of modernity" were eating away at established values. He saw in Theodore Roosevelt's campaign of 1912 the first concerted political effort to respond to the challenge of the industrial order, but his enthusiasm for Roosevelt waned with Roosevelt's reversion to jingoism. Thereafter, Woodrow Wilson became for Lippmann and his friends the hope of Americans, if not mankind as a whole. Drift

---

2 This and all works by Walter Lippmann are listed chronologically, with full publication data, beginning on p. 141 herein.

and planless action in the democracies threatened society. Representative government was imperiled by failure to organize the nation's resources to respond effectively to changing problems in accordance with well-defined purpose. The congressional system had become defective and required restructuring. Long before the great 1970s debate over the presidency, Lippmann warned of feverish activity at the center and a cold inertia in all its parts. The president was weighed down with all the tasks of a benevolent despot but denied the means to make authority effective. Lippmann wrote:

> We expect of one man that he shall speak for the nation, formulate its needs, translate them into a program. We expect that man to instill these purposes and this program into a parasitic party system, drive his own party to enact them, and create an untainted administrative hierarchy through which to realize his plans. We expect him to oversee the routine, dominate group interests, prepare for the future, and take stock of possible emergencies. No man can do it.[3]

Apparently, the guiding faith in his early writings rested on the Socialist belief in the essential role of planning, a reflection of the spirit of the times. Beneath this popular view, the bedrock of Lippmann's thought was an essential conservatism, a preference for order, and a deep faith in reason. He remained firm in these views through his final great work, *The Public Philosophy* (1955). (The book paradoxically received few favorable reviews.) In reviewing this work, with its inspired pleas for objective standards undergirding all political action, Hans J. Morgenthau observed:

> This book is animated by a noble and moving faith, reminiscent of the rationalistic idealism of the eighteenth century, in the self-sustaining power of reason to transform the philosophy by which men live and, through it, their very lives. Mr. Lippmann believes that men in their political thoughts and actions can be "sincerely and lucidly rational," and he considers this rationality the very foundation of the public philosophy. Herbert Butterfield, Reinhold Niebuhr, myself and others have tried to show how much more ambiguous and involved the relations between reason and politics are than is suggested by this simple rationalistic faith.[4]

3 Lippmann, *Early Writings*, ix, x–xi.
4 Hans J. Morgenthau, *Politics in the Twentieth Century* (3 vols.; Chicago: University of Chicago Press, 1962), III, 66.

Morgenthau acknowledged that his criticism was overstated to make a point. Yet Lippmann's political rationalism is fundamental to all his writings. His essay in the founding issue of the *New Republic* began: "Every sane person knows it is a greater thing to build a city than to bombard it, to plough a field rather than to trample it, to serve mankind than to conquer it."[5] Man's hope, he reasoned, is in ideas, not in guns or cannons. Man's thoughts are the only persistently effective weapons in controlling the exercise of force. Man's brain conceives the guns and determines the formation and use of mighty armies. Men bring into being vast arsenals of destruction, which have expanded beyond their control. For the future, man can master war only through the resolve to end it; he must control civilization so that no machine can turn traitor to it. Although it takes as much brainpower to make a sword as it does a plowshare, it requires a grasp of higher human values to prefer the plowshare.

Lippmann's intellectual journey had its birth in the regnant ideas on which the *New Republic* was founded: socialism, Wilsonianism, and opposition to the balance of power. On January 27, 1917, he wrote: "Peace has never been secured in Europe by that method [a teetering balance of power] and never will be."[6] He was chosen secretary of the Inquiry, a group of experts appointed by President Woodrow Wilson to prepare for the peace settlement after World War I. He joined in the formulation of the Fourteen Points and helped write the official interpretation used by Colonel House in prearmistice negotiations. He accepted President Wilson's view that the aim of the Allies should be "peace without victory" with Germany and that the postwar settlement should be based on a concert of power, not a balance of power.

On February 17, 1917, less than a month after his first statement on political aims and the organization of the peace, Lippmann tried to warn the president that legalism and moralism were not enough. An operative political strategy for war and peace was required. "It is a weak nation that would dribble into war," he continued, "not knowing why, or how, or whether." No one could question that both the blockade by the British and submarine warfare by the Germans were terrible weap-

---

5 Lippmann, *Early Writings*, 3.
6 *Ibid.*

ons, since war itself was terrible. However, in choosing between them, the United States would not be choosing between legality and illegality, or even between cruelty and mercy. Instead, he maintained: "It is because we cannot permit a German triumph that we have accepted the closure of the seas to Germany and the opening of them to the Allies." In language that foreshadowed Kennan, Lippmann declared: "We are an inveterately legalistic people, and have veiled our real intentions behind a mass of technicalities. . . . We have wanted to assist the Allies and hamper Germany, but we have wanted also to keep out of war. Our government therefore has been driven to stretch technicalities to the breaking point. We have clothed the most unneutral purposes in the language of neutrality."[7]

Lippmann's conviction was that the safety of the Atlantic was something for which Americans should fight.

> Why? Because on the two shores of the Atlantic there has grown up a profound web of interest which joins together the western world. Britain, France, Italy, even Spain, Belgium, Holland, the Scandinavian nations, and Pan America are in the main one community in their deepest needs. . . . They have a common interest in the ocean which unites them. . . . But if that community were destroyed we should know what we had lost. We should understand then the meaning of the unfortified Canadian frontier, of the common protection given Latin America by the British and American fleets.[8]

Once Germany had carried the war into the Atlantic by violating the neutrality of Belgium in its invasion of France, by striking against Britain, and by attempting to disrupt the United States, neutrality in spirit or action was out of the question. German victory on the high seas would have allowed Germany to become the leader of the East against the West and the leader in the long run of a German-Russian-Japanese coalition against the Atlantic world. The balance of power would have been overturned. Such an eventuality had to be unacceptable to the United States.

Two years later, on September 3, 1919, Lippmann's break with Wil-

7 *Ibid.*, 69, 71.
8 *Ibid.*, 73.

son was complete. Although isolationism for Americans was a thing of the past, Lippmann wanted to know what was to be put in its place. Wilson had declared: "It has come about by no plan of our conceiving, but by the hand of God. . . . We cannot turn back. We can only go forward with lifted eyes and freshened spirit, to follow the vision." For Lippmann, such counsel was like telling a twenty-one-year-old that he cannot turn back but must go forward and follow his visions. But what vision, and where? In his most pointed language directed at the president, Lippmann explained:

> One of the most serious aspects of the new dogma of non-isolation is that it so easily becomes a form of fatalism. The old dogma at least had the virtue of landmarks. The new dogma can easily become just a general drift, and that, I think, is what it has become within the last year. Having learned that we must "participate," we are forgetting to specify. We are resolved to take part in world affairs, but in our exhilaration we are inclined to omit the inquiry as to what part.[9]

This theme was to recur in Lippmann's later criticism of the containment of communism around the world.

Lippmann spoke with a voice of reason in a dark and angry world of unreason. Two other abiding characteristics of his work also deserve mention—his recognition of change and continuity. He once described his mission as an effort to come to terms with the mounting disorder in Western society. He reopened great questions and reexamined basic assumptions, including his own. He struggled in an anarchic century, where "whirl is king" (Aristophanes), to provide anchors for men's thought. He looked for those enduring truths that make up the public philosophy.

He was beyond question the best and quite possibly the most influential journalist in the history of the American republic. As Arthur Schlesinger, Jr., observed, no one had written for newspapers and magazines (notably in Lippmann's column, "Today and Tomorrow") with such devotion to the language, with such searching concern for the substance of issues, with such unfaltering instinct for the long view, and with such determination to educate the public on the great ques-

9 *Ibid.*, 86–87, 97.

tions of national and foreign policy. No one proceeded so firmly to describe the force of tradition and change, to rekindle respect for the values that had survived the ages, and to portray the complexities of modern life that had transformed the social and political context in which living values were reshaped and reformulated.

A rationalist through and through, Lippmann consistently sought to clarify and illuminate the dilemmas of the age without pretending he had the power to cut the Gordian knot. In his syndicated columns for the New York *Herald Tribune*, he did not presume to offer final answers. His running commentaries on public policies of the day produced a sense in his readers that existing policies were misconceived, misapplied, and likely to produce ills that exceeded the disease they were designed to cure. Yet Lippmann understood the play of contingent factors and the mysteries of political consequences in the historic process. Although he scorned irrationality and emotionalism, he was not a computer, devoid of human frailties and feelings. *Men of Destiny* (1927) included Lippmann's penetrating yet entertaining appraisals of Sinclair Lewis and H. L. Mencken and some of his best literary criticism and demonstrated his profound if sardonic view of the interplay of personalities and historical forces. His private conversations were suffused with perceptions of heroism and folly. He had written after the death of Franklin D. Roosevelt: "The final test of a leader is that he leaves behind him in other men the conviction and the will to carry on." If George F. Kennan could speak of Reinhold Niebuhr as "the father of all of us," no serious journalist after Lippmann could ignore the standards he set for intelligence and integrity in contemporary journalism.

At the same time, the weightier judgment of history must fall on his more extended interpretations of society and public policy. From his first explicit review, *The Stakes of Diplomacy* (1915), to his last writings on Soviet-American relations, *The Communist World and Ours* (1959) and *The Coming Test with Russia* (1961), and his writings on Western civilization including *Isolation and Alliances* (1952) and *Western Unity and the Common Market* (1962), he based almost all his thought on a single proposition. He was convinced that the United States throughout the twentieth century had lacked a settled and generally accepted foreign policy. Lacking this, America had been unable to prepare for war or to safeguard the peace. It was his working assumption that the United States had had a secure foreign policy from the decade following the War of 1812 to the end of the war with Spain in 1898. Politics throughout most of the nation's first century had stopped at the water's edge. However, in the presidential election of 1900, the nation became divided over the consequences of the war with Spain. Not since that date had an American president been able to rely upon the united support of the nation in the conduct of foreign affairs. From the promulgation of the Monroe Doctrine to the end of the war with Spain, the American people had not felt any urgent need to develop a foreign policy. Forgotten was the one self-evident principle of all foreign policy—which alone could settle discussion and controversy—that commitments and power must be brought into balance. Lippmann wrote: "Without the controlling principle that the nation must maintain its objectives and its power in equilibrium, its purposes within its means and its means equal to its purposes, its commitments related to its resources and its resources adequate to its commitments, it is impossible to think at all about foreign affairs." (Lippmann ended up hostile to every president from Theodore Roosevelt to Richard Nixon, and his most persistent criticism was their failure to employ this principle.) America has habitually divorced war and peace aims, ideals, interests, and commitments from discussion of armaments, strategic positions, potential allies, and probable enemies. In foreign policy, ends and means have to be balanced; nations must pay for what they want and want only what they are willing to pay for. Americans have failed because they are the victims "of a blinding prejudice that concern with our frontiers, our armaments and with alliances, is immoral and reactionary."[10] This was Woodrow Wilson's prejudice, but it had an even more profound effect on latter-day Wilsonians such as Cordell Hull.

Moreover, Lippmann was not willing to offer only a general criticism. He wrote with a clear and forceful definition of terms:

> I mean by a foreign commitment an obligation outside the continental limits of the United States, which may in the last analysis have to be met by waging war. I mean by power the force which is necessary to prevent

10 Walter Lippmann, *U.S. Foreign Policy: Shield of the Republic* (Boston: Little, Brown, 1943), 5.

such a war or to win it if it cannot be prevented. In the term necessary power I include the military force which can be mobilized effectively within the domestic territory of the United States and also the reinforcements which can be obtained from dependable allies.

Lippmann's primary thesis is that the essence of foreign policy is the balancing of a nation's commitments and power and the maintenance of a comfortable surplus of power in reserve: "In assaying ideals, interests and ambitions which are to be asserted abroad . . . [the policy maker's] measure of their validity will be the force he can muster at home combined with the support he can find abroad among other nations which have similar ideals, interests and ambitions."[11] The level at which a solvent balance may be struck may vary (as it does for the family who is poor, well-to-do, or rich), but the principle must be recognized and pursued if disaster is to be avoided.

The early history of the United States from 1789 to 1823 included deep and troubling dissension, so deep that President George Washington's farewell address dealt with his fear that factionalism would destroy the republic. Pro-French and pro-British factions had brought the republic to the verge of war, first with one and then with the other. Hovering over the nation's struggle for survival was the prospect of armed intervention by the combined great powers of central Europe. There were rumors of secession, particularly of the New England states; and there was an absence of unity over the ends and means of foreign policy, reflected dramatically in the crisis involving Citizen Genet.

In 1823 three Virginians—James Monroe, Thomas Jefferson, and James Madison—brought solvency and reason to American foreign policy. Through the Monroe Doctrine and a tacit but well-understood concert of power with Great Britain, they linked commitments and vital interests. Nor did the Virginians stand alone. John Adams' influence may have been even greater. Not by seeking popular approval or by responding to insistent ethnic or pressure groups, but by a statement of principles, they shaped a foreign policy that even a divided people could support. Vital interests, Lippmann explained, are those that a people agree must be defended at the risk of their lives. Widely different

11 *Ibid.*, 6.

cultures and nation-states place group above personal survival. Even Mahatma Gandhi, who practiced nonviolence, did not put the preservation of his own life above the defense of the community's vital interests. Such men are prepared to die in a hunger strike or at the hand of their enemy rather than abandon their principles.

The question follows: What are the vital interests of the United States? In Lippmann's earlier writings, he saw them as the defense of the nation's proven territory. Jefferson's admiration for France never obscured the threat of a French army encamped in New Orleans at the mouth of the Mississippi. In the Louisiana Purchase, the United States acquired the territory necessary to protect New Orleans. Jefferson recognized the realities of American interests, even though he was not upheld by the Supreme Court until twenty-five years later. Thereafter the larger continental homeland became stabilized as proven American territory, but in subsequent decades, the continental limits established at the Canadian and Mexican boundaries and extending from the Atlantic to the Pacific oceans required extracontinental outposts and territories for national defense. The French invasion of Mexico in 1861 was seen as a hostile act. Since 1873 the whole of the Western Hemisphere has been included in the proven territories. The Western Hemisphere became a security system and power constellation within a wider international order.

The United States is separated from its neighbors by what Lippmann called an ocean of water and air. North and South America are each islands in this ocean and islands in relation to one another. South America below the bulge of Brazil is closer to Africa and Europe than the United States is to the military centers in Europe. North America is more accessible to Britain, Western Europe, Russia, and Japan than to South America, China, or the South Pacific. Our nearest neighbors among the great powers are Britain, the Soviet Union, and Japan—along with Germany, the world's major military powers. Germany has twice threatened the system's equilibrium in trying to overrun one or more of the major powers and thereby becoming one of America's nearest neighbors. Hence, the defense of South America has become a vital interest of the United States. Since South America lacks a principal military power within its region, it can be threatened only by one of the great powers intruding on the Northern Hemisphere. To prevent a serious threat to Latin America, it is vital that the friends of the United States among the powers outweigh or at least balance its foes.

The United States is committed to defend at the risk of war the land, air, and water from Alaska to the Philippines and Australia and from Greenland to Brazil and Patagonia. With few exceptions, it has protected this area from the military dominance of any major outside power. Because the combined forces of the Old World would be overwhelmingly superior to those of the Western Hemisphere, America can never allow significant regions of this hemisphere to fall under the domination of a major controlling power or powers whose influence could spread over the United States. In order to protect the Western Hemisphere, it must help preserve a balance of power elsewhere in the world. Changing technology of warfare and realignments of the major powers may alter the shape of America's defense system. They may change the alliances it seeks for its security. However, "this is the system of power within which the United States is living and in which it still lives."[12]

In *U.S. War Aims* (1944), Lippmann argued that the discussion of war aims was not exhausted in the general principles of the Atlantic Charter and the Four Freedoms. Although these statements might be stars by which to set the nation's course, they were not signposts for the rough and broken country ahead. He wrote: "The only peace we can have is . . . the one now being wrought by waging the war, and we are presumptuous if we think that we can ignore this peace and make a different one." Peace depended on establishing firm relations among the Allies and recognizing the two emerging aggregates of power, the Atlantic community and the Russian orbit. Russia, he maintained, was as invulnerable in her land mass as the United States was at the core of the Atlantic community: "Between Russia and the Western world there is a distrust which is ancient and deep . . . as old as the great schism of the Dark Ages which divided Christendom between Rome and Byzantium." As war aims, the United States should: (1) consolidate the existing strategic and diplomatic connections of the Atlantic community; (2) recognize the strategic system of the Russian orbit, including the states east of Germany and west of the Soviet Union; (3) recognize China as

12 *Ibid.*, 70.

the center of a third strategic system destined to include the mainland of east Asia; (4) recognize that the Moslem and Hindu nations of North Africa (the Mahgreb), the Middle East, and south Asia will ultimately form strategic systems of their own; (5) make it the aim of any Far Eastern or European settlement that Japan and Germany not hold the balance between the other major powers in the regions; and (6) make the aim of a settlement following the war the disarming of the war party and the protection of the peace party by making defeat irrevocable and peace acceptable. Lippmann argued that in the peace settlement after World War I Georges Clemenceau was right and Woodrow Wilson was wrong: "By preferring peace in general to a specific peace, President Wilson in effect forgot about Germany." Wilson "dissolved the coalition which had won the war and could alone have perpetuated the settlement. He engendered a useless and pernicious quarrel with Italy over the insignificant port of Fiume."[13] Through this dispute, exploited by Gabriele d'Annunzio, Italian fascism got its start. After World War II, Lippmann maintained that peace had to be established specifically and directly in the world as it existed then. Peace would rest on the combined power of the Allies.

In *The Cold War* (1947), Lippmann confronted the faulty assumptions of the Truman Doctrine and the famous "Mr. X" article by George F. Kennan in *Foreign Affairs*. He agreed with Kennan that Soviet power was destined to expand unless opposed by "contrary force" at points of America's choosing. However, containment proposed to meet Soviet power on grounds favorable to the Soviets, surrendered the initiative to the Russians, envisaged a use of American military power to which it was unsuited, and threatened America's relationships with its natural allies in the Atlantic community. A more constructive policy would seek to remove all alien armies from the European continent; the presence of the Red Army in the center of Europe was the crux of the problem. Withdrawal was the sole means of testing Russian intentions and restoring the independence of European states. Lippmann favored the Marshall Plan but opposed the Truman Doctrine as a "strategic monstrosity."

Isolation and Alliances (1952) called for a deeper understanding of the

---

13 Walter Lippmann, *U.S. War Aims* (Boston: Little, Brown, 1945), 6, 152, 162–63.

profound changes in the world affecting American foreign policy since 1940. American and British interests had become so enmeshed that Winston S. Churchill spoke to a 1951 joint session of the two houses of Congress as a minister seeking a vote of confidence from a reluctant House. American foreign policy had moved through two phases. The first phase—isolation—lasted until the beginning of World War II and involved the advance of American power across the continent to the Philippines and the islands of the Pacific. The second phase—emergence as a primary world power—gave the United States responsibility for building a new coalition. The defense and security of free Europe became essential to America's national security. The twin aims of policy were the consolidation of Europe and a solution to the problem of Germany, which lay at the heart of the Cold War.

In *The Public Philosophy* (1955), Lippmann returned to his perennial concern—the decline and revival of Western society. He wrote of the malady of democratic states, the derangement of powers, and the public interest. He appealed for the defense of civility and the renewal of the public philosophy. He called on Americans to rediscover their heritage of ideals and universal laws. Although his final work was attacked as too closely attuned to certain doctrines of natural law, he succeeded in calling attention to common interests shared by Americans and friends abroad as expressed in an underlying faith in the inviolability of the human spirit.

In 1966 Lippmann left Washington after twenty-eight years and returned to New York, where he remained until his death in 1974. Lippmann wrote very little during these later years, but policy makers continued to respect his clear formulation of views, even those with which they sometimes differed. In the 1950s, although he had first supported action by the United Nations in Korea, Lippmann soon urged an armistice and political settlement and opposed General Douglas MacArthur's advance to the Yalu River. In Vietnam, he feared from the start that American involvement would entail a land war on the mainland of China. He returned to his conception of a regional power system and questioned America's tendency to become overcommitted beyond the sphere of its vital interests. His views were unacceptable to successive presidents and secretaries of state, although he remained a member in good standing of the establishment, and at least some of his warnings appear to have been vindicated by history. His strength lay in the principles he enunciated more than the tactics he proposed. Because he was outside the operating foreign policy elite centered at the New York Council on Foreign Relations, he sustained his independence of thought perhaps more than any other prominent writer or journalist. He set standards for commentators that few if any have matched. Richard Rovere wrote in 1975: "As a stylist, he should be studied not only by other journalists but by anyone interested in English prose, for he was surely as much a master of it as any modern American writer." As to the substance of his work, Rovere remarked: "Reviewing his work as a whole, I found most of it stood up far better than I had expected it to." He foresaw the military and political presence of the Soviet Union from the Baltic to the Balkans. He prophesied the instability of the Chinese Nationalist regime. He anticipated the problems that arose from the universalism of the Truman Doctrine. Yet historians cannot fully measure his worth if they judge him exclusively as a pillar of social and political wisdom: "He embodied most of what was best in the liberal and humanist tradition and brought a new dignity to American journalism."[14] It would be difficult indeed to point to anyone who has taken his place.

WORKS BY WALTER LIPPMANN

1913

A Preface to Politics. New York: Macmillan.

1914

Drift and Mastery. New York: M. Kennerly.

1915

The Stakes of Diplomacy. New York: Henry Holt.

1919

The Political Scene. New York: Henry Holt.

1920

Liberty and the News. New York: Harcourt, Brace & Howe.

1927

Men of Destiny. New York: Macmillan.

1928

American Inquisitors. New York: Macmillan.

1929

A Preface to Morals. New York: Macmillan.

14 Richard Rovere, "Walter Lippmann," *American Scholar*, XLIV (Autumn, 1975), 602, 603.

1932

Interpretations, 1931–1932. Edited by Allan Nevins. New York: Macmillan.

1933

The United States in World Affairs. With William O. Scroggs. 3rd ed. New York: Harper Brothers, for the Council on Foreign Relations.

1934

The Method of Freedom. New York: Macmillan.

1935

The New Imperative. New York: Macmillan.

1936

Interpretations, 1933–1935. Edited by Allan Nevins. New York: Macmillan.

1937

The Good Society. London: Allen & Unwin.

1940

Some Notes on War and Peace. New York: Macmillan.

1943

U.S. Foreign Policy: Shield of the Republic. Boston: Little, Brown.

1945

U.S. War Aims. Boston: Little, Brown.

1947

The Cold War: A Study in U.S. Foreign Policy. New York: Harper Brothers.

1952

Isolation and Alliances. Boston: Little, Brown.

1955

The Public Philosophy. Boston: Little, Brown.

1959

The Communist World and Ours. Boston: Little, Brown.

1961

The Coming Test with Russia. Boston: Little, Brown.

1962

Western Unity and the Common Market. Boston: Little, Brown.

1963

The Essential Lippmann. Edited by Clinton Rossiter and James Lare. New York: Random House.

1970

Early Writings. With an Introduction and Annotations by Arthur Schlesinger, Jr. New York: Liveright.

WORKS ABOUT WALTER LIPPMANN

Childs, Marquis, and James Reston, eds. *Walter Lippmann and His Times.* New York: Arno Press, 1959.

Rovere, Richard. "Walter Lippmann." *American Scholar*, XLIV (Autumn, 1975).

GEORGE F. KENNAN (1904–   )

The War on Legalism and Moralism

George F. Kennan was born in Milwaukee, Wisconsin, on February 16, 1904. His mother died soon after his birth, leaving him (in his words) scarred for life. His father's ancestors were pioneer farmers who came to the United States in the early eighteenth century from Ireland, stopping in Vermont before moving on to upper New York State and then to Wisconsin. Their outstanding characteristic was an obdurate, tight-lipped independence and a determined defense of individual freedom. Neither rich nor poor, they never saw themselves as employers or employees. As a result, the young Kennan was unable to identify in his own mind with the exploiters or the exploited in Marxian terms or to accept other Marxist assumptions. Kennan's grandfather and his father, born in 1851, preferred the eighteenth to the nineteenth century. Absorbing part of their values, Kennan maintained a certain detachment from twentieth-century commitments and manners. A cousin of his grandfather—a namesake, George Kennan—rather than his father, provided a model for the younger Kennan. They were born on the same day of the year and pursued parallel careers involving a focus on Russian affairs. The memory of the elder Kennan inspired George F. Kennan to found the Kennan Institute for Advanced Russian Studies in Washington, D.C., associated with the Smithsonian Institution.

The younger Kennan attended elementary school in Milwaukee and St. John's Military Academy in Delafield, Wisconsin. Its dean, Henry Holt, inspired him to seek a foreign service career, as did his reading of F. Scott Fitzgerald's *This Side of Paradise*. Entering Princeton in September, 1921, he found himself awed by its Gothic structures, self-conscious of the awkwardness of his youth and his unpolished midwestern ways, shy and aloof, yet too proud and sensitive to ask for help. Two professors left their imprint on his thinking—Raymond Sontag in diplomatic history and Joseph C. Green, who later designed the examination system for the foreign service. Their influence stemmed from intellectual power, not personal contact. Kennan left Princeton lonely and with few friends, a dreamer who had done little to understand the complexities of university organization or the opportunities of social and cultural life and who remained shielded from personal and group conflicts by a congenital dislike of confrontations. While at Princeton, Kennan recognized as a strength his reasonably lucid and open intellect—passive until challenged, sensitive to the world of thought, and free of intellectual preconceptions. His love of literature, including the English classics, had been nourished, along with his interest in modern history and politics. (His special love for the grand historic prose of writers such as Edward Gibbon is reflected in such Kennan phrases as: "Power is the medium in which we work.") He graduated from Princeton in 1925, prepared for future intellectual growth, not fully awakened but "with the promptings of a vague Wilsonian liberalism; a regret that the Senate had rejected American membership in the League of Nations; a belief in laissez-faire economics and the values of competition; and a corresponding aversion to high tariffs."[1] His Princeton education had served to identify these concerns, not to cast them in rigid ideologies beyond the reach of critical thought.

To his surprise, Kennan was one of seventeen successful candidates for appointment in the foreign service. (The oral examination panel was headed by Undersecretary of State Joseph C. Grew.) After training at the Foreign Service School in Washington, he was sent on temporary assignment to the consulate general in Geneva and then as vice-consul in Hamburg, Germany. (He had visited Germany first as a child and again before taking his examinations and was able to speak German fluently.) In the summer of 1928, he entered training as a Russian specialist and spent the next five and a half years in Berlin and the Baltic capitals of Tallinn and Riga. Thereafter, Kennan served as language officer in Berlin in 1929; third secretary in Riga in 1931; third secretary in Moscow in 1934; consul in Vienna in 1935; second secretary in Moscow in 1935; second secretary in 1938 and consul in 1939 in Prague; second secretary in 1939 and first secretary in 1940 in Berlin;

1 George F. Kennan, *Memoirs, 1925–1950* (Boston: Little, Brown, 1967), I, 16.

counselor of legation in Lisbon in 1942; counselor to the American
delegation of the European Advisory Commission in London in 1944;
minister counselor in Moscow in 1945; deputy director for foreign affairs at the National War College in Washington in 1946; director of
the policy planning staff of the Department of State in 1947; U.S.
ambassador to the U.S.S.R. in 1952; and ambassador to Yugoslavia
from 1961 to 1963. His public career was interrupted when he became
a member of the Institute for Advanced Study at Princeton from 1950
to 1952. After retiring from the foreign service in 1953, he became a
permanent professor at the institute until his retirement as professor
emeritus in 1974. Kennan's career has combined diplomacy and scholarship at a level unmatched by any other public servant. Like his uncle
before him, his command of Russian affairs played a large part in his
advancement.

In the late 1920s and 1930s, he was one of a small group of foreign
service officers chosen for training in Russian language, history, and
culture. His companions included Charles "Chip" Bohlen and Llewelyn
Thompson, both destined to represent their country as ambassadors to
the Soviet Union in crucial periods of the Cold War. Highly practical
men, Bohlen and Thompson commended themselves to the policy makers in the Department of State and to successive chief executives. Both
become adept at working within the bureaucratic system. Kennan, who
was the most thoughtful of the three, continued to be intimidated by
organizational structures and to exhibit a curious blending of the professional diplomat, policy planner, and political prophet. His friends observed more than a streak of the romantic in him. In the 1950s, he
talked of seeking public office as a congressman and was prepared to
throw aside his foreign relations responsibilities to lead a popular movement to rejuvenate the decaying cities. Alternately, he has exaggerated
and then underestimated the weight of his influence, which has led to
the contradictory criticisms that he was too arrogant or too humble. In
describing his personal failings as a student, Kennan had written of
"pride, oversensitivity, a sullen refusal to be comforted, an insistence on
knowing and experiencing the worst in order to be the more deserving
of sympathy."[2] However much Kennan has conquered the self-acknowl-

2 *Ibid.*, 10.

edged failings of his youth, he has never—with the possible exception of leadership in the Princeton institute—risen to the heights that his superb moral and intellectual endowments entitled him.

His professional career was from the start marked by both success and failure. Although his writings are among the strongest justifications in any language for professionalism in public service, his career points up the limitations of realizing such goals in practice. Or to put it more precisely, Kennan the prophet and romanticist has always been at war with Kennan the professional, as though he were counseling fellow professionals: "Do as I say, not as I do." In 1952 the Russians asked that he be recalled as American ambassador after an interview at the Berlin airport, in which he had compared the heavy constraints of living in the Soviet Union with those in Hitler's Germany. Earlier in 1950, Secretary of State Dean Acheson sent Kennan to South America, as Louis Halle remembered, "to get his sometimes adversary out of his hair." As an outgrowth of his travels, Kennan wrote a memorandum on the government and politics of Latin America, which remains to this day a faithful if melancholy portrayal of certain dominant forces and trends in that troubled continent. The assumptions and findings of the report were so sharply at variance with the controlling assumptions of American foreign policy and imparted so vividly their author's despair about the region that extra copies were ordered shredded and destroyed and the original text buried in the State Department archives. In it, Kennan had warned: "The shadow of a terrible helplessness and impotence falls today over most of the Latin American world." South American leaders were unable or unwilling to confront reality. He discovered in every capital an exaggerated self-centeredness and egotism and a pathetic urge to create the illusion of cleverness and virility and the fiction of extraordinary human achievement. "Latin American society lives by . . . a species of make-believe not the systematized, purposeful make-believe of Russian communism, but a highly personalized anarchical make-believe, in which each individual spins around him, like a cocoon, his own little world of pretense." Mexico City made a violent, explosive impression on him: "I felt that it never slept at night (perhaps because I didn't)." Caracas was a "grotesque crevice of urbanization . . . jammed in among its billious-yellow mountains." "Rio [was] too repulsive" and

Sao Paulo "still worse." Everywhere Kennan went he was affected with "a curious sense of mingled apprehension and melancholy." Looking back, he was to observe: "The very fact that I, travelling around and reacting to stimuli could not help but write such passages, whereas the Department of State, being what it was and facing the tasks it faced, could not help but reject them and refuse to take cognizance of them . . . [showed] the logic that was now bringing to an end the usefulness of my career as a Washington official and forcing me out into a life where the deeper and more painful ranges of analysis and speculation could be . . . more safely indulged."[3]

Even when President John F. Kennedy called Kennan out of retirement to become ambassador to Yugoslavia in 1961, his effectiveness was dimmed by the hesitancy of Washington to respond to his urgings that the example of a dissenting Communist state be exploited fully in Eastern Europe. Kennan wished to go further in normalizing relations and building a network of cultural and economic ties with Yugoslavia than his superiors were ready to accept. Throughout his career, Kennan was almost invariably ahead of his time. He was persuaded that the two superpowers need not be enemies but could not be friends. He found Harry Hopkins' conciliatory views mere eyewash.

Kennan differed sharply with Secretary of State Dean Acheson, John Foster Dulles (then Acheson's assistant), Assistant Secretary Dean Rusk, and Ambassador Philip Jessup on the admission of Communist China to the United Nations. The issue in the summer of 1950 was whether admitting Communist China would have positive or negative results. Kennan discovered himself "for the most part in a lonely position of single opposition to the view of . . . associates" in arguing that such admission would only serve to register an existing situation of fact. It would, he believed, relieve the confusion and uncertainty in Asia about American intentions. It would undercut the charge of at least some Asians who suspected the United States of an imperialist design to restore Chiang Kai-shek to control on the mainland. During the debate, Kennan proposed not that America recognize China or even vote for its seating but that it "state frankly that in our opinion the Peking regime

3 *Ibid.*, 476, 477, 478, 479, 481, 482.

had not shown a due sense of responsibility for its international obligations; that its international behavior had been offensive . . . that we,
for these reasons, had not recognized it and saw no reason to do so."
However, since "our motives in this matter [of China's United Nation's
membership] had been widely questioned and since it had been alleged
that we had ulterior purposes, we were prepared . . . to abstain completely from all further participation . . . in the consideration of this
problem in the United Nations bodies, from any voting on the subject,
and from any sort of pressure or intervention with any other power on
the way it should vote." Kennan's views were shouted down by Dulles
in particular, who feared that such a stand would only confuse the
American public and weaken support for the president's defense program. Kennan elaborated:

> With Rusk and some of the others I think there was a real sense of moral
> indignation about the Chinese Communists. These people, after all, are
> treading now the paths which we old Russian hands were treading over
> twenty years ago in our first experiences with the Soviet dictatorship. We
> were not unaware then, and we are not unaware now, of the fundamental
> ethical conflict between their ideals and ours. But we view the handling of
> our end, in this conflict, as a practical matter similar to many other matters
> with which diplomacy has had to deal through . . . the centuries. We
> have learned not to recoil from the struggle for power as something shock-
> ing or abnormal. It is the medium in which we work . . . and we will not
> improve our performance by trying to dress it up as something else.[4]

In its conscience, America might be convinced that it was right. In
international politics, however, it was but one of many nation-states
seeking to achieve national security and to safeguard national interests.
These drives and ambitions, including those of America's enemies,
could not be made to disappear behind a putative common legal or
philosophical system. So deep were the differences in the debate over
China that after the discussion Dulles was quoted as telling a journalist
that, whereas he had once thought highly of George Kennan, he had
now concluded that Kennan was a very dangerous man because he ad-
vocated the admission of Communist China to the United Nations

4 Ibid., 493, 494.

and a cessation of United States military action in Korea at the 38th parallel.

If there are lessons to be drawn from this debate, they may be suggested by three pointed questions: Would the history of American foreign policy in Asia have been different if Kennan's views had prevailed? Is it safe to assume that in debates over particular foreign policies intellectuals whose arguments encompass subtleties of thought and ambiguities almost invariably come out second best? Is it significant that Kennan suucceeded in influencing foreign policy in a direct and measurable way only in the following two policy proposals—his containment doctrine, set forth in his February 22, 1946, telegram of eight thousand words from Moscow, and the "Mr. X" article, which appeared in the influential journal *Foreign Affairs* (July, 1946) under the title, "The Sources of Soviet Conduct"? The New York *Times* journalist, Arthur Krock, by comparing the two arguments, identified the journal article as having been written by the author of the long telegram. Kennan himself was to note that the two papers suffered from three deficiencies: failure to mention the satellite area of Eastern Europe and its effects on the possible decline of Soviet power; failure to make clear that what was meant by the containment of Soviet power was not containment by military means of a military threat but political containment of a political threat; and failure to make clear that this containment was not necessarily containment to be imposed everywhere, as expressed in the Truman Doctrine, but rather in geographic areas vital to American security. The reference that provoked the greatest controversy in the "Mr. X" article was the need to confront the Russians with unalterable counterforce "at every point where they show signs of encroaching upon the interests of a peaceful world."[5]

There followed criticism of Kennan by Walter Lippmann, in a series of twelve articles published in book form as *The Cold War*. Lippmann urged a concentration on the vital countries of Europe and mutual withdrawal of Soviet, American, and British forces from Europe and warned of any attempt to make a truncated West Germany into an ally in an anti-Soviet coalition. Each of Lippmann's proposals was to figure prom-

---

5 George F. Kennan, "The Sources of Soviet Conduct," *Foreign Affairs*, XXV (July, 1947), 581.

inently in all of Kennan's later writings and his belated attempt at clarification. The die was cast, however. In early 1946, following Kennan's long telegram, Secretary of the Navy James Forrestal helped to bring Kennan back to Washington to the National War College and influenced Secretary of State George C. Marshall to name Kennan to head the policy planning staff. It mattered little that Kennan questioned the sweeping nature of the commitments implied in the Truman Doctrine, which universalized the concept of containment. Kennan wrote: "I have been struck by the congenital aversion of Americans to taking specific decisions on specific problems, and by their persistent urge to seek universal formulae or doctrines in which to clothe and justify particular actions." Six months earlier or six months later, Kennan's two statements might have had less effect. In Kennan's words: "All this only goes to show that more important than the observable nature of external reality, when it comes to the determination of Washington's view of the world, is the subjective state of readiness on the part of Washington officialdom to recognize this or that feature of it."[6] Kennan's partial view of reality expressed in his own containment writings remains his dominant influence on postwar American foreign policy. Thereafter, he sensed he was becoming progressively out of touch.

The essence of his thinking on Soviet-American relations and the requirements of American foreign policy was expressed in a subsequent exchange with Secretary of State Henry Kissinger. The subject was the containment of the Kremlin. In a speech on February 3, 1976, Secretary Kissinger stated that "for the first time in history the Soviet Union could threaten distant places beyond the Eurasian land mass—including the United States." With nuclear technology and decolonization of the international system, the Soviet Union "for the first time has begun to define its interests and objectives in global terms thrusting into the Middle East, Africa, and Asia." (What is surprising is that a historian as able as Kissinger would have forgotten Iran and Mossadegh, Korea and Vietnam, Nasser's Egypt and the Cuban missile crisis.) However, choosing his words to fit Soviet direct action, Kissinger asserted: "Angola represents the first time that the Soviets have moved militarily at

6 Kennan, *Memoirs*, 295, 322.

long distance to impose a regime of their choice. It is the first time that the United States has failed to respond to Soviet military moves outside the immediate Soviet orbit. And it is the first time that Congress has halted national action in the middle of a crisis." The consequences, according to Kissinger, were grave. By failure to act, the United States would set an ominous precedent and would have to make harder choices at higher costs in the future: "To claim that Angola is not an important country, or that the United States has no important interests there, begs the principal question. If the United States is seen to waiver in the face of massive Soviet and Cuban intervention, what will be the perception of leaders around the world as they make decisions concerning their future security? And what conclusions will an unopposed superpower draw when the next opportunity for intervention beckons?"[7]

Mr. Kennan's response was measured, respectful, and sympathetic and was framed in the language of principle devoid of any play on the strengths or weaknesses of personalities. He praised Kissinger for a "thoughtful and statesmanlike speech," acknowledged the differences in applying containment to Soviet expansionism at present as compared with 1947 when the concept came into use, and admitted "that the Soviet Union has a far greater capacity for making this strength felt in regions far from its own shores than was the case 30 years ago." He reminded Kissinger, however, that official United States military estimates are prone to exaggerate the capacity of an adversary. Rather gently, Kennan introduced certain qualifications, nuances, and reservations that could usefully be added to what Kissinger had to say. "First of all, it is important to recognize that not all places are of equal importance from this standpoint." Korea and Cuba have high strategic importance, affecting not only American interests but those of other great powers. Distant countries may have local strategic interests without affecting the world balance of power. Second, the observer has to assess the gains and losses to a great power in undertaking to establish its influence in an area remote from its borders. Short of total occupation of the territory and suppression of indigenous government, the attempt

---

7 Henry Kissinger and George F. Kennan, "Containment of the Kremlin," Washington *Post*, February 16, 1976, p. A15.

to turn the resources of that territory to the exclusive benefit of the outside power is subject to a host of complications. By these standards, Cuba has been a financial millstone around the Soviet neck, and Egypt was hardly a resounding success: "There is no reason the United States should feel itself obliged to protect any other power from the assumption of responsibilities that are going to be an awkward burden to it." Third, it is essential to consider what allies and forces America can work with. In circumstances of civil strife, American involvement can be restricted to aiding a particular group or faction: "The limits of the quality of that faction as a military or political factor . . . became the limits of the effectiveness of our action. If there is any one factor, the ignoring of which has gone farthest to frustrate previous efforts of this sort on our part (consider Chiang Kai-shek's China and Vietnam), it is this. It is not everyone who can be made successful, even with the greatest effort of outside aid." Finally, there are situations in which what the United States seeks to accomplish can be done only with the support of world, or at least regional, opinion. America risks losing this if it casts itself in the same light as the opponents: "People are of course sensitive to the show of strength; but they are sensitive to other things, too."[8]

The root principles of Kennan's approach are not to be found in policy debates (he acknowledges that he is by temperament and talents ill-equipped in this area) but in numerous books of enduring value. In *American Diplomacy, 1900–1950* (1951),[9] delivered as the Charles R. Walgreen Lectures at the University of Chicago during his first year away from the Department of State, he posed a single fundamental question: What was the cause of the failures of American foreign policy in the first half of the twentieth century? He found an answer in America's legalistic-moralistic approach to the baffling and troublesome issues of the external world. Being a nation largely satisfied with the existing international system and the laws by which it was ordered, the United States could not conceive that others would seek through force to upset that order. Not only did the United States cloak its defense of

---

8 *Ibid.*
9 This and all books by George F. Kennan are listed chronologically, with full publication data, beginning on p. 000 herein.

the status quo in legalistic terms, but it compounded the difficulties by adding moralistic justifications. Instead of accepting the reality of awkward conflicts of national interest and seeking solutions least unsettling to international life, America looked for formal legal criteria to resolve disputes. Yet law in the half-anarchic international society was too abstract and inflexible and less adapted than diplomacy to the accommodation of conflicting interests. Law was of little value in protecting the satellite countries of Eastern Europe or in controlling the spread of civil wars. It overestimated the possibility of international sanctions and the prospects of military action by a coalition of states. Why then had law prevailed in American foreign policy? First, American success in establishing the rule of law within its national boundaries led Americans to believe a similar achievement was possible for the international community. Second, lawyers had been a dominant group shaping foreign policy, both because they appeared to introduce precision and certainty into an uncertain realm and because they were freer to move in and out of government.

More serious still for Kennan than legalism was moralism—the carrying over into the affairs of state concepts of absolute right and wrong. Those who claim there is a law of nations are indignant against the lawbreaker and feel moral superiority over him. Where a spirit of indignation controls military policy, the lawful and moral state demands unconditional surrender and undertakes to reduce the lawbreaker to complete submissiveness. Ironically, a war fought in the name of high moral principle intensifies violence and is more destructive of political stability than a war based on national interest. Total war and unconditional surrender are the price of a legalistic-moralistic approach. Historically, wars for limited objectives had limited the conduct of war. When objectives are moral and ideological and seek to change the attitudes and traditions of an entire people or the personality of a regime, victory lies beyond the reach of military action. Law may be for nations "a gentle civilizer of events," but it is better for leaders to recognize that national interest may be the most they are capable of knowing and understanding. If purposes at home are decent ones, unsullied by arrogance or hostility toward other people or delusions of superiority, this contributes more to a better and more peaceful world than claims of universal law or absolute moral principles.

Realities of American Foreign Policy (1954) contained Kennan's Stafford Little Lectures at Princeton University. Foreign policy, he argued, is a means not an end. What matters most is what happens on American territory. What are the ends and the objects of American society? First, they involve a government that protects the individual in the exercise of certain rights—life, liberty, and the pursuit of happiness—and, going back to the philosophy of his pioneer-farmer forebears, the right to hold and dispose of property. The individual is capable of the rational pursuit of his own self-interest, and the role of government is mainly but not exclusively that of a "benevolent watchdog." (Later, Kennan was to warn that the state had responsibility to resist the environmental deterioration in the society.) The end of government is to assist in achieving the objectives of organized society. From this, it follows that the two basic purposes of foreign policy are the protection of the nation from military and political intrusion and the protection of Americans engaged in private pursuits abroad. These two purposes are the only ones that result from the original goals of American society. In early American history, they led to a conception of foreign policy that was limited, modest, and restrained. Such purposes provide scant basis for international benevolence, lofty pretensions, or moral superiority. They do not make America the world's savior or a society whose social reforms provide a universal panacea. These original purposes, however, came to be replaced by the American dream, marked by a fateful combination of innocence and ignorance about the rest of the world.

Between the turn of the century and the 1930s, America occupied itself with worldwide arbitration and conciliation agreements and the framing of ninety-seven international agreements of which only two were invoked. Meanwhile, Hitler came to power largely unnoticed, and Americans took part in an endless round of disarmament talks and plans for outlawing aggression. Again during World War II, America planned for a world organization, unmindful that the Soviet Union was emerging as a new threat to the equilibrium of Europe. With the outbreak of the Cold War, Americans suddenly became aware—for the first time, or so it seemed—of the horrible reality of the postwar world, of the fact that its earnest and smiling partner had vanished and that in his place America faced another great and inexplicable monster, more threatening than all the others and commanding half the world's resources. This is one reality for American foreign policy—a world of raw power and rivalry with the Communist order. The other reality is more comfortable—the non-Communist world where people speak in familiar languages. In that world there is still a place for the American dream. In the Communist world, there is only unremitting strife and the law of the jungle. In such a world, Kennan asked, how can America find a unifying principle capable of bringing these two realities together to end the confusion and schizophrenia?

"If there is any great lesson we Americans need to learn with regard to the methodology of foreign policy," Kennan wrote, "it is that we must be gardeners and not mechanics in our approach to foreign affairs. We must come to think of the development of international life as an organic and not a mechanical process."[10] Americans did not create all the forces at work in the world. Americans must learn to perceive these forces for what they are and to make them work successfully with us and for us. Americans need to learn patience; they should not expect the world's problems to yield to forced and ill-considered measures. Some assume that Americans influence the Russians only by acting against them directly. Kennan insisted that just the opposite is true. The Russians watch and are influenced by what Americans do at home and by what Americans do more than by what they say.

In *Russia, the Atom and the West* (1957), Kennan discussed the Soviet Union in the nuclear age. He reminded his listeners in Britain (where he delivered the Reith Lectures on which the book was based) and America that the purpose of military strength and the threat of the atom was to provide a shield behind which Western societies would develop a new sense of direction and purpose. British and American defenses might also allow these countries to buy time for change to take place within the borders of their mighty totalitarian adversary. The London *Times* editorialized: "A single man, by strength of mind and feeling, has by himself produced a political change, a current of movement under the ice."[11] He had called for greater Anglo-American and European unity and the mutual withdrawal of forces from the heart of Europe. The problem of Germany lay at the core of any European settlement, and

10 George F. Kennan, *Realities of American Foreign Policy* (Princeton, N.J.: Princeton University Press, 1954), 93.
11 Editorial, London *Sunday Times*, February 16, 1958, p. 7.

Kennan argued for flexibility and openness on the future of Germany. Kennan's colleagues in the Department of State were less charitable when they argued that any attempt to pull back Western troops would leave Europe defenseless against a Soviet advance. By his proposals, he infuriated West German leaders and set off his foremost intellectual adversary, Secretary of State Dean Acheson, prompting James Reston to write: "Next to the Lincoln Memorial in moonlight the sight of Mr. Dean Acheson blowing his top is without doubt the most impressive view in the capital."[12] Yet West Germans have lived to see a policy of *ost-politik*, and the Americans have signed the Helsinki Accords, which recognize the legitimate spheres of influence of East and West. Kennan's thinking on Europe was apparently more prophetic than his critics, and his judgments more soundly based.

Kennan's books on Russia represent a large investment of his time and are more appropriate for Soviet specialists. Kennan received the Bancroft and Pulitzer prizes and the National Book Award for *Russia Leaves the War* (1956), the first volume of *Soviet-American Relations, 1917–1920*, followed by the second volume, *Decision to Intervene* (1958). He has continued his research on late nineteenth-century diplomatic history and is speaking less frequently on issues of contemporary importance. In the late 1960s, he debated students of the radical left in *Democracy and the Student Left* (1968), charging them with a lack of constructive purpose. Two volumes of his *Memoirs* appeared, the first in 1967 and the second in 1972, and overnight they became a much-quoted source in debates on the Cold War.

In *The Cloud of Danger: Current Realities of American Foreign Policy* (1977), Kennan submitted his recommendations on foreign policy to the incoming Carter administration. The overarching concern of this work is Soviet-American relations. Kennan unequivocally called for a more determined effort to break out of the straitjacket of military rivalry, seek every possible advance toward disarmament, and dissolve the cloud of danger hanging over mankind. He discussed foreign policy problems in the major world regions and urgent current problems, such

---

12 James Reston, "New Proposals for Old Disposals: Review of George F. Kennan's *Russia, the Atom and the West*," *New York Times Book Review* (March 2, 1958), 26.

as the SALT talks, human rights, and detente. Kennan sought to distill a coherent grand design from the varied approaches to American foreign policy. If he is viewed as successful, he has helped to provide a road map for future policy makers. Even if he has failed, he has set forth general ideas and principles conspicuously lacking in an age of specialists.

Kennan's continuing preoccupation has been with the impact of a hydra-headed public opinion on foreign policy. Bismarck had favored a limitation on legislative debates of foreign policy and had ruled out any discussion by parliaments of military estimates. This approach, he predicted, would reduce military budgets by 10 to 20 percent. For Kennan, as paradoxically for President Dwight D. Eisenhower, the enemy of a prudent foreign policy is the military-industrial complex. However, Kennan has confessed that he sees no solution to the problem within the American political system. America can't manage its external relations without allies, yet such relations are enormously complicated by congressional and public debates conducted in the spirit of military and political crusades.

Despite his strictures against moralism, Kennan is a deeply moral person. His closest friends see him as a man of far greater warmth and personal loyalty than is publicly perceived. Although taciturn and reserved, he is deeply committed to those he trusts and respects. Above all, no one questions that his is a mind of highest intelligence and originality. His grasp of foreign policy has seldom if ever been matched in American thought and practice.

WORKS BY GEORGE F. KENNAN

1951

American Diplomacy, 1900–1950. Chicago: University of Chicago Press.

1954

Realities of American Foreign Policy. Princeton, N.J.: Princeton University Press.

Das Amerikanisch Russische Verhaltnis. Stuttgart: Deutsche-Verlags-Anstalt.

1956

Russia Leaves the War. Princeton N.J.: Princeton University Press. Vol. I of *Soviet-American Relations, 1917–1920.*

1958

Decision to Intervene. Princeton, N.J.: Princeton University Press. Vol. II of *Soviet-American Relations, 1917–1920.*

Russia, the Atom and the West. New York: Harper & Row.

1961

Russia and the West Under Lenin and Stalin. Boston: Little, Brown.

1964

On Dealing with the Communist World. New York: Harper & Row, for the Council on Foreign Relations.

1967

Memoirs, 1925–1950. Vol. I. Boston: Little, Brown.

1968

From Prague After Munich. Princeton, N.J.: Princeton University Press.

Democracy and the Student Left. Boston: Little, Brown.

1971

The Marquis de Custine and His Russia in 1839. Princeton, N.J.: Princeton University Press.

1972

Memoirs, 1950–1963. Vol. II. Boston: Little, Brown.

1977

The Cloud of Danger: Current Realities of American Foreign Policy. Boston: Little, Brown.

LOUIS J. HALLE, Jr. (1910–)

The Crisis as Viewed Through History

Louis J. Halle, Jr., was born into a wealthy family on November 17, 1910, in New York City. He received a bachelor's degree from Harvard College in 1932, majoring in history, government, and economics. He worked for a railway company in Central America, and this early interest in South America continued through his years of public service. He was employed in an editorial capacity for a book-publishing firm, spent one year studying anthropology at the Harvard Graduate School, and served briefly in the army. Late in 1941 he joined the Department of State and remained there until 1954, except for a period in the Coast Guard.

Halle's role in the Department of State can be divided into two major activities. Until the summer of 1951, he was primarily concerned with Latin American affairs, in particular technical cooperation and the development of long-range policy for the whole of Latin America. In August, 1951, he was assigned to the National War College where he attracted the attention of George F. Kennan and Joseph E. Johnson, who was to become president of the Carnegie Endowment for International Peace. He became a member of the policy planning staff of the State Department, served under both George F. Kennan and Paul H. Nitze, and was intimately associated with Secretary of State Dean Acheson. His responsibilities spanned the entire range of United States foreign policy, and he was primarily involved with its conceptualization, development, and planning. He brought to this task the qualities of the generalist, for which his broad cultural background and wide political experience provided nearly ideal preparation.

In August of 1954, after John Foster Dulles became secretary of state, Halle left the State Department to accept an appointment as research professor in the Woodrow Wilson Department of Foreign Affairs at the University of Virginia. Here a period of reflection and study enabled him to launch a distinguished and productive scholarly career, which led to the publication of some ten books in foreign policy and international relations. At Virginia, he brought to his seminars a blend of historical imagination and realistic foreign policy analysis which identified him as one of the most thoughtful policy analysts in the Western world. By temperament and style, he preferred the life of the independent scholar, never seeking to fit his talents to the newly emergent trends of behavioral studies.

In 1954 he left the United States at the invitation of Jacques Freymond to become professor of American foreign policy at the Graduate Institute of International Studies in Geneva, Switzerland, where he remained until retirement. In 1977 he became a Swiss citizen, having long since made the decision to pursue his academic career in Geneva and to view American foreign policy from the vantage point of Europe. He lectured periodically in the United States and at centers in Europe but resisted frequent opportunities to return to the United States. It was in Geneva that Halle completed most of his writings. For a time, he turned his attention to the main questions of strategic foreign policy which drew on historical and contemporary periods in Western history. His seminars provided the vehicle for exploring and experimenting with new ideas. A new book emerged from nearly all of his famed Geneva seminars.

Halle's publication of sixteen books came as no surprise to those who knew his early writings. He began his career as a naturalist, publishing books of exquisite charm and grace, such as *Birds Against Men* (1938), *River of Ruins* (1941), and *Spring in Washington* (1947), which remains a minor classic.[1] His vivid portrayal of birdlife and nature reflected not only his ability to write but his interest in the world around him. If he had been less committed, he could have spent his years in the family's comfortable surroundings in upper Westchester County. His earliest political writings may have been too measured, discursive, and philosophical to place him at the center of the public controversies that

---

1 These and all works by Louis J. Halle are listed chronologically, with full publication data, beginning on p. 168 herein.

swirled around the more outspoken and often polemical writings of Kennan, Morgenthau, and Niebuhr. Yet for those with a taste for historical interpretation, no book on the postwar period is more important than his *Cold War as History* (1967). Those who know these earlier writings and Halle's broad cultural interests and unquenchable intellectual curiosity will not be surprised that in later years he turned to a vision of universal order arising from concern with the underlying chaos of the times.

Between his books in natural history and his monumental effort in universal history, *Out of Chaos*, Halle wrote a series of challenging volumes that illuminate various aspects of foreign policy, their theoretical basis and their cultural and historical background. Of these, *Civilization and Foreign Policy* (1952), which was described by Secretary of State Dean Acheson as "a book of illumination," provided an approach and a method for thinking about foreign policy. In this early study, Halle searched for general principles of foreign policy to answer the question: "Why a foreign policy?" He also discussed the elements of power, control of power, force or consent, and leadership or dominion. In his introduction, Secretary Acheson commented: "We Americans in our study and writing on international relations, have tended to shun theory and logical philosophic analysis of historical material—certainly in this century—in favor of narrative exposition and absorption in the problems of international organization." Halle's goal in *Civilization and Foreign Policy* was to established such a theory. As Acheson put it: "Mr. Halle believes that a new generation may be arising who have found in their intense and practical experience that our theoretics are of no help, and who are bringing their great gifts and experience to making good this deficiency." This generation, whom both Halle and Acheson lauded, numbers men such as George F. Kennan, Paul Nitze, and C. B. Marshall. With Halle, they were "the reviewers and critics of accepted policies, the reappraisers of problems, the prognosticators of new ones, the instigators of new synthesis and direction of effort to meet the emerging future."[2] To do so, they required an applicable body of theory in the area where philosophic and scientific thought approach

2 Louis J. Halle, Jr., *Civilization and Foreign Policy* (New York: Harper & Brothers, 1952), xvi, xix.

one another. To be relevant, the theorist, in Acheson's words, had to have one foot in the clouds and the other in the mud. Halle's book contained some of both of these elements. It helped the reader see the world scene steadily and whole, an objective which undergirds all of Halle's writings.

This book's major significance lies in the distinctions it makes between responsibility and thought. On one side, in Acheson's words: "The direction of the conduct of the foreign relations of the United States rests and must rest with the President of the United States. In him and upon him are the power and responsibility for decision." However widely the president may range for advice, the secretary of state must be his principal adviser. Therefore, "the Secretary . . . should be privy to all his thoughts and to him should be given the last clear chance for advice before action." To give such advice, the secretary needs help. "The formulation of judgment as to facts, probabilities, policy, and action calls for institutional effort, for which there is at the Secretary's hands one of the most effective instruments in the world—the Department of State." No single mind or group of minds can provide the basis for judgments that are so interrelated and complex. "Too much must be held in suspension awaiting the catalyst of decision."[3] The press of daily work makes the long view difficult. Courses of action are continued after their reasons for being have ceased to exist. The immediate obscures the horizon. Therefore, on the other side of action, someone or some group responsible to the secretary must keep the State Department's vision in focus. This was the task Halle and his colleagues undertook. *Civilization and Foreign Policy*, among other things, is a book about policy planning and the long view and about the challenge to civilization posed by the conflict between Western civilization and its foes.

Civilization and Foreign Policy was a different book in substance and in style than Halle's writings that immediately preceded and followed it. *On Facing the World* (1950) was a letter to his son John in several chapters meant to convey his personal philosophy. *Choice for Survival* (1958) began as a historical inquiry into the question of political choice

3 *Ibid.*, xvii, xviii.

and proceeded to confront the effects of the nuclear revolution on contemporary choices. This revolution has "increased the possibilities and the likelihood of averting unlimited war . . . [but also] has increased the penalty for failure to avert it." *Dream and Reality* (1958) spotlighted the human nature of foreign policy. Its primary thesis was that governments are people who are imperfect and fallible in perceptions, dominated by fears and subject to cycles of hope and disillusionment or dream and reality. Although Halle was concerned with the histories of other states, he dealt most directly with the United States plunged into a world of power politics in 1898, seeking for half a century to reconcile a policy of isolationism with imperial commitments overseas. Step by step, the course of American thought and action led, as in a Shakespearian tragedy, to Pearl Harbor. With the formulation of postwar American policies, Halle believed that Americans were beginning to adjust dreams with realities. He sounded a note of optimism, which he was not to sustain in the 1960s and 1970s: "The fifty years of floundering are over and we see our nation acting, at last, with a degree of worldly wisdom unmatched since the days of the Founding Fathers."[4]

Halle's next three volumes furthered his inquiries into fundamental issues of political and international philosophy. In *Men and Nations* (1962), he explored the philosophical foundations of man's common thought. In *The Society of Man* (1965), Halle turned to the theme of theory and practice in politics—how men seek to reconcile the orderly conceptual world of thought with the chaotic existential world. When life in the two worlds is marked by excessive divergence, such as Halle asserted was true for the Marxist-Leninist ideology, the consequences are tragic. However, through an evolutionary process leading to the worldwide organization of society, man may be driven forward by reciprocal action in the dual world of thought and action toward a new world society.

In *The Cold War as History* (1967), Halle undertook, in the spirit of Thucydides—a participant-observer in the Peloponnesian War—to describe a recent period of history as though it were a hundred years in

---

4 Louis J. Halle, Jr., *Choice for Survival* (New York: Harper & Brothers, 1958), 142; Louis J. Halle, Jr., *Dream and Reality* (New York: Harper & Brothers, 1958), 301.

the past. From the standpoint of its possible effect on the attitudes toward the present crisis, this book may have the most lasting effect of all Halle's writings. In it he reviewed the origins, underlying forces and trends, principal events, and vital participants in the conflict with a detachment from the views of those who viewed the Cold War as armageddon for America and those who asserted that there was nothing at stake. He traced the roots of Soviet policy back to historic Russian attitudes and goals and indicated that American behavior was an outgrowth of a historic experience which was the direct opposite of the Russians'. (No enemy had swept across American borders generation after generation; Americans had resisted centralization and repression, rather than giving passive approval to its establishment out of fear and custom.) Halle deftly sketched the power vacuums on either side of Russia into which it has tended to expand throughout its history. He analyzed Russia's postwar intentions in Eastern Europe, the tragedy of Poland, and the fall of Romania, Hungary, Bulgaria, and Czechoslovakia, as well as the American response through the Truman Doctrine, the Marshall Plan, and NATO. He carried his history through Nikita Khrushchev's era, coexistence, Cuba, and the beginnings of Vietnam and portrayed the Cold War as a human drama in which strong and weak leaders struggled to master the historical forces surrounding them. The story, as it unfolded for Halle, was not one of virtue struggling to overcome evil but instead one of irony, tragedy, and apparently inevitable conflict. Both sides are caught up in a condition of absolute predicament or irreducible dilemma; the proper attitude for the observer is sympathy for both parties.

Louis J. Halle's *Out of Chaos* (1977) is a work of epic proportions written with the same motivation and commitment that inspired Arnold J. Toynbee, Oswald Spengler, and Jacob Burckhardt. Underlying their several approaches is the same restless and brooding concern that segmental and specialized knowledge may be obscuring the search for life's meaning. Historians seek principally to report and describe past events; philosophers of history explore why events took place as they did and try to fathom history's patterns. From Thucydides to Halle, the aim of such philosophers was to establish certain viable principles of history and an organizing theme around which each study is built.

Toynbee's theme was his belief that world civilizations "may all reveal the same plot, if we analyze them rightly." That plot for him could be followed through three Acts, described as growth and development; crisis, breakdown, and rally; and final dissolution. The respected British historian, H. A. L. Fisher, himself a skeptic about political prediction, wrote of Toynbee: He "does not wholly confine himself to facts. He is fertile in large historical ideas and suggestive comparisons. . . . We do not think that his volume loses in practical value . . . [for he] keeps an impartial mind." Jacob Burckhardt, another scientific historian, also placed fact and spirit at the core of his historical writing: "The task of history as a whole is to show its twin aspects, distinct yet identical, proceeding from the fact that, firstly, the spiritual, in whatever domain it is perceived, has a historical aspect under which it appears as change . . . which forms part of a vast whole beyond our power to divine, and that, secondly, every event has a spiritual aspect by which it partakes of immortality." Man in history is both creature and creator, subject to forces he can only partly control but capable as no other living being of shaping them to his ends." That fact prompted Spengler's controlling view: "Man has become the creator of his technics of living—that is his grandeur and his doom. And the inner force of this creativeness we call culture."[5]

Out of Chaos is significantly different in origins, intent, and structure from the histories of Toynbee, Burckhardt, and Spengler. In 1922 Toynbee at age thirty-three began to outline his monumental *A Study of History*. Halle was nearly twice that age and the author of sixteen somewhat diverse books on foreign policy, politics, philosophy, and natural history when he began his magnum opus. Toynbee and his predecessors had confined themselves to the historian's craft and to the more traditional historical subject matter; but Halle, with breathtaking audacity, undertook to survey the whole of basic knowledge. To prepare himself, he studied treatises in the physical and biological sciences and entered into painstaking correspondence with authors of the leading

5 Arnold J. Toynbee, *The Tragedy of Greece* (London: Oxford University Press, 1931), 6; Royal Institute of International Affairs, *Survey of International Affairs, 1924* (Oxford: Oxford University Press, 1926), v–vi; Jacob Burckhart, *Force and Freedom* (New York: Pantheon Books, 1943), 83; Oswald Spengler, *Man and Technics* (New York: Alfred A. Knopf, 1932), 30–31.

texts. Through self-education, Halle pursued the ideal of the Renaissance man; and by every standard available to me, he has nobly attained his goal. The first two parts of the 650-page book are an awesome demonstration of the ability of a richly endowed mind in the humanities to encompass the complexities of the physical universe and of the origins and development of life on the planet. To have accomplished such mastery as a member of an interdisciplinary research team would have been noteworthy enough. Not only, however, has the integration of vast bodies of a specialized knowledge been achieved by an individual mind, but in their exposition Halle has written with a clarity that calls to mind James Reston's review of an early book by one of Halle's closest friends, George F. Kennan: "He had an idea and he could write. . . . He had not been living in a university long enough . . . to smother his ideas in clouds of academic jargon."[6]

Throughout the book, Halle has probed areas of human experience few humanists have dared to approach. Part III on the mind is subdivided into "The Origin of Mind," "The Coming of Man," "The Evolution of Brains," "The Beginnings of Human Culture," "Promethean Man," "Imagination," and "Language." Parts IV, V, and VI, and a conclusion entitled "Implications" are more characteristically the work of the philosopher of history, but with at least one conspicuous difference. The themes of the first three parts, which are drawn most heavily from the physical and biological sciences, are recapitulated and applied throughout the discussion of cultural and political history. Science is invoked not to bring a superficial respectability to Halle's work but to support and enrich it with the knowledge that science has contributed to human understanding. But it is science as creative theory, mathematics, and synthesis, not science as ever-narrower research, that captures Halle's thinking: "A research scientist disassembles a watch to measure and catalogue its parts; whereas a theoretical scientist, seeing a chaotic variety of scattered parts, puts them together in his imagination to make a single whole."[7]

Halle's major thesis is that men in historical civilizations over the

6 James Reston, "New Proposals for Old Disposals: Review of George F. Kennan's *Russia, the Atom and the West*," *New York Times Book Review* (March 2, 1958), 1.
7 Louis J. Halle, Jr., *Out of Chaos* (Boston: Houghton Mifflin, 1977), 583.

past six thousand years have brought order out of chaos through the application of mind and spirit and the establishment of a normative order. Every civilization is the product of an inspiration associated with some normative order of the mind that takes the form of a religion or an ideology. Civilizations, like any living organism, have life histories, extending from infancy through youth to old age and death. Halle implies that the current civilization, which has spread to the ends of the earth through the influence of science and technology, is entering old age. The birth of Western civilization coincided with the ending in about 1000 A.D. of the Dark Ages. Its vision was based on its aspiration to infinity (the Gothic cathedral), its complex balance of forces (the arch as contrasted with the Greek column and lintel), and its polarities and tensions. Throughout history, civilizations have broken down when their normative vision has been weakened and replaced by sheer military force. Tyranny and Caesarism or the police state has been the last-ditch response to growing social anarchy expressed in the expansion of military empires that become overextended and collapse.

At such a moment in history, Halle offers two predictions concerning the unknown future: it will not be what anybody has anticipated, and it may entail the loss of all cultural moorings and the shattering of psychological security for mankind. Hitherto, men in the West have been able to conduct their lives, regulate their behavior, and make their decisions on the basis of a normative order founded on tradition, deriving its authority from custom and moral consensus and providing an established hierarchy of values for distinguishing good from bad or right from wrong. When the conditions of life to which traditions and customs are bound change overnight, people lose their moorings without having gained new values and are prey to outlandish fashions, political demagogues, and convulsive mass movements. Because the pace of change is too rapid for tradition and custom to keep up, Halle believes that the next two or three centuries will be a period of unprecedented chaos and disorder, more damaging because nuclear weapons, the most lethal powers of destruction, could in a few days annihilate a large part of conscious life on what would become an essentially uninhabitable earth.

Halle, like Toynbee, asks what the outcome will be and if mankind can find a way out. Toynbee, believing with Halle that Western civilization is in decline but refusing to accept Spengler's pessimistic determinism, suspended judgment on prospects for the West, and so in considerable measure does Halle. Toynbee took hope for the more immediate future in the possibility of a realistic political settlement between East and West and ultimately in world government. Halle sees some chance of the former but none for world government at present. Toynbee was persuaded that the movements of civilizations have been recurrent, but "the continuous upward movement of religion may be served and promoted by the cyclical movement of civilizations round the cycle of birth, death, birth." Religion, particularly Christianity, provides the ultimate hope for Toynbee. Halle concludes his monumental work with words reminiscent of Toynbee: "With one exception, we can have absolute knowledge of nothing. The exception was stated by Decartes. . . . I think, therefore I am. . . . My thoughts encompass divinity, there divinity is. The divinity that my thoughts encompass is associated with the order that arises out of chaos. . . . As we expand our knowledge of this realm, we . . . see it in terms of one sublime order that awaits full realization."[8]

WORKS BY LOUIS J. HALLE, JR.

1936

Transcaribbean: A Travel Book of Guatemala, El Salvador, British Honduras. New York & Toronto: Longmans Green.

1938

Birds Against Men. New York: Viking Press.

1941

River of Ruins. New York: Henry Holt.

1947

Spring in Washington. New York: Harper & Brothers.

1950

On Facing the World. New York: William Sloane Associates.

1952

Civilization and Foreign Policy. New York: Harper & Brothers.

1958

Choice for Survival. New York: Harper & Brothers.

Dream and Reality. New York: Harper & Brothers.

8 Arnold J. Toynbee, *Civilization on Trial* (New York: Oxford University Press, 1948), 236; Halle, *Out of Chaos,* 646.

LOUIS J. HALLE, JR.

1962

Men and Nations. Princeton, N.J.: Princeton University Press.

1963

Sedge. New York: Praeger.

1965

The Society of Man. London: Chatto & Windus.

1967

The Cold War as History. New York: Harper & Row.

1972

The Ideological Imagination. Chicago: Quadrangle Books.

1973

The Sea and the Ice: A Naturalist in Antarctica. Boston: Houghton Mifflin, for the National Audubon Society.

1977

Out of Chaos. Boston: Houghton Mifflin.

1978

Foreign Policy and the Democratic Process: The Geneva Papers. Edited by Louis J. Halle and Kenneth W. Thompson. Washington, D.C.: University Press of America.

RAYMOND ARON (1905–)

Conflict and the Sociological Imagination

Raymond Aron was born March 14, 1905, in Paris, France, the son of Gustave Emile and Suzanne Aron. His father was a professor of law. The younger Aron attended the École Normale Superieure in Paris. He earned his *agregation de philosophie* in 1928 (graduating first in his class followed by Jean-Paul Sartre) and his *doctorat en lettres* in 1938. He was a lecturer at the University of Cologne in Germany from 1930 to 1931; a member of the staff of the French Institute in Berlin from 1931 to 1933; a professor of philosophy at the Lycee in Havre, France, from 1933 to 1934; secretary of the Center of Social Information at the École Normale Superieure in Paris from 1934 to 1949; professor of sociology at the University of Toulouse in France in 1939; editor of *La France Libre* in London, England, from 1940 to 1944; and a pilot for the Free French in World War II. During the war, he was an associate of General Charles de Gaulle. In the postwar era, it was said that Aron was the only political scientist whom the general read with any consistency. Aron has also enjoyed a wide readership in America. Noted for his skepticism and liberal realism, Aron has often been compared with Walter Lippmann. Herbert G. Nicholas called him the "indispensable intellectual conferencier" and "the cool distiller of passion and interest into order and light."

Within France, Aron's double reputation has been that of distinguished political sociologist—he has been professor of sociology at the College de France since 1970 and professor in the Faculté des Lettres at the Sorbonne from 1955 to 1968—and columnist and pundit, whether as cofounder of *Les Tempes Modernes*, member of the staff of *Combat* in 1946, or regular columnist of *Figaro* since 1947. He has eschewed lasting political and religious affiliations, but his essentially conservative political outlook has led him to engage in fierce debates with Marxist thinkers (he was burned in effigy during the Vietnam War).

Events have shaped his philosophy. From his early Kantian optimism modified by a direct experience with the rise of totalitarianism in Germany, Aron ceased to believe in progressive history. Examiners asked when he presented his doctoral thesis if there were personal reasons to explain his melancholy perspective. He answered that a sense of imminent catastrophe hardly inspired mirth. In the late 1930s and after, Aron became identified with the realistic school of social thought. His focus has been on the present more than on the past or the future. Stanley Hoffmann has argued that Aron's intellectual masters were Baron de Montesquieu and Max Weber more than Karl Marx or Immanuel Kant, but Aron has observed that for thirty years he read and criticized Marx and that his interest in Montesquieu and Alexis de Tocqueville came late in his career.

Aron belongs to the mainstream of contemporary European, rather than Anglo-American, political and social thought. This heritage has placed him at the center of the great debate between classical and scientific viewpoints. European sociologists in the late 1800s reacted to the scientific pretensions of Auguste Comte and criticized the application of narrow scientific methodologies to the human sciences. Like other European writers, Aron has tended to consider sociology and the philosophy of history as nearly interchangeable spheres of thought. In his doctoral dissertation, he made a strong argument for historical relativism. Historical perception moves through three separate stages: first, fiction, myth, and legend; second, scientific history; and third, critical analysis, which does not reject the scientific method but seeks rather to point up the limits of historical science. Aron's doctoral thesis, *Introduction to the Philosophy of History* (1961), had the subtitle: *The Limits of Historical Objectivity*.[1]

Aron's first important work following his doctoral thesis was *German Sociology* (1964), a discussion of Max Weber's approach to the social sciences and Weber's attempt to arrive at universally valid propositions of fact and causality. Science for Weber did not consist of eternal truths but progress toward truth. True science has the possibility of universally

---

1 This and all works by Raymond Aron are listed chronologically, with full publication data, beginning on p. 177 herein.

valid knowledge, but the prospect of this in the human sciences is debatable. In the natural sciences, segments of reality may be isolated and measured, but historical events can only be understood through combinations and synthesis. Both Weber and Aron rejected the claims of Comte and his followers that all studies must be scientific. However, Weber offered a radical distinction between facts and values, which from Aron's perspective was too far-reaching. Weber believed that social realities were fragmentary and irregular but that social scientists were able to impose on such realities an objective method that could produce universally valid answers. Aron criticized this purported universality since he doubted that the initial subjectivity of the observer could ever be wholly purged. Historical conditions for Weber were facts that existed independently of values. Aron questioned whether this distinction was wholly acceptable.

Aron's *Century of Total War* (1954) examined the transformation of warfare from Sarajevo to Hiroshima. For limited wars in the eighteenth century, soldiers had no need to know why they fought. By the twentieth century, however, the soldier and citizen had become interchangeable; the public mobilized for war had to be infused with a spirit of moral righteousness. Once war ended, mass passions and secular religions destroyed the traditional institutions that might have brought stability instead of violence. With World War II, Europe entered the century of total war; it had lost control of its history and was dragged along by the contradictory promptings of techniques and passions. A national war was followed by an imperial war, and Aron plainly feared that nations would be carried into a third world war by the chain reactions of violence.

Aron asked how men were to control the forces let loose by a century of total war. Toynbee had prophesied that peace would come as societies were exhausted by violence and as a universal empire emerged that subjected belligerent states to its laws. Only Marx wrote of understanding history in order to change it. The influence of Europe in the Third World has been weakened by the appeal and prestige of the Marxist theory of imperialism, according to which Western economies are driven to seek colonial empires to avert social and economic collapse. Yet Aron, continuing his thirty-year criticism of Marxism, observed that economic need had little effect on colonialism, especially for France: "It will not be denied that capitalism tends to incorporate underdeveloped territories into its system. . . . [Yet] neither the First nor the Second World War originated directly in a conflict over colonies." Political and diplomatic interests came first, and economics followed: "Modern economy creates solidarity among the nations. The idea of sharing spoils, of seizing treasures, belongs to another age. In the century of industry and trade, war would deal a fatal blow to everyone, victors and vanquished."[2] Even Hitler had always placed political over economic interests.

The present century has ushered in wars by total states. Wars always resemble the societies that wage them. The supreme laws of the nation at war may be summed up in two words: organization and rationalization. In wartime, administrative centralization becomes irresistible. Two groups of men take control of the state: generals and industrialists. Group autonomy, freedom of judgment, and expression of opinions become luxuries. Total mobilization approaches the totalitarian order. State monopoly of publicity and ideology stems from the need to "organize enthusiasm." World War I created the opportunity grasped by the Bolsheviks to seize power in Russia, much as the economic crisis of 1929 in Germany brought the National Socialists to power. Because war and peace following World War II are not two distinct and separate conditions, the Cold War has condemned the democracies to permanent mobilization: "Let the Cold War be prolonged for some years and all countries will be transformed into fortified camps, unless they prefer the certainties of nonresistance to the uncertainties of effort and struggle."[3]

In these circumstances, Aron called for "faith without illusions." Comparing individual rights or the possibility of political opposition or the effect of production on the welfare of the masses, the American and Russian systems are direct opposites of one another. In determining the fate of Western civilization, their rivalry is not negligible, neutralists notwithstanding. The question to be answered is whether the struggle can be viewed in the same terms in Africa and Asia. Differences between

2 Raymond Aron, *The Century of Total War* (Garden City, N.Y.: Doubleday, 1954), 58.
3 *Ibid.*, 92.

developed and underdeveloped countries will persist, not for decades but for centuries. For them suffering or famine is the penalty for not making the most of existing resources. Aron felt that material progress was possible in the developing world, but he had greater doubts that social or spiritual progress would automatically follow scientific progress. The French worker, though receiving higher wages for shorter hours, had come to doubt (with his doubts being fed by intellectuals) that he had anything to defend: "Social envy . . . is in danger of damaging the cohesion of collectivities which make material success the supreme aim." Aron took heart in discovering "a dawning suspicion that other institutions [than economic production] are also important— the rule of law . . . a career open to initiative or talent, mutual confidence between the different elements of the community, the development of science through freedom of research." Technical science is morally neutral. Although violence has increased due to the power of science as employed by modern states, so has healing through medicine. Barbarism was not created by the Industrial Revolution: "The population of Germany after the Thirty Years' War had fallen by more than half. That of Western Europe has risen by ten percent since 1939." The Romans sold slaves, and the ancient Chinese perfected torture. Science does not teach man to abuse his fellow man; it merely affords him more lethal means to do so: "Humanity is not doomed to lose itself in the conquest of nature and in forgetfulness of itself."[4]

A novelist wrote concerning the struggle between democracy and communism that the former was defending a half-truth against a total lie. Soviet society claims to be on the march toward perfection, and people are always ashamed of reality when they compare it with the ideal. Some look to a universal Communist empire as they would to utopia, but for Aron, "such an empire is no longer a dream but a nightmare." The cultures of the world are too diverse and the nationalisms spread by Europeans across the continents are too ardent for the establishment of universal empire. For the West: "The right to choose one's God, the right to seek truth freely, and the right not to be at the mercy of the police, of officials, or of psycho-technicians, are, or should be for

4 *Ibid.*, 361, 362, 365.

them values as unconditional as the triumph of the Soviet Union for the Stalinists." In the long run, fidelity to such traditional values may prove to have exerted a greater hold than the fury of fanaticism. The totalitarians, in practice, bring back "a secular despotism, a bureaucratic hierarchy . . . and it has not been proved that the totalitarian regimes are any more an episode in the age of wars. The survival of hope depends on the victory of the liberal communities."[5]

These goals are the substantive hopes that Aron has offered an embattled world, and their source is essentially his sociological imagination. He has accepted Weber's plea for adventurous choices in the midst of contradictory values, which are conflicting but not inherently irreconcilable. For nations that must survive in a Hobbesian world, the ethics of responsibility as defined by Weber are more directly relevant than the ethics of conviction. Political decisions must heed both the demands of conscience and what Aron called reasonable choice. Prudence and compromise can reconcile the two ethical approaches. Science, which for Weber had little or no connection with political choice, can help in the analysis of the conditions of choice. The state of nature is the distinguishing feature of international relations, and a rational theory must take this into account, as discussed in *Peace and War* (1970). What differentiates the international field from all others is the legitimacy of the use of military force. In international relations, the state is required to take justice into its own hands. The state of nature is the state of war, for international political relations are conducted in the shadow of war. Aron agreed with Montesquieu, however, in describing war as a social not a natural phenomenon. The statesman's aim, therefore, must be to mitigate and moderate, not to eliminate war. In peace, nations should do the most good possible to one another; and in war, the least harm. International relations thus possess a dual social and antisocial character. There is more to such relations than conflict, but conflict will never disappear.

Normative theory, as distinguished from rational theory, is dependent upon choices that include history, the limits of knowledge or doctrine, and the requirements of rationality. The conditions of choice, as

5 *Ibid.*, 365, 366.

Aron viewed them, are bounded by theory and practice, the two forces of normative theory in international affairs. There is no simple route from theory as science to theory as action. Indeed, the counsels of action or precepts for foreign policy derive not from science but from moral theories. The application of theory to practice is limited by the fact that ends are indeterminate, means cannot be measured, and unique circumstances cannot be compared. Diplomacy is indeterminate. The statesman who abides by the rules risks defeat by those who show less commitment to their observance.

Prudence in foreign policy represents a synthesis of the social and antisocial requirements of normative theory. It cannot resolve the antinomies of the dual character of morality; it strives to reach a compromise. The first condition of moral choice among nations is the recognition of the leader's responsibility for the security of the state. Though idealists reject the use of force, the statesman is obliged to accept its function for self-preservation. Prudence demands action in accordance with the concrete facts of the international situation rather than out of passive obedience to abstract goals. Prudence prefers to limit violence to punishment of the aggressor, which too often amounts to a meaningless search for the guilty party. The goal of normative theory in practice is the establishment of concrete and accessible moral objectives, not the search for limitless moral objectives. Identifying moral precepts can create a moral framework. Prudence means acting in the realm of irreducible indeterminacy, recognizing the legitimacy of the use of force, and seeking points of compromise in the law, rather than engaging in frequent a priori condemnation of violence.

Does Aron's point of view allow him to think and write within a moral framework, or does his position lead to the abandonment of morality in the face of persistent conflict? In more general terms, is prudence a means of building a moral viewpoint or a denial of moral principles? Theoretically, Aron's approach is one of instrumental rationality, which involves interpreting facts, adapting politics to the accessible facts, and searching for the moral content in factual situations. Normatively, Aron rejects the ethics of conviction as an immediate guide to action and chooses instead the ethics of responsibility. More specifically, in foreign policy for the Cold War, the ethics of responsibility requires that the West must survive the challenge of the Soviet Union, must reject any strategy calling for the conquest by the West of Eastern Europe, and must maintain both a nuclear and a conventional balance with the Soviet Union. In military strategy for the Cold War, the ethics of responsibility demand sufficient military preparedness and strength to safeguard the West in war and sufficient deterrent strength to prevent war if possible.

In evaluating the ultimate values of the West in the struggle with the Soviet Union, Aron proceeds on two levels. Although both sides claim to represent certain democratic values, sociological evaluation shows that the Soviet Union employs democratic values only in a rhetorical sense. The sociologist is able to discover little liberty in the Soviet Union. From the standpoint of philosophical analysis, Aron rejects as an absurdity the argument of the Communists that historical determinism gives moral validity to their political ambitions. Historically, regimes claiming absolute truth as the basis for molding society end in repression and totalitarianism. The Soviet Union is no exception.

Lastly, Aron is skeptical about the prospects of universal peace. A radical transformation of international society is unlikely. A more human and moral course for national leaders is to strive for moderation, look for reasonable choices, and follow the path of prudence.

WORKS BY RAYMOND ARON

1946

L'Homme contre Les Tyrans. 2nd ed. Paris: Gallimard.

1948

Le Grand Schisme. 13th ed. Paris: Gallimard.

1954

The Century of Total War. Garden City, N.Y.: Doubleday.

1955

Polémiques. 5th ed. Paris: Gallimard.

1958

War and Industrial Society. Translated by Mary Bottomore. London: Oxford University Press.

1959

Imperialism and Colonialism. Leeds, England: University of Leeds.

1961

Introduction to the Philosophy of History. Translated by George J. Irwin. Boston: Beacon Press.

The Dawn of Universal History. Translated by Dorothy Pickles. New York: Frederick A. Praeger.

Dimensions de la Conscience Historique. Paris: Librairie Plon.

1962

The Opium of the Intellectuals. Translated by Terence Kilmartin. New York: W. W. Norton.

1963

World Technology and Human Destiny. Ann Arbor: University of Michigan Press.

1964

German Sociology. Translated by Mary and Thomas Bottomore. New York: Free Press of Glencoe.

La Philosophie Critique de L'Histoire: Essai sur une Théorie Allemande de L'Histoire. 3rd ed. Paris: Librairie Philosophique J. Vrin.

1965

Democracy and Totalitarianism. Translated by Valence Ionescu. New York: Frederick A. Praeger.

The Great Debate: Theories of Nuclear Strategy. Translated by Ernst Pawel. Garden City, N.Y.: Doubleday.

Auguste Comte et Alexis de Tocqueville. Oxford: Clarendon Press.

1967

The Industrial Society: Three Essays on Ideology and Development. New York: Frederick A. Praeger.

1968

"The Anarchical Order of Power." *Daedalus,* XCV (Spring, 1966), 479–502.

On War. Translated by Terence Kilmartin. New York: W. W. Norton.

Progress and Disillusion: The Dialectics of Modern Society. New York: New American Library.

1969

Marxism and the Existentialists. Translated by Helen Weater, Robert Addis, and John Weighman. New York: Harper & Row.

The Elusive Revolution: Anatomy of a Student Revolt. Translated by Gordon Clough. New York: Praeger.

1970

Main Currents in Sociological Thought. Vol. II. Translated by Richard Howard and Helen Weaver. Garden City, N.Y.: Doubleday.

An Essay on Freedom. Translated by Helen Weaver. New York: World Publishing Co.

Peace and War: A Theory of International Relations. Translated by Richard Howard and Annette Baker Fox. New York: Praeger.

1974

The Imperial Republic: The United States and the World, 1945–1973. Translated by Frank Jellinek. Cambridge, Mass.: Winthrop Publishers.

1975

History and the Dialectic of Violence: An Analysis of Sartre's Critique de la Raison Dialectique. Translated by Barry Cooper. Oxford: Blackwells.

1976

Penser La Guerre, Clausewitz. 2 vols. Paris: Gallimard.

1978

Politics and History: Selected Essays by Raymond Aron. Edited and translated by Miriam Bernheim Conant. New York: Free Press.

PART IV

World Order Theorists

A treatise on international thought that ignored world order theorists would be fragmentary and incomplete. The world scene invites broadly conceived study and analysis of the forces of nationalism and internationalism. The literature of contemporary international studies reflects the dual nature of national competition and international cooperation. The majority of thinkers discussed in the first three parts have emphasized the forces of national sovereignty, although not to the exclusion of common international interests. Other thinkers have placed greater emphasis on emerging worldwide interests and have endeavored to construct theories of world order. Like the writers already discussed, a list of preeminent world-order theorists is bound to be selective and incomplete. International lawyers, political scientists, and historians who have been the architects of new approaches to world order have influenced others who continue to develop new perspectives and approaches in the 1970s. The Institute for the Study of World Order, headed by Saul Mendlowitz, and the Institute for the Study of World Politics, which I have directed, are present-day expressions of scholarly interest in world order.

Any list of world order theorists must include thinkers such as Quincy Wright, David Mitrany, Charles de Visscher, and Arnold J. Toynbee. Their writings surpass in scholarly content and theoretical rigor the action-oriented writings of the leaders of such movements as Peace Through Law or the World Federalists. However noble and inspiring, these movements have lost much of their relevance in the 1970s, but the works of men such as Wright and Mitrany will endure and cannot be ignored by present-day scholars.

Quincy Wright helped to found the Chicago School and created the first interdisciplinary committee on international relations in any American university. His students included Harold Lasswell, William T. R. Fox, Frederick Schuman, Nathan Leites, Richard Falk, Marcus Raskin, and many who established centers of international studies at other universities. Wright was both the scholar par excellence—probing every existing discipline for the light it threw on problems of war and peace—and the tireless reformer of the international system. Every major scholarly and professional organization turned to him for leadership. His *Study of War* remains the most far-ranging and encyclopedic review of war and peace in the English language.

David Mitrany had fewer scholarly credentials, but his theory of functionalism underlies most of the later writings on transnationalism and interdependence. His *Working Peace System* called attention to activities between nations that tended to build international community. Whereas other writers stressed international politics, Mitrany highlighted the importance of international cooperation through international waterways and postal and telegraphic communications. These efforts, he hoped, might ultimately lead to the erosion of national sovereignty as international functionalism spilled over into the realm of international political cooperation.

Of all the publicists, jurists, and scholars writing on international law, the Belgian jurist Charles de Visscher may have the most lasting influence. European legal writers and American scholars, such as Percy Corbett (who translated into English de Visscher's classic *Theory and Reality in Public International Law*), Philip Jessup, and Myres Mc-

Dougal, have testified to the formative influence of de Visscher's work. De Visscher discussed the relation of theory and practice in international law, the connections between national and international morality and international law, and the problems of enforcement. Charles de Visscher was both a moral philosopher and an international jurist.

Arnold J. Toynbee sought as a historian to explain the rise and fall of world civilizations and the possibilities of world order. He was more a philosopher of history than a historian. He traced the histories of twenty-one known civilizations and constructed a theory of history to account for their birth and death. He predicted the future of Western civilization and its implications for present-day world order. His multi-volume *Study of History* remains the most ambitious contemporary analysis of universal history—an appropriate conclusion for this study of master thinkers.

QUINCY WRIGHT (1890–1970)

Beyond the Study of War

Quincy Wright was born on December 28, 1890, in Medford, Massachusetts, one of three sons of Philip and Elizabeth Wright. His family and ancestors comprised an impressive body of scientists and scholars. His great-grandfather Elizur Wright, a leading actuarial authority, was called the father of scientific life insurance. His father, Philip Green Wright, who began his career as a mathematician, widened his interests to include astronomy, economics, and literature. As a professor at Lombard College in Galesburg, Illinois, he was remembered by Carl Sandburg as an inspiring teacher and the man responsible for the publication of Sandburg's first book. Philip Wright did economic research for the Brookings Institution on the tariff, international economics, and foreign trade and published a 1932 report on unemployment entitled, "Outcasts of Efficiency." Strong family interests in science were also evident in the careers of Quincy's two brothers. Sewell applied mathematical models to the study of population genetics, and a younger brother, Theodore, made major contributions to aviation engineering and aviation production. That Quincy shared this commitment to science was evident throughout his *Study of War* (1942) and in particular in his applications of the statistical studies of Lewis Richardson, who used mathematics to analyze war and other international phenomena. Quincy received the bachelor's degree from Lombard College in 1912 and the master's and doctorate degrees in 1913 and 1915 from the University of Illinois.

Along with his interest in science, Wright also demonstrated an early commitment to normative concerns and to reform of the international system. In 1907 he wrote a prize-winning essay entitled "The Christ of the Andes," analyzing the arbitration of the bitter boundary dispute between Chile and Argentina (the title referred to the monument erected to memorialize that settlement). Throughout his career, Wright was to uphold the need for reform and rational change in international law, organization, and politics. As both a scholar with the highest reputation for objectivity and the prophet of a new world order, he combined rigorous social science with vigorous social reform. He championed the new international law in his writings and as a close advisor to Justice Robert Jackson at the Nuremberg trials. As one of the founders of the Commission to Study the Organization of the Peace, he helped plan the postwar structure of the United Nations. He was active at both the national and grassroots levels as a leader of the United Nations Association in the United States. He was the only American scholar to attain the presidencies of the American Society of International Law, American Political Science Association, International Political Science Association, and American Association of University Professors. In personal recollection of Quincy Wright, I am struck by the extent to which he combined broad theoretical interests and concern for policies and problem-oriented studies.

The criticism is frequently made by reviewers of the corpus of international relations literature that theorists are indifferent to problems and students of foreign policy care little for scientific or philosophical generalizations. The dominant motif in much present-day writing is a separation of theory and practice. It divides age groups, methods of approach, and leading writers in the field. Often policy studies are reserved for pundits and observers courageous or foolhardy enough to undertake the study of a complex problem. It is the thesis of this personal recollection of Quincy Wright that to a considerable extent he represented a different outlook on theory and problems. His lectures were interspersed with frequent and extended discussions of policy questions. The first three lectures I ever heard him give dealt with Soviet-American relations, the Nuremberg trials, and the role and limitations of the United Nations.

The nature of international relations in the first half of the twentieth century determined that leading figures such as Wright would be both scholarly and practical. The international relations community asked them to serve as members of arbitration panels and advisers to international organizations and courts and to study practical problems. The gap between those who make foreign policy and those who write about it had not become as great as it is today. This was particularly the case after the United States Senate rejected the League of Nations. Men like Wright spearheaded the attempt to link foreign policy to organizations like the League. They were the moral spokesmen for the reformation of international society. They called upon legislators and policy makers to reconsider the relation of the United States to the League of Nations. Because they had a single, simple proposition for transforming international society, they received a hearing by policy makers. Their influence was heightened by the evangelical quality of their reforms. Policy makers could not ignore scholars who had generated a following among students and the concerned public. Some of the new international studies centers, such as Brookings, helped to give them even greater outreach through publications that dealt with policy problems.

As late as 1945, Wright shuttled back and forth between Chicago and Washington, seeking to influence foreign policy. There was little, if any, stigma attached to relationships with government. Indeed, the aura of the man of affairs surrounded Wright and gave greater credibility to his theories. The consensus on foreign policy goals and methods was greater by far then than it is in the 1970s. I cannot recall reference to Wright's working within the system because in fact the intellectual community was itself an integrated system. Even the debates at the University of Chicago between Wright and Hans J. Morgenthau went on within a particular framework and system. The absence of deep divisons helped to encourage scholars to look at political questions.

Wrights's scholarly output was enormous—1,155 published titles including 21 books, 141 chapters in or introductions to books by others, 392 journal articles, 123 encyclopedia articles, 423 book reviews, and 55 published radio broadcasts. Given his dual interest in normative and scientific concerns, it is not surprising that half of his 1,155 titles appeared in legal or international journals, and the other half were published in social science, philosophical, and historical journals. His writing, though scholarly and erudite, was clear and practical.

Wright's magnum opus was *A Study of War*, first published in 1942 and republished in 1965 with a commentary on wars since 1942.[1] (His

---

1 This and all works by Quincy Wright are listed chronologically, with full publication data, beginning on p. 201 herein.

wife, Louise Wright, also published an abridged, one-volume edition in paperback in 1965.) *A Study of War* is a work of forty chapters totaling 1,080 pages, plus an additional 420 pages of forty-four scholarly appendixes on multidisciplinary approaches to war, peace, and international relations with critical analyses of the assumptions and axioms underlying each of the disciplines. Not only is *A Study of War* a major contribution to an understanding of war, but it also contains some of Wright's most important views on the social sciences and international studies. Yet Quincy Wright's importance as a theorist of world order is not exhausted in his role as a social scientist and a normative thinker. His approach to international politics and organization and to peace and war can also be illumined by examples from his teaching. In fact, Professor Wright's teaching may be at least as important as his monumental output of scholarly writings. In his teaching, some of Wright's major conceptions of war and peace, international organization, and foreign policy were made concrete and explicit.

As early as the 1930s, Quincy Wright addressed himself to the problem of war in his lectures and researches. He saw war as a continuing social and political institution. Although disagreeing with Karl von Clausewitz's dictum that war is the continuance of politics by other means, he did recognize that domestic policy and international strategy are intrinsically linked. As others have noted, Wright was involved in a significant intellectual movement at Chicago. The political science department, of which he was a member, sought to mobilize the total resources of the social sciences to bring them to bear on political and social problems. It was natural, therefore, that Wright, although an international lawyer, should from the start seek to rally colleagues from neighboring and sometimes remote disciplines to help him in the study of war. *A Study of War* is encyclopedic in scope since he turned to the biologist and botanist for insights on war in the natural order, the psychologist and psychiatrist for guidance on the pathology of war, and the anthropologist and archaeologist for lessons from ancient cultures and peoples. *A Study of War* included quotations from Warder C. Allee, Bruno Bettelheim, Lewis F. Richardson, and Carl Rogers. The University of Chicago in his time was as rich in aggregate intellectual resources as any university in the country. Even the professional schools were recruiting grounds for Wright, and he turned to the faculties of law and medicine to discover individuals who were concerned with conflict, aggression, and violence. Later scholars credited Wright with having provided early hints and propositions that guided their work.

One value of Wright's *Study of War* may be the historical evidence it produced that neither the League of Nations nor the United Nations nor any international agreement had ever successfully outlawed or eliminated war among nations. The patient study of conflict resolution taken up in the 1960s by a new generation of social scientists and natural scientists has its model in his work. No one would be justified in saying today that mankind has exhausted the study of war or the search for the modalities of peace, for conflict is present on every side—in the Communist and the non-Communist world and among the newly independent states and the more ancient ones.

Curiously Wright's study is more in tune with our times than it was with the prevailing spirit of the post–World War I era. At that time, the United States had just rejected the League of Nations, which Woodrow Wilson had helped to structure through speeches and writings. A nation had turned on its prophet. The Senate and a "handful of willful men" had rejected internationalism. In response, activists and scholars girded themselves for a great crusade to establish an international organization that would do away with war. Secretary of State Cordell Hull was to speak of the United Nations as the instrument for eliminating once and for all national rivalries and power politics. The cause of war was assumed to be known—it was the product of one form of international relationship, which a new international organization would eradicate. It should not be surprising, therefore, that many international lawyers and fledgling social scientists were anxious to get on with the study of peace. Some idealists were impatient with *A Study of War* because of its concentration on the social and psychological aspects of aggression, discussion of innate instincts, and research into the motivations of nations and their historic conflicts. They wanted to concentrate on creating an international institution that would eliminate war, not to study war's recurrence in history. Wright too was strongly in favor of the League of Nations and the United Nations, but he was attempting to determine the conditions of peace through a deepening understanding of the causes of war.

Wright as a historian was fortunate to be writing in the 1930s and 1940s rather than the 1960s. It was not *infra dig* in those days to take an example from the Congress of Vienna or from the diplomacy of the Italian city-states. There was a respect for history that was subsequently to disappear. Hans J. Morgenthau was himself the product of a classical training in European history, yet I often marveled that Wright and Morgenthau were almost equally conversant with details of twelfth-century or sixteenth-century diplomatic history. With all his zeal for the reformation of international society, Wright understood that men and nations had passed this way before. He wanted to discover and report how men thought and acted in earlier periods of history. He was often reminded of analogies from history. Although wary of some analogies, he often found them suggestive. He documented the evolving character of warfare—history and war, origin of war, primitive warfare, historic warfare, and fluctuations in the intensity of modern war—with the historian's discipline and skills. It goes without saying that he made use of the historical research of others. No single scholar could have done all the original research for a work like *A Study of War*.

In all of this, Wright felt an affinity with Arnold Toynbee. Wright first suggested to some of his students the relevance of philosophies of history to contemporary international relations. What bothered him about Toynbee was Toynbee's overgeneralization not supported by evidence. Wright was in one sense more closely wedded to the tentative and cautious practicing historian, but at the same time his broadmindedness and eclecticism led him to urge others to delve into the philosophy of history. In at least one limited field, he was a bold theorist of history. His ideas about warfare and the control of warfare represent a certain limited philosophy of history. His generalizations offended more specialized scholars, yet they were supported by documentation and scholarship. He could not bring himself to take the strong line that Toynbee did as philosopher of history, but he was challenged and excited by this approach.

Institutional history came into its own in Quincy Wright's day. People were beginning to write about the Congress of Vienna, the European system, and the first stages of the League of Nations. The evidence was available on the workings of certain reformist organizations

187

that grew out of the Hague conferences at the turn of the century. Wright was eager to find out how given institutions had worked, what the effects of new structures and codes had been on practice, and why certain organizations were used more often than others in international politics. He was interested in the Department of State as an institution and examined it through his research and through consulting. He encouraged the work of the Brookings Institution, which under Leo Pasvolsky began basic studies on a broad range of international organizations.

For another reason, however, Wright made his contribution at least partly as an institutionalist. He found himself curiously in the center and yet at the periphery of those reformist institutionalists like Robert Hutchins, Mortimer Adler, and the Borgeses at the University of Chicago. Hutchins was convinced that new institutions could transform human behavior. In his debate with Reinhold Niebuhr, Hutchins had argued that, although the extent of world community necessary and essential for the support of a world government did not exist, world government interacting with community could bring it into being. World government was necessary and therefore possible in Hutchins' view. Wright had some of this vision in his own outlook, but his historical and institutional grounding made him skeptical about Hutchins' version. At the same time, Wright was sympathetic with Hutchins' observations, so once again he became involved in a fascinating interchange with first-class minds pursuing common objectives from different angles of vision. He was a sometime speaker and commentator in the panels that Hutchins organized. He himself brought together various groups for week-long symposia under the auspices of the Norman Wait Harris Foundation to discuss world community, international institutions, and the United Nations. He teamed up with William Fielding Ogburn and Louis Wirth, the distinguished Chicago sociologists, to spur discussions on the relation between society, community, and institutions. He was endlessly intrigued by the question of how much community was necessary for what kinds of institutions in society. No one could say that he was a narrow institutionalist who looked at organizations divorced from their social, economic, and political context. Yet he was an institutionalist; institutions were the primary focus of his writings and studies on institutional history, political studies, and organizational theory (he encouraged the early work of Herbert Simon, Nathan Leites, and Harold Lasswell). When the present anti-institutionalism lessens, scholars may once more come back to Wright's institutionalism, as well as to his historical and legal approaches, for new insights on current problems. And more important still, his example of a theorist concerned with policy problems holds lessons for all those who in some manner are a part of today's divorce between theory and practice.

Wright's approach to conflict and war is still valuable because the problems to which he rallied the combined intellectual resources of the social sciences, natural sciences, and professional schools still persist. He recognized that war has its roots in the underlying nature of man and of societies—the struggle for natural resources, the persistence of insecurity in personal and international relationships, and the inadequacies of the machinery of law and order on the international scene. This was prophetic, not only for the 1940s, but almost certainly for the 1970s and the 1980s as well.

Quincy Wright studied world order and international organization through detailed empirical scholarship. Much can be learned concerning his approach through examining his views of a specific international body in *Mandates Under the League of Nations* (1930) and in a 1946 lecture on the Trusteeship Council. Wright noted in his lecture that the Trusteeship Council is one of the five principal organs of the United Nations and that the problems it addresses have deep historical roots. Even in the fifteenth and sixteenth centuries, dependent territories were on the international agenda: one expedition after another sailed from Europe to explore and colonize Asia, Africa, and America. In 1946 one-fourth of the world's territory and one-fifth of its population were still politically dependent. Their size and number were declining, but Wright was realistic enough to know that new forms of dependency would emerge. He warned that countries could be equal in law but satellites in fact. Wright pointed out that the ways dependent people were dealt with, even by international organizations, varied. In some colonies, a governor was sent to rule native peoples who had no residual right to independent status. Another pattern was that of the protectorate, in which the state had certain rights but was not all-powerful.

In these patterns, certain principles were recognized. First, the government of dependent people ought to be for the benefit of the governed. The rulers were to accept "the white man's burden" and rule without benefit to themselves. Education was to be provided. Of course, practice was frequently different; the lot of the dependent peoples was often one of slavery or forced labor. Second, dependent people ought to become independent eventually, or at least equal in status to the ruling government. Sir Cecil Hurst said that all British colonies were on a ladder climbing to dominion status. All dependent peoples were equally entitled to move in this direction. This tendency had manifested itself as early as the assertion of independence by the United States. Dominion status developed most rapidly in the nineteenth century for India, Pakistan, Burma, Malaya, and the Dutch East Indies. A great number of states became independent before, during, and shortly after World War II. Of the fifty-seven members of the United Nations in 1946, thirty-three had been dependent territories in the middle of the eighteenth century, and six continued in that status at the outbreak of World War II. Third, the ruling state should not monopolize the trade of its dependencies (the open door policy). Because Britain pursued this principle, its colonies became a network of interdependent economic interests that limited monopoly tendencies at the center. Fourth, dependent countries should be ruled under broad international responsibility. The maintenance of this relationship should depend, not on the choice of the ruler, but on international treaties and international institutions. Hence, ruling states had mandates, which in 1946 became trusteeships.

As early as 1885, many of these principles were recognized in a declaration of the Berlin Conference. They were brought together in Article 22 of the League of Nations Covenant. The covenant, according to Wright, was a compromise. Some nations wished to annex neighboring dependencies, but Woodrow Wilson's Fourteen Points opposed this; some wanted them to become independent; others wished them returned to their former owners. The compromise adopted was a system of mandates suggested by the elder statesman from South Africa, Jan Christian Smuts. A commission was appointed to rule by established principles with well-defined benefits prescribed for the governed. Most of these territories remained mandates until after World War II. The system was most successful in the 1920s. As the League of Nations grew weaker, its ability to maintain the broad principles of the mandates declined. There were abuses by aggressive governments, especially by Japan, which prepared its mandated islands for war. The birth of the United Nations brought a similar problem and a comparable solution.

The trusteeship system of the United Nations closely resembled the mandate system, although certain differences exist. The use of the words *trust* and *tutelage* in Article 22 of the League of Nations Covenant implied that the territory was to be administered for the good of the governed and was to be led toward eventual national maturity and independence. The emphasis in the United Nations Charter was again on trusteeship. All dependent peoples were to be governed for the good of the country itself, not only for those formally under trusteeship (Chapter XII) but for all "non-self-governing territories" (Chapter XI). States governing the latter were required to render reports: for instance, the United States on Puerto Rico. Reference was made in the article on nonself-governing territories to development "toward self-government." Wright concluded that the constitutional structure of the Trusteeship Council and its political makeup assured that it would be a powerful influence toward the independence of dependent people. This has proven to be the case.

Even in dealing with a so-called specialized agency or nonsecurity unit of the United Nations, Wright evaluated it in the light of international politics as well as international law. He examined the potential of the United Nations in terms of constitutional provisions in the charter and external political realities. In addition, he was more aware than many of his contemporaries of the controlling influence of history. The United Nations was not unrelated to the structures of the League of Nations. The problems that confronted the new organization had their roots in the successes and failures of the old. It was fashionable at the time to stress the novelty of international organization, but by and large Wright eschewed this approach. This meant that both his teaching, which reflected his approach to immediate problems, and his writings, which were fashioned with an eye to long-term problems, continue to have relevance even when the forces of history have changed.

In 1946, immediately after World War II, Wright offered courses on the conduct of American foreign relations. As early as 1922, he had published *Control of American Foreign Relations*. The central theme of his courses after World War II was the beginnings of the Cold War. I am struck, in reviewing my notes from these courses, with the comprehensiveness, foresight, and objectivity of his analysis. He began his discussions of Soviet foreign policy by noting the contradictory elements underlying it. One factor was the impact of Stalinism on the doctrinaire Marxist-Leninist line. Another was the fluctuation of Soviet policy. In the 1920s, the Soviet Union was against the League of Nations; in the 1930s, it was one of its most dedicated members. Thereafter, following the dispute over sanctions, the Russians were voted out of the League. The role of public opinion in Russia was different from that in the West, Wright argued. Public opinion was not an autonomous and independent force, but one largely created by the press in conformity with party policy. As the party line shifted, the official line of the press also changed, and public opinion changed with it.

Wright discussed major approaches to relationships with the Soviets in 1946–1947. At this time, the proponent of firmness against an inevitably expanding Russia was Secretary of State James Byrnes, while Henry Wallace championed a policy of conciliation with a misunderstood friend. Wright observed that the policy of Byrnes won out; the Marshall Plan and NATO followed, and the Cold War intensified. He went on to say that views of Soviet tactics would be based on differing interpretations of Soviet aims, like the "Mr. X" article in *Foreign Affairs*, July, 1947. Wright cited, not without some sympathy, George Kennan's views (for Wright as a consultant to the Department of State was one of the first to know of Kennan's identity as Mr. X) that firmness in dealing with Russia was necessary. Because of its ideology and present structure, the Soviet Union was forced to emphasize to its people the continual danger they faced from attack by Western powers. Extreme dictatorship and tight controls over the press could not be sustained unless there was a credible fear of foreign aggression, so the Kremlin was obliged to keep this fear alive. Kennan maintained that as long as it continued, the Soviet Union would find it hard to believe in conciliation as a realistic policy. Hence, a policy of containment was necessary to meet the Russian advance. Wright also cited the interpretation of

Waldemar Gurian of Notre Dame, who argued that the Soviet Union was following a flexible but rational policy directed at world conquest. Gurian explained that the Soviets were suspicious people, pessimistic by nature, fearful of the city slicker as rural people sometimes are, but possessing peasant instincts of shrewdness.

Out of these theories Wright extracted two broad views—that Soviet policy was essentially aggressive and driven toward world conquest and that any Soviet advances were merely part of a quest for security. I remember quite vividly his attempt to reconcile these views. The student of Soviet policy must consider both the dynamics of aggression and the quest for security. All countries have some expansionist and some security elements built into their policies. The Soviets wished both to survive and to expand. The wellsprings of these two motivations were Russian nationalism and world Communist ambition. The Russian element, which derived partly from traditional Czarist policies, provided that the Russian Communist people must have a territorial base and a power complex if their position in the world was to be upheld. To survive, in fact, the Soviets had to play traditional power politics. In the absence of an effective world organization, they found it necessary to increase national power and to take new strategic positions. Especially was this true in the two-power world. Each power, East and West, sought to become a little stronger than the other. However difficult power might be to measure, the endless quest for it was ever present. The Soviet fear of a "Cordon Sanitaire" after World War I recurred after World War II in their fear of a ring of United States satellites in Asia and Western Europe.

No less powerful than traditional Russian aims was the revolutionary ideology to which the Soviet Union was heir. Not only were the Russians convinced that the acceptance of a Communist economy would advance human welfare, in that a more equitable distribution of the benefits of production would improve the lot of the common man (a thesis defended in E. H. Carr's *Soviet Impact on the Western World*); they were also convinced that capitalism carried within it the seeds of its own destruction. Eventually, communism would triumph through strength, though violence would be needed to overcome the resistance of the last adherents of the dying capitalist order.

Wright suggested that history seemed to offer some support for the

Soviet view. Leaders such as Stalin could recall that a tiny handful of insignificant men had begun their movement. Marx worked largely unnoticed in the British Museum, and at one point even the librarian was unsure of what had happened to him. In thirty years this tiny movement had gained ruling power over a huge nation, won two military victories, added satellites, achieved visible expansion, and became one of the two great world powers. It also had major political parties aligned with it in France, Italy, and Eastern Europe.

The combination of maintaining a territorial complex and propagating an ideology has ample precedent. It occurred in the Arab empire in the seventh century, in the French Crusades in the Middle Ages, and in the Habsburg Empire at the time of the Reformation, especially in its defense of Catholicism in the Thirty Years War. Wright maintained that it was even found in the United States, in the test under Abraham Lincoln of the republic's ability to survive. Both security and manifest destiny were considerations then, as they were in 1822 in James Monroe's message of sympathy for the struggling Greeks. By and large, the dynamism of ideologies wanes in the course of revolutionary change, as it did in the case of the French Revolution and in the United States' retreat from the struggle to spread democracy. Whether this would happen to the Soviet ideology remained to be seen.

The growing strength of the Soviet Union did not, in any case, lead Wright to recognize Russia as the greatest power. The United States had the atomic bomb, a growing economy, and control of the Security Council vote by a nine-to-two margin. There was support for a free economy in the United States and little willingness to settle back to await a depression. Therefore, strong as the adversary might be, Wright saw that Russia was not strong enough to threaten American independence.

Russia also had certain weaknesses, which were especially apparent in the period after World War II. It was highly centralized, causing inevitable inflexibility. Soviet diplomats were rather wooden, like automatons controlled by the Kremlin. The center of government was swamped with numerous burdens; requests for instructions too often were buried. The standard of living in the United States was ten times that in the Soviet Union. The Russians were a poverty-stricken people trying desperately to rebuild the ruins of their country, two-thirds of which had been devastated by the war. Their internal discontent was indicated by the existence of a police state and recurrent purges. As Wright saw it, this discontent was not accidental but inevitable. (In fact, according to the theories of Soviet expansionism that Wright discussed, communism springs not so much from the roots of a dying capitalism as from human misery, and it actually needs a continuance of that misery in order to gain support. Therefore, the Western powers could best fight communism by reducing human misery.)

In this context, Wright anticipated that Soviet policies would work themselves out. Some kind of satellite relationship was inevitable for Eastern Europe. In 1944 Winston Churchill and Sir Anthony Eden had offered a sphere of influence to Joseph Stalin, excluding only Greece. Roosevelt had opposed this initially and tried to stop it at Yalta. One of Wright's students, Frederick Schuman, maintained that Russian leaders believed that the Yalta agreements had assigned them unquestioned domination in Eastern Europe. Thus, Russia felt that the West's objections to the manhandling of Soviet satellites were unjustified. The Russians sought to build support in Eastern Europe and eventually in Greece and Turkey. They followed a similar line in northern Asia, seeking to maintain or establish their interest in northern China, Iran, Mongolia, and North Korea. India, Indonesia, and other colonial areas were additional arenas for Soviet propaganda. Thus, Russia appeared as a champion of self-determination. In the United Nations they held to their veto. Although they discussed breaking the deadlock in the talks on developing peaceful uses of the atom bomb, they did little more than discuss it.

In short, Wright understood the manifold elements and forces at work in determining Soviet policies. He saw clearly the dangers and problems inherent in revolutionary extremism, but he believed that time would moderate this extremism. He stressed that stability under law was essential in a shrinking world and that, to this end, states needed to be tolerant of ideological differences to develop what President John F. Kennedy called "a world safe for diversity."

The catholic approach of Quincy Wright, which is apparent in his study of war as a social phenomenon, is also typical of his study of the international organization in the transitional period from a world of dependent peoples to one of predominantly independent states. Wright faced the realities of the mid–twentieth century, comprehending the continuing influences of the eighteenth and nineteenth centuries and projecting the forces of history through contemporary times and into the future. Although a political scientists and an international lawyer by trade, he had the historian's sense of continuity—his protection against a utopianism that would offer too little guidance for contemporary policy makers. There is an eclectic quality to Wright's approach to foreign relations that combines the outlooks of the legalist, the realpolitiker, and the political theorist.

In his analysis of the rise of the Soviet Union as an international superpower, he paid heed to the interrelationships of historic, social, and psychological forces. Russian policy was based on the historic insecurity of the Russians. It also took its direction from the unique expansionist creed of Marxist-Leninist ideology as translated by Stalin. In his later writings, Quincy Wright was ready for the shifts in Soviet policy reflected in Nikita Khrushchev's attempts at normalization of relations with the West. His very eclecticism and the open system in which he operated made Wright attentive to both the continuing and the novel features in a nation's policies.

In the same way Wright tried to see international institutions as providing continuity in a changing social and political order; for example, the transition from the mandate system of the League of Nations to the trusteeship system of the United Nations. The end of the colonial world led to the acceleration of the trusteeship system, accentuating and cutting short the preparation for independence. The United Nations Trusteeship Council became the center from which the traumatic march toward independence was directed and controlled. There is a prophetic ring in Wright's 1946 theory that the council had constitutional power if the nations or a majority of them were prepared to grant it full use of its powers; for the meteoric rise of the influence of new nations in the United Nations assured that the Trusteeship Council would in fact be used to bring about the full realization of national self-determination. Whether the council contributed in equal measure to assuring the capacity of these newly independent states to exist as self-governing units is another question, which Wright was still seeking to answer. Indeed, one of the blessings of his intellectual journey is the fact that it was such a long and fruitful one.

Finally, he contributed to the understanding of war and peace by bringing all dimensions of the problem into focus. *A Study of War* is a vast reservoir for all present-day students. Some of the research and certain of the methods have been rendered obsolete by scientific advances, and there is work going on today that supplants findings on which Wright relied; but none of this destroys the value and the grandeur of his achievement. The fact that he is today the most footnoted social scientist dealing with all aspects of conflict and war may be his most enduring tribute. In all the areas discussed, his steadfast devotion to research and study and his openness to new intellectual discoveries were the hallmarks of his work. For this reason, we are likely to return to his writings for guidance and inspiration during the coming decades.

Much has been said about the irrelevance of the legalists' approach to the conduct of foreign relations. The point has been made that legalism, with its stress on what ought to be and on abstract codes of international behavior, has obscured the harsh realities of making foreign policy. It has misled the "outs" into thinking that the "ins" were merely cynical and perverse in their determination to do what was best for the nation. It has led to the naive conclusion that replacing cynics with idealists would put everything right. In a word, legalism has ignored the primacy of national interest and the ambiguities of decision making and choice.

This criticism has been leveled at Quincy Wright by some if not all of us in the field. In reviewing his work, we have not hesitated to point to the difficulties that arose in applying some of his principles. Among them has been the problem of assuring that nations would follow the legal code that Wright and others laid down. In fact, the legal precepts he set forth have more often than not fallen just beyond the reach of those responsible for the course of national policy. This has been true in what Wright has written on universality of membership in international organization, on the place of the individual in international law, on the Nuremberg judgment as it applied to the responsibility of individuals for the actions of states, and on the possibilities of transcending the use of force in foreign policy. In fairness to Wright, it should be noted that in these and other instances he came to recognize that his principles were more idealistic than realistic in terms of application. In fact, there is evidence that with the years he grew more and more pessimistic about state behavior. I felt this was particularly true when men he had known and respected in private life followed policies in public life that he considered a breach of principles. When I talked with him in his later years, I sensed a feeling of sadness more than of righteous indignation when he talked about Vietnam or China policy or the decline of the United Nations. This could have been a result of age; I felt it was also the reaction of a once-burning idealist discouraged by the shortcomings and failures of events in international life.

Yet the story of Wright's legalism is only partly told if one brackets him with those denounced as legalists and moralists. For at least three reasons, Wright was a far more practical legalist than those who spearheaded the movement. First, he was forever in dialogue, through his students or directly, with Hans Morgenthau and his followers. Perhaps never in the history of international studies has so stimulating a dialogue occurred. Their debates were an instance of two powerful minds meeting in serious exchange, not passing one another unnoticed in the night. There was enough community of interest so that their differences brought significant clarifications for them both. The impact of one on the other was not hard to ascertain. They had mutual respect and affection, even while challenging each other with vigor and great force. A personal recollection will expand this point. My first introduction to the graduate student body at the University of Chicago occurred at a Sunday brunch at the Windermere Hotel, when I noticed a group of twelve or fifteen students at a larger table locked in the kind of disputation that occurs only in those rare moments when contending doctrines dominate human life. I mistakenly thought the debate had to do with some aspect of their personal lives or that year's World Series. On the contrary, half of them were Wright's students, the other half Morgenthau's. Their discussion reminded me of the debates that must have taken place at the time of the Reformation or the French Revolution. This experience disclosed the living reality of a serious intellectual clash between a legalist and a realist. It was clear that the legalist grew to be more pragmatic out of the dynamics of their interaction.

Second, Wright was insatiable in assimilating vast bodies of human knowledge. He was forever exploring the work of scientists, humanists, psychologists, and public interpreters. Because of his limitless curiosity about the application of knowledge from all spheres to international relations, Wright's theories and his approach have about them an all-inclusive, eclectic quality that significantly distinguishes him from the "hard" theorists. Single-factor analysis cannot be found in Wright. He sometimes links together ideas and data that seem at first glance to have little if any interrelationship, causing scholars to raise questions of consistency or to wonder whether Wright fully grasped the latest example drawn from his most recent seminars and reading. I often felt that way about the interpretations he drew from political philosophy and theology (I grumbled under my breath that Locke or Kant or Niebuhr would not recognize their views in Wright). Yet the important thing was that Wright's tireless examination of the vast storehouse of knowledge kept him continuously open to new alternatives and able to live and think in concrete terms.

Wright's tentativeness about his own theories was a further antidote to his legalism. He had a disarming way of listing four possible approaches of which one was usually his own. The critic might say that he had done this to set up straw men to support his own choice of theory. My point here would be that the process of examining alternative approaches helped Wright keep his own approaches in perspective. It guarded him against fanaticism or the belief that his view was the only possible one on a problem. It helped him to keep his own legal preferences in perspective.

All this was reinforced by the fact that he was a painstaking and indefatigable scholar. His footnotes often occupied three-quarters of a page, with the text tucked away in four or five lines at the top. He was forever finding the adverse example or case. He avoided tying himself to one legal precedent by poring over all the other precedents, including the one in that morning's New York *Times*. His office was a shambles of dog-eared books and papers, nearly all of which he had looked at in the month's reading. He was congenitally unable to begin any conversation with a simple proposition; he preferred to talk about the evidence or the precedents that might lead you or him to the formulation of a conclusion or a principle. His learning was prodigious, but continually evolving. Since it spanned and extended far beyond legal thought, it was impossible for him to remain a legalist in any narrow definition.

Third, he was a member of the Chicago school of political science, and this in itself kept him close to practical political realities. Every third quotation in a discussion of politics was likely to involve Charles E. Merriam. He had a running dialogue with Merriam, Harold Lasswell, Walter Johnson, and their followers. The comparison between municipal and international law came naturally to Wright, partly because the ground had been covered in faculty lunches with Merriam and others. If this connection with a group who saw politics as enclosed in a legal framework was sometimes misleading, it was also a broadening force for Wright. He gained from Merriam and Merriam's associates another body of experience that drew heavily from practical politics. The inner workings of the Chicago City Council were Byzantine and conspiratorial as Merriam described them. There were ever-present ambiguities and clashes of interest. To talk of the pure theory of law in this setting was a practical impossibility, and Wright must have sensed that what was true within a defined municipal constitutional framework was true *a fortiori* in the lawless world that existed internationally. His fervor to build law into this world never took him too far from the Chicago political scene.

Wright's other great work, *The Study of International Relations* (1955), is similar to *A Study of War*, although its scope is more limited. In it, Wright explored the multidisciplinary basis of international studies and the differing approaches to war and peace. His approach in the book reflected his 1931 experience at the University of Chicago in forming an interdisciplinary Committee on International Relations, the first of its kind to offer degrees that involved the applied and scientific cross-disciplinary attack on international problems.

Wright must therefore be seen as the theorist and designer of the study and the reform of international relations. Because he kept norms and science in relative proximity, his influence persists in the 1970s. Yet any objective assessment of Wright's influence must recognize the limits of his contribution. Many of the topics he discussed have disappeared from the international agenda: the outlawry of war, collective security, and the new international law. His determination to be prophet and reformer led him to misjudge the perennial problems of international politics. More than writers such as Martin Wight, Hans J. Morgenthau, and Louis J. Halle, he attached his enormous scholarly prestige to transient reformist causes. In his later years, he was sometimes dismissed as a rather garrulous old spokesman for grand designs more relevant to the past than to the present or the future. He was not always discriminating in the policies and theories that he defended, and some of his bold visions led not to international progress but to a succession of blind alleys. His buoyantly optimistic spirit and his lack of a coherent political philosophy were seen as weaknesses rather than strengths. Because he touched every problem, his analysis of specific problems often lacked profundity and depth. He appeared to some as the Don Quixote of international thought rather than as a systematic thinker.

Yet until the final hours of his immensely productive eighty years, he remained an inspiring and vital figure of unflagging energy and hope. He was a shining example to his students of the scholar-statesman, following the path as he saw it to a better world order. For those whose lives were touched by Quincy Wright—whether in the United States, India, Turkey, or east Africa—he remains a source of inspiration and hope.

WORKS BY QUINCY WRIGHT

1922

The Control of American Foreign Relations. New York: Macmillan.

1930

Mandates Under the League of Nations. Chicago: University of Chicago Press.

Research in International Law Since the War. Washington, D.C.: Carnegie Endowment for International Peace.

1942

A Study of War. 2 vols. Chicago: University of Chicago Press. Abridged edition by Louise Wright, 1964.

1955

The Study of International Relations. New York: Appleton-Century-Crofts.

1960

The Strengthening of International Law. The Hague: Academy of International Law.

International Law and the United States. Bombay and New York: Asia Publishing House.

1961

The Role of International Law in the Elimination of War. Manchester, Eng.: Manchester University Press; New York: Oceana Publications.

DAVID MITRANY (1888–1977)

Transcending Politics Through Functionalism

David Mitrany was born on January 1, 1888, in Bucharest, Rumania, a son of Moscu and Jeannette Mitrany. His education in political science and international relations took place at the London School of Economics and Political Science. His earliest firsthand exposure to world affairs occurred as a member of the editorial staff of the Manchester *Guardian* from 1919 to 1922. He was a visiting professor or lecturer at Harvard and Yale universities and at Smith College. From 1922 to 1929, he served as assistant European editor of the *Economic and Social History of the World War*, sponsored by the Carnegie Endowment for International Peace. In 1933 he was appointed professor in the School of Economics and Politics at the Princeton Institute for Advanced Study and, in 1943, adviser on international affairs to the Board of Unilever and Lever Brothers, Ltd.

Mitrany's fame derived from his writings on functionalism; but he also wrote *The Problem of International Sanctions* (1925), *Marx Against the Peasant* (1951), *The Progress of International Government* (1934), and several books on southeastern Europe.[1] His celebrated works on functionalism included the classic *A Working Peace System: An Argument for the Functional Development of International Organization* (1944) and *The Functional Theory of Politics* (1975) and numerous essays and reviews. Mitrany's standing is unusual in the field of international relations. He was never the denizen of a major professional chair in a British or American university, although he was recognized through distinguished appointments at the Princeton Institute for Advanced Study and at Harvard and Yale. Until rather late in life, he did not attract even a modest

---

1 These and all books by David Mitrany are listed chronologically, with full publication data, beginning on p. 215 herein.

academic following, although serious scholars belatedly and rather un-ashamedly used his writings as a point of departure. Thus, well-known political scientists were more likely to describe themselves as neofunc-tionalists or integrationists rather than functionalists, which was Mi-trany's term.

Mitrany's roots were not found in a single philosophical position or professional discipline. He drew his inspiration from liberalism, radi-calism, syndicalism, Fabian socialism, nineteenth-century rationalism, theories of the mixed economy, and New Deal experiments such as the TVA. He was a wartime intelligence researcher, a journalist and foreign correspondent, a postwar planner, a seminar-and-discussion group leader, a political adviser to a powerful international business concern, and a fairly traditional political theorist. He never headed a research center, he was without a generation or more of formal students, and he did not found a scholarly or popular journal. Yet his influence has been far-reaching.

The reason for Mitrany's influence is not readily apparent. What was it that caused Reinhold Niebuhr to describe *A Working Peace System* as "the best I have seen on the subject" or Hans J. Morgenthau to assert that "the future of the civilized world is intimately tied to the functional approach to international organization"? Why should the *Times Literary Supplement* proclaim in July, 1974, that "if Functionalism does not work no other approach will"? What is it about the outlook of functionalism that has challenged the interests and talents of scholars and observers of widely divergent viewpoints and methods? An inquiry into its contri-butions, limitations, and problems may answer this question.

Functionalism's contribution to international thought is at least threefold: (1) it proves a useful framework for viewing efforts at inter-national cooperation in rudimentary social and economic areas; (2) it offers a plausible approach to problems of world order and to bridging the gulf between international anarchy and world community; and (3) it adds a new dimension to international thinking, which has tradition-ally been confined to political, diplomatic, and legal questions. Func-tionalism's limitations as a rational and coherent theory arise not so much from these valid contributions as from its utopian, antipolitical, and noninstitutional character—limitations reflecting positive points of emphasis that nevertheless are imperiled by their excesses. Functionalism's problems derive from its failures in historical prediction, its disparagement of ideas, and its lack of intellectual and scientific rigor—failures in no way unique to functionalism but nonetheless damaging to its historical and theoretical integrity.

It will not do to praise functionalism and to ignore its limitations and the problems arising from them, any more than criticism of functionalism justifies overlooking the valid and significant role it plays in international studies. One such study—to examine functionalism's relevance to higher education for development—will be explored in detail. The findings of this study stem from a twelve-agency review of higher education for development in Africa, Asia, and Latin America. The agencies include the World Bank, Inter-American Development Bank, UNESCO, the United Nations Development Program (UNDP), UNICEF, United States Agency for International Development (USAID), the French Ministry of Foreign Affairs, the British Overseas Development Administration (ODA), the Canadian International Development Agency (CIDA), Canada's International Development Research Centre (IDRC), and the Ford and Rockefeller foundations. Fieldwork in the study was conducted by three regional teams made up of African, Asian, and Latin American educators. The teams were headed by Aklilu Habte, then minister of youth and culture of Ethiopia, now head of the Educational Divison of the World Bank and formerly president of the National University of Ethiopia; Puey Ungphakorn, then rector of Thammasat University in Bangkok, Thailand; and Alfonso Ocampo, former minister of health in Colombia and rector of Universidad del Valle in Cali, Colombia. Together these groups undertook twenty-three case studies of important experiments in which higher education provided significant responses to urgent development needs, such as increased food production, public health services, educational and cultural development, population control.[2]

The first question worthy of attention is: Of what value is function-

---

2 The case studies and conclusions have been published in Kenneth W. Thompson and Barbara Fogel, *Higher Education and Social Change* (2 vols.; New York: Praeger, 1976, 1977). These themes are also discussed in Kenneth W. Thompson, *Foreign Assistance: A View from the Private Sector* (Notre Dame, Ind.: University of Notre Dame Press, 1972).

alism and what contribution does it make to understanding an inquiry into international education and social development? Subordinate to this are the questions: Does functionalism provide a useful framework of thought for approaching international education? Does it offer a new perspective for education and world order? Does it add a new theoretical dimension? Because the guidelines of the twelve-donor agencies emphasized various national educational experiments, functionalism must be examined within well-defined boundaries and not considered on a global basis. Nevertheless, it is possible to offer some tentative impressions on the relevance of functionalism that deserve further discussion and study. As an intellectual framework, functionalism comes closer to fitting the problem area being considered than does any alternative framework. In one sense, it achieves its usefulness by default. Political realism is too much concerned with power and statecraft to be directly relevant on any overall basis. Idealism, which advocates that global solutions be undertaken immediately, bears little relation to what the developing countries are now seeking in higher education. Most important, education, though it has its political, legal, and diplomatic aspects, is a social and increasingly an economic enterprise. Among theories propounded, only functionalism deals with such a trend. Its controlling assumptions are therefore closer to the problems of higher education than is any competing theoretical approach.

It must also be recognized that the quest for world order in education is more likely to be achieved through the efforts of national educators working steadfastly on common problems than through ambitious theorizing on global education. Repeatedly, educators serving on regional teams queried other regions on new approaches to such fundamental issues as improved health delivery systems or increased food production. The Africans wanted to know more about the health sciences in general or about Candelaria (an experimental program for health care for the poor) in Cali, Colombia. Latin Americans, in turn, wondered about subprofessional training in engineering and accounting and technical training at the Ngee Ann Technical College in Singapore, one of the few educational institutions anywhere that voluntarily downgraded itself from degree-granting to certificate-granting status in response to manpower planning needs. The Asians, for their part, asked about the use of artisans and technicians from the community in such institutions in Africa as Ahmadu Bello University in northern Nigeria and the University of Science and Technology in Ghana. Whether political theorists concerned with the nation-state know it or not, there is an emerging international community of scientists and educators who share common concerns and are grappling with similar if not identical problems. Many such scientists and educators have taken their inspiration from and legitimized their experiments through Western experience and institutions. But these practices are becoming a thing of the past. For the future, these thinkers are turning more to one another's programs, especially as these relate to urgent Third World problems.

Finally, functionalism's most positive contribution may be in offering a striking new dimension to international thinking. Education has played a subordinate role in most of the writing on war and diplomacy. For the scholars of war and peace, the reigning question has been how effectively education has created a stronger sense of nationalism or alternatively a true world outlook. The UNESCO project on national histories illustrates this concern. Functionalism, by contrast, views education as a sectoral problem addressing itself to specific issues and defined areas, an approach that comes much closer to the dominant outlook in a higher education study. It would be farfetched to insist that the agronomists, physicians, and educators who studied or were the focus of study in the higher education project were primarily interested in nationalism or globalism as such. Given the urgency of the needs within relatively poor and hard-pressed countries or societies (an exception such as Singapore notwithstanding), they were unlikely to have written or thought much about the broader issues that have been the main concern of political scientists like Mitrany. The key question is whether a functional interest in education promotes a spirit of internationalism in actions and programs.

Functionalism's limitations stem from its utopian, antipolitical, and noninstitutional character. Its utopianism stems from a belief that successful functional cooperation will affect political and legal areas, gradually eroding the tenacious hold that national sovereignty has exerted on diplomats and statesmen. On one rather modest level, some evidence for this can be derived from the aforementioned study. Regional team members brought ministers and national development specialists into at least some of their discussions. Their findings suggest that narrow nationalism is an obstacle to strong educational development within the smaller developing countries. Without exception, the regional teams called for more international exchange and heralded the value for education of foreign technical assistance.

At the same time, however, especially on the question of importing overall educational solutions, all three regional teams expressed skepticism and concern. Too often, outside experts came to lecture, not to listen. The larger technical assistance agencies have a tendency to "package" the prevailing educational approach as the single answer to unique and particular problems. If the Third World was ever prepared to accept "Made in the United States" or "Made in Great Britain" answers to their problems, that day has now passed.

Furthermore, the processes begun in facing local community problems tend, to the degree that they are successful, to heighten national pride and a sense of national identity. The Cameroon, with one of the most successful centers in the health sciences in Africa, sees that center as a dramatically successful national effort, not one that lessens the force of its government. Indeed, the loyalty and commitment of national governments in general may well be the foremost ingredient required for a good educational recipe. If functionalism assumes an inevitable spillover from educational internationalism to political internationalism, UNESCO's failure to involve ministers of education to discuss successful educational experiments objectively, without constant reference to national pride, punctures the utopian balloon of functionalism.

The second limitation of functionalism reinforces this trend. It assumes that national and international politics will become less important as nonpolitical cooperation proceeds. Once again, the higher education study tends not to support this thesis. Governments in the developing countries see education as unmistakably political.[3] They

---

3 Other countries also see education as unmistakably political. Certainly this is the case in Communist countries. Moreover, even in some European states, there are strong linkages between the governments and the universities. Professors have civil service status, and the budget is determined by the Ministry of Education. As a rule, the *ordinarius* has an independent position, but there are subtle ways to influence trends in education from above. *Numerus clausus* is generally practiced in medical schools. This is what the Ngee Ann Technical College is doing in Singapore.

maintain that educational theories which presuppose a separation of government and universities are Western ideas, not applicable to meeting the desperate needs of poorer countries. In Tanzania ministers and government officials constitute 37 percent of the governing board of the university at Dar es Salaam. In Mali the so-called university is comprised of a series of institutes stemming from and dependent on such important ministries as agriculture, education, and the interior. The Ngee Ann Technical College in Singapore trains only the precise number of technicians called for by government planners. At least in the developing countries, it is simply not the case that a functional enterprise such as education leads to an erosion of national sovereignty. Quite the contrary is true.

Functionalism is a victim of yet another limitation. It has little to say about institutions and their comparability and interaction across national boundaries. "Function determines form" is functionalism's mandate. Pushed to an extreme, every unique function for every unique national problem will require a unique institutional form. Not only is this approach in conflict with the aims of organizational theory to achieve certain generalizable views about institutions; in the field of education, it also detracts from the concerns of comparative education. In the present study, it was found that national educational systems in the Third World were significantly influenced by their educational heritage, even when they were reacting to and revolting against it. It is simply not possible to discuss higher education in Africa without referring to the institutional legacy of the British, the French, or the Americans. Perhaps the functionalist's mandate should be reformulated as "function ought to determine form." In fact, however, historical antecedents make this relation between function and form impossible in many cases. The functionalist may need to recognize that history has a way of causing shipwreck for almost every simplifying social theory. All this is not to deny the value or the usefulness of the functionalist perspective but merely to warn the historian of some of its limitations, as Jacob Burkhardt did in calling attention to the self-deception of the "grand simplifiers."

Functionalism's failures are a result of its shortcomings in historical prediction, its disparagement of ideas, and its lack of scientific and intellectual rigor. These failures, it should be pointed out, are in no way its monopoly. They occur and recur with almost every important social viewpoint and theory. The annals of history are strewn with man's failures to foresee historical developments. Few if any on-the-spot observers anticipated the French or Russian revolutions. Building on his observations of social experiments such as the New Deal, Mitrany foresaw similar experiments of a functional or regional type that would break down national loyalties in international affairs. Some viewed the specialized agencies of the United Nations in this respect after World War II. Whatever the value of lessons learned and functions performed by these bodies, their net effect has been to highlight national struggles and rivalries. In a similar way, functionalism in higher education has not led, generally speaking, to a diminution of national sympathies. In fairness, this criticism cannot be leveled at the worldwide network of international agriculture institutes, which come close to substantiating the functional prediction. However, the same cannot be said of higher education in east and west Africa, whose institutions have had greater contact with metropolitan countries than with one another. In some parts of Africa, the trend has been toward a devolution of educational functions, as with the substitution of national educational systems in Francophone Africa for education under one uniform French system. The breakup of the University of East Africa and the failure to achieve a federated system of higher education in southern Africa and Central America are further evidences of the failure of the functionalist prediction.

Functionalism has to a certain extent cleared the air by showing that functional experience was more likely to bring international cooperation than rhetoric and ideas. Yet as Max Lerner once wrote, "Men have thoughts; ideas have men." There is a certain contradiction inherent in the functionalist's disparagement of ideas that divide more than they unite and in Mitrany's faith in the power of the functionalist creed. It may also be true that an important idea, such as the concept of a rural health service in medical education, may be as significant as the creation of readily accessible rural health clinics. A mystique just as often surrounds an announced educational creed as it does an innovative educational experiment, and to ignore one while praising the other may be as great an error as is overstressing abstract educational ideas without furnishing practical examples.

Finally, functionalism comes under fire from those who say it does not possess sufficient scientific and intellectual rigor. It is an approach of the most general sort, not a well-tested and refined social theory. To a certain extent, this criticism comes through in *Higher Education and Social Change*. It is relatively simple to conclude that education is a functional endeavor, but far more complex to show that so general an approach provides any meaningful guidance on what to do or what to expect from cooperative endeavors in health education, agricultural education, or teacher education. For example, one has only to ask what functionalism tells about rural health stations as distinct from regional or provincial hospitals in Cameroon or Colombia to recognize the problem. There is a certain impreciseness and remoteness from urgent problems within given sectors of higher education that may illustrate these questions of intellectual rigor. Functionalism is similar to a Kantian category empty of specific content and therefore hard to use in actual social and political circumstances. To this, the functionalist will no doubt answer that this is its strength and significance. The failure is one, nonetheless, that supporters and critics must recognize more fully and more to clarify before seeing functionalism as a utopia or a panacea.

The test of a theory of international relations rests on its usefulness for more than one segment of social experience. Higher education in the developing countries falls, broadly speaking, within the overall sector that David Mitrany defines as social and economic. Yet the linkages between education and the political system are close. Education touches some of the most sensitive areas of a nation's life—the loyalties of the young and the building of manpower capacity. It would be surprising if governments, especially in poorer countries, were prepared to trust vital educational processes to others. The leader of Tanzania, Julius Nyerere, once told me when I asked about outside assistance to Tanzania's primary and secondary school system: "Unless I can provide for the education of our young people, my people will turn out my government and me."

Nevertheless, functionalism is at least as appropriate for interpreting international cooperation in higher education as is any other theory. It is true that higher educators, especially those with professional competence, do constitute an international community of scholars who find it relatively easy to work together, free of overwhelming political constraints. I had little or no difficulty locating two dozen educators in less-developed countries who were competent to join in the study of higher education for development. Their professional reputations were evident to anyone in the field; and it was clear that whatever the political differences among their respective countries, they would have few problems working together. Although each of them had had some success in drawing in ministers and government officials—thus illustrating on a limited scale the spillover of the will to cooperate from nonpolitical to political subjects—they were effective because they were primarily educators, rather than promoters of transnational values among decision makers in government. Their work has provided object lessons for the less global minded of their associates; and there can be little doubt that in their governments' inner councils, men like G. L. Monekosso in the Cameroon, Aklilu Habte in Ethiopia, and Ambassador Soedjatmoko in Indonesia have provided sources of inspiration for international cooperation. Although functionalism emphasizes the transforming power of new social and economic processes and forces, the role of unique individuals embodying new funnctional approaches may be equally important.

Clearly, the relevance of the functionalist approach increases as problems are more specific and well defined. Agricultural development serves as a striking example, specifically the need to increase food production. International institutes for agricultural research are at work in Mexico, Colombia, the Philippines, India, Nigeria, and Kenya, each devoting resources and manpower to the search for new high-yield varieties of specific crops. To illustrate, the Philippines concentrates on rice, Mexico on corn and wheat, and India on foods for semiarid lands. Scientists from many countries work side by side, with little thought to differences of national origin. Successful experiments lead to multinational agreements on diversified programs in research and training. Far from hampering progress, a broadly based international effort stimulates scientific development and dissemination of results. International governing boards set policy for the institutes on the basis of regional, not

211

national, needs and priorities. Just as successful public health ventures in Africa, Asia, and Latin America helped pave the way for cooperation in international agriculture, these international institutes foster a spirit that is spreading to other fields. Third-World leaders have so often been subjected to promises without performance from the promoters of technical assistance that cooperative programs which bring results lead to additional endeavors. Success breeds success and a willingness to undertake new experiments within the broad spectrum of development.

Yet social and economic advancement proceeds along an extended timeline, seldom if ever yielding to instant solutions. The success stories of the international agriculture institutes are rooted in a quarter-century of progress in the Mexican Agriculture Program of the Rockefeller Foundation initiated in 1943. The conquest of tropical diseases by private and public international health agencies had its beginnings at the turn of the century. It will not do for functionalists to portray political advancement as painfully slow and social progress as immediate. Functional approaches offer no immediately visible payoffs; the side effects or unintended benefits may be as valuable and far-reaching as direct successes. Yet no one would deny that in certain social areas cooperation that had been thwarted by political allegiances had advanced apace in a functional context. The long-run effects of educational and scientific leaders grown accustomed to cooperative efforts, of regional or worldwide approaches and solutions in one area attracting notice in other areas, and of the experience of international bodies or boards in shaping transnational policies all combine to encourage respect for the functional approach.

Having said all this, experience in higher education dictates certain caveats to the functionalist idea. Higher education in general is wider and broader than a single problem. Functionalism and its assumptions fit agricultural education, specifically education and research for increasing food production. But higher education spans a far broader band of public policy, touching sensitive issues of national interest and class and society. Higher education is closely linked with government, especially in the Third World. Therefore, successful experiments in higher education involving international cooperation tend as often to reinforce as to reduce nationalism. National governments with hard decisions to make about the allocation of scarce resources reserve to themselves decisions on education, claim credit for any educational advances, and insist on a major role in the governance of universities. It is too much to expect that governments in less-developed countries will easily allow the control of higher education to pass to international bodies.

Finally, higher education is influenced in every country by the culture. It is not a single commodity that can be packaged and delivered from one country to the next. In one country, institutes of higher education stem from and are dependent upon their respective ministries of government. In another country, separate educational institutions are expected to produce only those graduates who fill a manpower need. In still other countries, the important role of independent institutions in liberal arts is slowly being recognized. To consider these several versions of higher education as examples of a single category is to prepare the way for misunderstanding and disillusionment. What is common to each of these distinctions is their focus on the relation of higher education to government. In many industrialized countries, the two are considered independent; in Third World countries, they are integral to the common national endeavor of promoting national development and alleviating poverty. This fact sets limits to functionalism's role but in no way detracts from the benefits of international cooperation in higher education.

Whatever the limitations of functionalism, it represents a unique approach to an emerging world order: "It involves a diagnosis of the problems or disorder in international society, and a prescription for ways of shaping a better world." Functionalism is bound not to any ideology or dogma but to the living realities of a world order of public welfare and international service. The functional perspective has become an established feature of the literature of international relations. It is more an approach than a tightly knit theory. The writings of most present-day theorists of transnationalism, such as Joseph Nye, Robert Keohane, Karl Deutsch, I. L. Claude, Ernst B. Haas, J. Patrick Sewell, and Leon N. Lindberg, can be traced back to the functionalist idea. Functionalism is about cooperation, collaboration, plowshares, and peace. It "stresses the plenitude of relationships of a legitimised character between all manner of diverse actors which form the very fabric of world society. . . . The billiard ball analogy of international society is rejected; greater significance is attached to the emergence of an increasing range of . . . interdependence; the term 'world politics' or 'world society' is preferred to 'international politics;' the role of governments is to be progressively reduced by indirect methods, and integration is to be encouraged by a variety of functionally based, crossnational ties."[4]

Mitrany's *Working Peace System* is the founding study, as were the early writings of Leonard Woolf, Norman Angell, Robert Cecil, and G. D. H. Cole. All these writings stressed economic development, the limits of state welfare programs, and the crisis of democratic individualism. They assumed that just as material self-sufficiency had brought peace and tranquility nationally, it could bring about international peace if the size of the units that evolved was commensurate with mankind's social and economic needs. Just as the family gave way to the state, the state must yield to larger international bodies designed to meet urgent economic and social needs. Technicians and specialists were better equipped to meet such needs than popularly elected national assemblies, although Mitrany called for specialist assemblies such as the assembly of the International Labor Organization, the consultative committee of the European Coal and Steel Community, and the special advisory groups of UNESCO. In the nineteenth century, postal and telegraphic communications and international commerce on rivers and waterways had been organized along functional lines. The specialized agencies were given substantial autonomy from the United Nations after World War II, as were regional organizations in Europe and the developing countries. Most impressive of all were the international nongovernmental organizations.

The success of functionalism in building the fabric of a working peace system remains open to further study at the theoretical, historical, and empirical levels. Mitrany's influence has highlighted the important contributions of international and regional functional organizations. The successes of such agencies in the industrial world have properly been described as "integrationist functionalism," but in the Third World,

4 A. J. R. Groom and Paul Taylor (eds.), *Functionalism: Theory and Practice in International Relations* (New York: Crane, Russak, 1975), 1, 2.

their work has more often served "developmental functionalism." Wherever functional cooperation has been pursued, it has demonstrated both strengths and limitations. Sectoral cooperation has not led, as Mitrany prophesied, to the erosion of national sovereignty when large-scale efforts have been pursued. A reverse spillover effect has occurred in functionalism as national politics and pressures have come to dominate functional organizations such as UNESCO. Functionalism has not overcome national loyalties; the more fundamental the areas of cooperation, the greater the impact of nationalism. World order evolves slowly, and persistent national attitudes and interests remain a part of the international landscape.

WORKS BY DAVID MITRANY

1914–1915

Rumania: Her History and Politics. London: Oxford University Press.

1915

The Balkans: A History of Bulgaria, Serbia, Greece, Rumania, Turkey. With Nevil Forbes, Arnold Toynbee, and D. G. Hogarth. Oxford: Clarendon Press.

1917

Greater Rumania: A Study in National Ideals. London: Hodder & Stoughton.

1925

The Problem of International Sanctions. London: Oxford University Press.

1930

The Land and the Peasant in Rumania: The War and Agrarian Reform, 1917–1921. New Haven, Conn.: Yale University Press.

1933

The Progress of International Government. New Haven, Conn.: Yale University Press.

1936

The Effect of the War in Southeastern Europe. New Haven, Conn.: Yale University Press.

1944

The Road to Security. London: National Peace Council.

A Working Peace System: An Argument for the Functional Development of International Organization. London: Royal Institute of International Affairs.

1951

Marx Against the Peasant: A Study in Social Dogmatism. Chapel Hill: University of North Carolina Press.

1954

Food and Freedom. London: Batchworth Press.

1975

Functionalism: Theory and Practice in International Relations. Edited by A. J. R. Groom and Paul Taylor. New York: Crane, Russak.

The Functional Theory of Politics. London: M. Robertson, for the London School of Economics and Political Science.

CHARLES DE VISSCHER (1884–1973)

World Order and Legal Realism

Charles de Visscher's approach to world order and legal realism reflected his personal experiences as a participant-observer in the development and analysis of contemporary international law and its periodic breakdowns. As a Belgian citizen, de Visscher had learned firsthand the possibilities and limitations of international law. Belgium's tenaciously held claim to the status of neutrality, established by the Belgian Guarantee Treaty of 1839, had not prevented it from being overrun in two world wars. Yet Belgium's long independence had also demonstrated to some degree the utility of international law, because it was in the French and British interest to see that Belgium remain a neutral country.

Charles de Visscher was born on August 2, 1884. He studied law, with particular emphasis on public and private international law. He subsequently became professor of international law at Louvain and Ghent universities. His first book, *Belgium's Case: A Judicial Enquiry* (1916), addressed the problems of Belgium's neutral status during World War I.[1] De Visscher's stature as a foremost authority on the major issues of international law stemmed from his scholarly publications—more than eighty in number. He delivered annual lectures at the Hague Academy of International Law in 1923, 1925, 1929, and 1935. He published papers in the *Revue de Droit International et de Legislation Comparée* and in the *American Journal of International Law*. His writings gained the respect of lawyers, historians, political scientists, and moral philosophers because of his broad outlook. For example, he wrote that law can grow and develop only when it is based on a moral social order.

---

1 This and all books by Charles de Visscher are listed chronologically, with full publication data, beginning on p. 224 herein.

De Visscher attained increasing recognition. Following World War I, he was asked to join in efforts to rebuild the international order. He was primarily concerned with the legal aspects of the League of Nations. He served as a member and rapporteur of the committee preparing amendments to the League Covenant and on the Committee for the Study of Conciliation Procedures. From 1923, he was a member of the Permanent Court of Abitration.[2] Because of the instability created by the war, de Visscher gave highest priority to the problem of stability. *The Stabilization of Europe* (1924) reflected his thinking on the subject. De Visscher demonstrated both a rigorous legal realism and a faith in the future. He believed that a better world was possible and that it was his duty to join in the common effort to bring the world closer to its potential as an international community.

In his later years, de Visscher's integrity and scholarship led distinguished educational and professional groups to honor him. He received honorary doctorates from various universities, including the Universities of Nancy and Montpellier. He was named to membership in the Royal Academy of Belgium, the Union Academique Internationale, the Institut de France, the Madrid Academy of Moral Science, and the Institute of Moral and Political Science of Rumania.

He participated in the activities of the Permanent Court of International Justice both as a lawyer and as a judge. He pleaded before the court in cases involving the European Commission of the Danube, the International Commission of the Oder, the access of Polish war vessels to the port of Danzig, the treatment of Polish nationals in Danzig, and the legal status of eastern Greenland. He was a member of the Committee of Jurists on the Corfu Channel case. He was elected judge of the Permanent Court (PCIJ) in 1937. In the interwar period, he was named to the Committee of Experts on the progressive codification of international law, was the Belgian delegate to the First Conference on the Codification of International Law, and served as rapporteur to the Third Committee of that conference. Thus he learned about international law as much from practice as from the text writers and publicists.

---

2 *International Court of Justice Yearbook, 1946–1947 (The Hague: International Court of Justice, 1947),* 48.

During World War II, Judge de Visscher was president of the Belgian Political Movement of Resistance, which kept in touch with the Belgian government-in-exile in London. His countrymen appointed him a member of the Belgian Government of Liberation in 1944–1945, and he represented Belgium in numerous international conferences during the immediate postwar period. In 1945 he was chosen by Belgium to serve on the Committee of Jurists to prepare a draft statute for the new International Court of Justice. He was present in San Francisco at the creation of the United Nations, and he was Belgium's delegate in early 1946 to the first session of the General Assembly of the United Nations.

In February, 1946, the General Assembly elected him to a six-year term on the International Court of Justice. He retired from the court in 1952, recognized for his lasting contribution to international law and for providing the International Court of Justice with a sense of continuity with its predecessor Permanent Court of International Justice. After his retirement, he maintained an active interest in international law as a teacher, adviser, and author. His numerous articles appeared in a multitude of journals, and he continued to write until his death in 1973. His most renowned work, *Theory and Reality in Public International Law*, first appeared in French in 1957 and has since gone through four editions and an English translation. It continues to be his most important contribution to international relations theory.

In the preface to his great work, de Visscher declared his intention to be "to increase the authority of international law by bringing back into it the values upon which it is founded and freeing it, in contact with life, from certain systemizations which under the guise of science or unity of method have isolated it from its social function." De Visscher criticized several erroneous conceptions of international law, particularly the "voluntarist, individualist, positivist" school, which viewed the state as the final arbiter of justice. Positivists, lacking any independent standard by which to judge the actions of states, bind themselves to a particular historical idea—the state—which is no longer an accurate reflection of reality. The first chapters of the book traced the course of international legal thought beginning with the initial period of the Christian commonwealth: "The idea of a Christian community lies at the origin of international law." Even during the rise of the European state and through the thought of Grotius, there was still present the notion of "a moral concept that refused to accept the greatness of the State as the sole end of public life."[3] The efficacy of international law is dependent on its moral foundations. In the early Christian period, the stress was on humanity rather than on nationalism. In the final analysis, international law must be based on certain controlling ideas of human nature and human need.

With the enormous growth of state power reinforced by the theories of Thomas Hobbes and Baruch Spinoza, the state took on its own morality, thereby displacing the medieval idea of a human community: "The natural-law tradition retains its vitality in theory, but becomes more and more remote from governmental practice, for which everything in the end comes down to power. The dogma of unlimited sovereignty killed the theory of just war." In place of the natural law tradition, positivism emerged declaring that law is law simply because the sovereign decrees it.

> Voluntarist positivism attained its full rigor and its narrowness only in the course of the nineteenth century when national movements had multiplied tenfold the power and exclusiveness of sovereign States. . . . But it achieved this strong systemization around the State only by sacrificing the idea of an objective order to a purely formal conception of international law. It excluded from law the higher considerations of reason, justice, and common utility which are its necessary foundations.[4]

With this absolute notion of state sovereignty came the idea of the balance of power. Although at times the practice of balancing power was intermittently "undeniably useful" in promoting moderation, it could not set up a true world order: "For the balance is like all concepts that rely solely upon force; not necessarily false, they are always inadequate, since force is good or bad according to the use made of it." The classical balance of power system established at the Congress of Vienna, although inspired by the virtue of moderation, foundered on the rocks of nationalism and the rise of industrial civilization. It lost its last vestiges of legitimacy with the outbreak of World War I, when the alli-

---

3 Charles de Visscher, *Theory and Reality in Public International Law*, trans. Percy Corbett (rev. ed.; Princeton, N.J.: Princeton University Press, 1968), vii, 4, 14.
4 *Ibid.*, 17, 21.

ances hardened, the small states went unprotected, and totalitarianism was unleashed. Positivism also revealed its weakness as a result of world war.

> As a reaction against a deformed and sterile law of nature, the positivist theories had the indisputable merit of offering a clear and generally true picture of international relations in the period of relative political stabilization that characterized the nineteenth century. Their irremissable weakness was their moral indifference to the human ends of power and their passive acceptance of the individualism of sovereignties. Cutting norms off from their deepest roots for the sole purpose of integrating them in a scientific but purely formal system, they constantly dessicated and impoverished them. This explains the discredit into which these theories fell.[5]

In place of this morally bankrupt and unreal view of international law, de Visscher proposed a teleological view of international law. This view did not seek to ignore the realities of power; in fact, it insisted on being grounded in reality. For de Visscher, the connection between this teleological view and reality was a matter of "scrutinizing the raison d'etre of norms, restoring the contact between the normative apparatus and the underlying realities." International law is not a fixed, static idea, determined by one period of history, but a dynamic, changing evolutionary idea capable of growth toward ordering power to serve human ends.

> It is pure illusion to expect from the mere arrangement of inter-State relations the establishment of a community order; this can find a solid foundation only in the development of the true international spirit in men. What concerns us is much less the principle of power than the position taken by the regime with regard to the very notion of power. What is decisive is the disposition within the State to keep its action within the limits assigned to it by a functional conception which orders power to human ends instead of dedicating it to its own indefinite extension.

Although de Visscher seemed to be attacking national sovereignty, he actually indicated that the development of an international spirit would not occur by systematically undermining state sovereignty.

> What we must understand, and have the courage to say, is that the transition from State to international morality will never take place by way of

5 *Ibid.*, 24, 54.

a mere spatial broadening of the present moral attitudes of men. The historical distribution of power has implanted group morals which are particular morals and the relations that spring from them rest neither on the perception of an extranational common good nor on the consciousness of a destiny common to all men. It is by other paths and on a different plane that man may perhaps one day attain a morality capable of supporting a world community.

What de Visscher asserted was the power of the idea, which most "realists" undervalued. By clinging to the concept that ideas have little power, realists actually may prevent beneficial developments in world history.

The international community is a potential order in the minds of men: it does not correspond to an effectively established order. It falls short of a legal community in that it lacks legal control of the use of force. . . . The human ends of power alone, can provide a moral basis for action. It is by a return to man, by linking the conception of State, organization and means, to the person who is its end, that we can find, on the plane of an impersonal but not extra-personal common good, the sole moral and legal justification of the obligatory character of international law. The idea of an international community belongs to those great intuitions, to those civilizing ideas which, though slow in their action and subject to eclipses, are nevertheless positive forces that generate political and social change. The most intransigent realist cannot deny their reality or their strength, for it is observation itself that establishes the refusal of man's active nature to consider itself subject to ineluctable laws and the unwillingness of his moral nature to regard as invariable just what is effectively imposed in fact.[6]

Thus, de Visscher in the end was both a practical man of affairs and a historical idealist. He wrote of the need to distinguish between those issues under the jurisdiction of international law and those dominated by nationalism. He warned of the constraints on international law in a century of nationalism beginning with the French Revolution. He recognized the force of the anarchic concept of unlimited sovereignty and what he called the national community of memories. The sovereign state and its exemplars evaluate issues from a political not a legal point of view. The contemporary international system operates within a ter-

6 *Ibid.*, 94, 97, 101, 404.

ritorial framework. International lawyers, to be effective, must make concessions to politics—concessions that are difficult for men of law. International treaties cannot escape the force of national sovereignty especially in disputes over their execution. The contemporary resort to force shows the limits of international law. Even within the United Nations, the admission of new members is dependent not only on legal standards but on changing combinations of political interests. In 1956 de Visscher wrote: "The present slowing down of judicial activities must be attributed much less to a deterioration in their spirit or to an imperfection in their methods than to external factors of a strictly political nature which paralyze the role of all international law in international relations." These factors included the abrupt entry of countries with civilizations foreign to the basis of international law and the intensity and duration of political tensions. Law depends on a minimum of stability in the international order. Order in peace remains the first requirement of the international community. Without a minimum of order, justice is powerless. Judge de Visscher quoted a fellow jurist, N. Politis: "It is thought that justice will bring peace because it is believed that justice can do away with war. It is rather the contrary which is true. The reign of justice presupposes peace. In an atmosphere saturated with passions, rivalries and hostile attitudes, the judge is powerless, because his weapon, the law, loses all value before force."[7]

Charles de Visscher stands almost alone among international lawyers in recognizing the intimate connection between law and a peaceful world order, thus linking him to Butterfield, Lippmann, and Morgenthau who wrote of the need for the peace-making processes of diplomacy. World order for de Visscher is inseparable from its normative foundations and from power and politics. Thus, de Visscher's theories remain relevant to urgent international problems to a degree often lacking in the writings of other world-order theorists. Yet de Visscher departed from the political realists in a number of important respects. De Visscher and the realists would agree that the separation of international law from its social, political, and moral circumstances was a mistake:

7 Charles de Visscher, "Reflections on the Present Prospects of International Adjudication," *American Journal of International Law* L (July, 1956), 474.

"The distinction between ethical and legal categories, reasonable in itself and in many ways necessary, must not be pushed to the point of completely separating law from the primary moral notions." To pretend that men confined within close-knit national communities were likely to take a universal moral outlook was wrong. In de Visscher's words: "Merely to invoke the idea of an international community, as the habit is, is immediately to move into a vicious circle, for it is to postualte in men, shut in their national compartments, something that they still largely lack, namely the community spirit, the deliberate adherence to supranational values." From one other standpoint, de Visscher and the realists hold a common view articulated by him when he maintained: "The central problem of the normative order is henceforth much less the legal validity of the formal process of elaborating international law than the obstacles confronting its extension."[8] Although Visscher was sensitive to the limitations of present-day international law, he pressed more forcefully than any of the realists for the International Court of Justice and for a network of international institutions that would serve the human person. Realists had looked with skepticism on the immense commitment of time and energy given to drafting international legal conventions and promoting the spread of principles of law when the resolution of conflict is more often determined by nonlegal means. They distrusted the disproportionate influence of lawyers in shaping American foreign policy and criticized the tendency of lawyers to be defenders of the status quo. It would be far better, they felt, to examine the political and social situation promoting a nation's observance of legal undertakings than to laud formal legal arrangements that are often observed more in the breach than in the keeping. De Visscher agreed with much of this criticism, but so profound was his commitment to a world order serving humanity that in the end he chose to defend another intellectual position. He can appropriately be considered a world order theorist and an idealist without illusions.

8 De Visscher, *Theory and Reality in Public International Law*, 98.

WORKS BY CHARLES DE VISSCHER

1916

Belgium's Case: A Judicial Enquiry. Translated by E. F. Jourdain. London: Hodder & Stoughton.

1923

La responsabilité des états; cours professé à L'Académie de droit international de la Haye. Juillet.

1924

The Stabilization of Europe. Chicago: University of Chicago Press.

1957

Theory and Reality in Public International Law. Translated by Percy Corbett. Princeton, N.J.: Princeton University Press. Revised edition, 1968.

1963

Problèmes d'interprétation judiciaire en droit international public. Paris: A. Pedone.

1966

Aspects rècents du droit procedural de la Cour Internationale de Justice. Paris: A. Pedone.

1967

Les Effectivités du droit international public. Paris: A. Pedone.

1972

De L'equité dans le reglement arbitral au judiciare des litiges de droit international public. Paris: A. Pedone.

ARNOLD J. TOYNBEE (1889–1975)

World Civilizations and World Politics

Arnold J. Toynbee was born in London on April 14, 1889, the son of Harry Toynbee, a social worker, and Sarah Marshall Toynbee, one of the first women in Britain to receive a college degree. He was named for an uncle who had died at the age of thirty but whose notes were the basis for *The Industrial Revolution* (1884). The nephew wrote in the preface to the 1956 edition of this book: "I was named for him because I happened to be the first male child bearing his name to be born into his immediate family after his death in 1883."[1] Toynbee never had the opportunity to know his uncle, but he followed him at Balliol College, Oxford, where his uncle had been a tutorial fellow. Toynbee caught a vision of simplicity in his uncle and an unmistakable note of greatness. When Arnold J. Toynbee died, he was described as an amiable and simple man, who had an offhand, rather than professional, manner and who would engage almost anyone in conversation. Toynbee Hall, a London settlement house where university students could learn firsthand about the poor, was built as a memorial to the elder Toynbee.

The younger Toynbee was raised in an atmosphere that encouraged childhood reading about Greece and Rome and a concern for human need. His education took him to Winchester and then to Balliol College, Oxford. In contrast with E. H. Carr or David Mitrany, who represented the loyal opposition to Britain's foreign-policy elite and spoke for the disinherited and disadvantaged, Toynbee pursued a thoroughgoing British classical education and way of life. He continued his studies in Greece, was trained at the British Archeological School in Athens, and began to ponder the mortality of civilizations including his own on

---

1 Arnold J. Toynbee, *The Industrial Revolution* (1884; reprinted, Boston: Beacon Press, 1956), x.

walking tours among the ruins of classical Greece and Crete. Returning to Britain in 1912, he was named tutor in ancient history at Balliol. From 1915 to 1919, he was drawn into wartime service for his government, and in April, 1918, he was appointed to the Political Intelligence Department of the Foreign Office. He was a member of the Middle Eastern section of the British delegation to the Paris Peace Conference in 1919 and again in 1946 after World War II was a member of the British delegation to the peace conference in Paris. His fluency in five languages and knowledge of the Middle East made him a valued public servant. From 1919 to 1924, he was Koraes Professor of Byzantine and Modern Greek Language, Literature, and History at London University. From 1939 to 1943, he was director of foreign research and press service of the Royal Institute of International Affairs and from 1943 to 1946, director of the Research Department of the Foreign Office. He continued his association with Chatham House (the Royal Institute of International Affairs) after World War II as Stevenson Research Professor of International History and director of studies until his retirement from this dual appointment in 1955. He received numerous honorary degrees (Oxford, Birmingham, Columbia, and Princeton) and in 1968 was named an associate member of the Academy of Moral and Political Sciences of the Institut de France. His monumental *Study of History* (1934–1961) first gained recognition in the United States. It was ignored by the *English Historical Review*, which deferred its first review until 1956, and apparently offended the editors of the prestigious *Cambridge Modern History* because of its attacks on parochial history (it was said that the joint authors of the *Cambridge Modern History* considered his one-man adventure in historical synthesis an act of immense presumptuousness). American reviewers, including the eminent Charles A. Beard, reviewed the first three volumes immediately in 1935 in the *American Historical Review*. Another American reviewer described it as the most provocative work on historical theory written in England since Karl Marx's *Das Kapital*.

A dual problem confronts anyone who proposes to discuss and evaluate historical writing. First, he must be certain of the objective that underlies the work. One useful guide is the distinction between historical writing and the philosophy of history. In general, historians seek to

226

report and describe past events. Philosophers of history, however, ordinarily accept an additional task. They consider the problem of why events took place as they did and attempt to fathom the meaning and formulate the principles of history. It is not always possible to draw a sharp line between these two approaches, but the standards of a historian are unlikely to correspond at all points with those of a philosopher. Although both Thucydides and Augustine formulated principles of history, only the former wrote narrative history. The historian is judged by the accuracy with which he portrays the past; the philosopher is judged by the value of his world view for understanding and interpreting the present. There are philosophers of history who boldly set about casting horoscopes of the future. Indirectly, all philosophies of history have this aim. Although Toynbee repeatedly disavowed any intention of his historical prophecy,[2] numerous references and analogies—indeed the whole character of his major work—suggested that he kept an anxious eye toward the future. He applied an underlying philosophy to the facts of history and wrote of a time span that approached the universal. On this account, we must judge him not merely as a historian but as a philosopher of history. Philosophy of history, however, has three possible meanings. It may refer to the methodology of history or the metaphysics of history or the logic of history. That is, any philosophy of history may be construed as a *method* for dealing with the complexities of history or an interpretation of the *meaning* of history or a statement of the *laws* of history. This discussion will be confined to Toynbee's historical method, which will indirectly reveal his conception of the meaning and laws of history.

For Toynbee, history and the techniques for studying it are a curious blend of science and fiction. Most social studies are planned and designed either to treat a subject systematically by scrupulously precise and scientific procedures or in an opposite sense to illuminate some profound myth or spiritual truth through poetry and fable. The notion of joining these techniques and using the one to supply deficiencies in the other is so uncommon that almost no one has challenged Toynbee

---

2 "While we can speculate with profit on the general shape of things to come, we can foresee the precise shadow of particular coming events only a very short way ahead." Arnold J. Toynbee, *Civilization on Trial* (New York: Oxford University Press, 1948), 204.

in terms of this fundamental dualism. Instead, empiricists and social scientists have consistently challenged his mysticism and humanists his scientism.[3] It is important, therefore, to examine the relative place given to each as twin pillars supporting his method of history.

Toynbee's stress on the scientific method would at first seem to place him in the tradition of Henry T. Buckle, Vilfredo Pareto, and Ellsworth Huntington. There have been few scholars as sanguine as Buckle regarding the creation of a science of society and human behavior. He was convinced that any human phenomenon could be isolated and studied "by observations so numerous as to eliminate the disturbances." Statistics had "thrown more light on the study of human nature" than all past or present approaches. No aspect of behavior need be outside this province.

> When we perform an action we perform it in consequence of some motive or motives. . . . Those motives are the results of some antecedents. . . . Therefore, if we are acquainted with the whole of the antecedents, and with all the laws of the movements, we could with unerring certainty predict the whole of their immediate results. . . . If, for example, I am intimately acquainted with the character of any person, I can frequently tell how he will act under some given circumstance. Should I fail in this prediction, I must ascribe my error not to the arbitrary and capricious freedom of his will, nor to any super-natural prearrangement, for of neither of these things have we the slightest proof; but I must be content to suppose either that I had been misinformed as to some of the circumstances in which he was placed, or else that I had not sufficiently studied the ordinary operations of his mind.

Although Pareto was less expansive regarding universal scientific laws and principles, he was equally convinced that truth can be uncovered only through scientific testing and probing. The sole legitimate field of study is "the field of experience and observation strictly. We use those terms in the meanings they have in the natural sciences such as astronomy, chemistry, physiology, and so on."[4]

---

3 The most devastating and intelligent of these attacks was by R. H. S. Crossman, "Mystic World of Arnold Toynbee," *New Republic*, July 14, 1947, pp. 24–26.

4 Henry T. Buckle, *Introductions to the History of Civilization in England* (New York: Albert & Charles Boni, 1925), I, 10–11, 18, 90–91; Vilfredo Pareto, *The Mind and Society* (New York: Harcourt Brace, 1935), I, 33.

228

These are merely two examples of methodologies that in differing degrees have been founded upon principles derived from the natural sciences. The natural scientist seeks to deal with separate, discrete factors neatly defined. Then he proceeds to consider the relations between these individual units. Toynbee put his separate, discrete civilizations through their paces in roughly the same way, for he observed:

> In methodology what I am trying to do is to apply the scientific notion of "law," "regularity" and "recurrence" to the history of human affairs and find out experimentally how far this way of looking at things will go in this field. . . . I do think that the scientific apparatus can be applied fruitfully to human affairs to some extent, e.g., where they are considerably affected by the physical environment and where it is the subconscious part of the psyche more than the will and the intellect that is in command.[5]

An early source of inspiration for Toynbee was the comparative history of E. A. Freeman. In *A Study of History*, Toynbee acknowledged that "he owes a greater debt than he can repay to the reading of Freeman's *Historical Essays* as a boy." It was Freeman's contention that societies could be studied and compared as separate and distinct units. In Toynbee's system, "the comparative method of studying analogies and parallels" is consistently pursued. He contrasted the methods used in contemporary business with those of historical writing:

> While our Western historians are disputing the possibility of making a comparative study of historical facts, our Western men of business are all the time making their living out of a comparative study of the facts of life around them. The perfect example of such a comparative study for practical ends is the collection and analysis of the statistics on which the business transactions of insurance companies are based; and some such study, in which statistics are collected and averages taken for the purpose of making forecasts, is at the basis of almost all profitable business. . . . In this adventure, at any rate, we need not hesitate to follow the lead of our latter-day masters.[6]

The course of history for Toynbee is a consequence of man's relation to his geographical environment, as well as to his fellow men. The

---

5 Arnold J. Toynbee to Kenneth W. Thompson, September 22, 1949.
6 Arnold J. Toynbee, *A Study of History* (6 vols.; London: Oxford University Press, 1934–61), I, 34, 180–81, 339.

influence of geography on history is a topic for scientific or pseudoscientific study. Here Toynbee acknowledged his dependence upon the tradition of Ellsworth Huntington, who is referred to as "one of our most distinguished and original minded students." Some statements raise doubts as to who is the pupil, who the teacher. For example, Toynbee asserts: "The cycle of the seasons governs life itself by governing our food supply."[7] Yet from Buckle to Huntington to Toynbee, there is a descending order of emphasis upon geography as the all-determinative force. What the three students had in common was a belief that to a greater or lesser degree man's destiny was shaped by the relatively permanent factors in his physical surroundings. How these can best be studied is a question the historian must answer. First, Toynbee called on scientific techniques through which correlations between a society's development and its geographical base might be established. He attempted to find out whether there were geographical factors common to societies with similar patterns of growth or decline.

But this attempt soon raised the question of whether geographic factors in particular, or measurable and predictable elements in general, could ever account fully for human conduct or for the birth, growth, and death of a society. The late Morris Cohen once issued a sharp warning on this point:

> To say that anything is determined by its environment is actually to say only that in order to explain anything we must look to its relationship with other things—which amounts to an undeniable tautology. The essential fact is that the environment of every human being and the context of every human act contain human and non-human elements inextricably intertwined. Only as we realize that the events of human history include both mind and matter as polar components can we escape the grosser errors of those who would spin the world out of ideas and those who look to earth, air, fire and water to explain all human phenomena.

In this vein, Toynbee maintained that ideas and myths, as well as more tangible factors, are a part of the historian's equipment. Quite consciously and deliberately he used myths as an instrument of scientific inquiry and a pointer to put reason on the right path. His geographical

7 *Ibid.*, 293; Toynbee, *Civilization on Trial*, 31.

determinism was thus never more than half-hearted. The scientific approach, which some writers had erected into a philosophy and pseudo-religion, became for him a useful but imperfect technique, which he questioned: "Have we not been guilty of applying to historical thought, which is a study of living creatures, a scientific method of thought which has been devised for thinking about Inanimate Nature? . . . Let us shut our eyes, for the moment, to formulae of Science in order to open our ears to the language of Mythology."[8]

Throughout *A Study of History*, the overriding influence of Toynbee's early grounding in Anglican Christian socialism is continually in evidence. As a young man he absorbed the ideas of Sir Frederick Maurice, Charles Kingsley, Canon Barnett, his uncle Arnold Toynbee, and his father-in-law Gilbert Murray; and these molded his social consciousness. But the prime source of Toynbee's individualism and mysticism stemmed from the influence of Henri Bergson, whose writings hit Toynbee "with the force of a revelation."[9] The ideas of creative and emergent evolution permeated the whole structure of Toynbee's philosophy of history. The emphasis on impermanence, on purpose in the midst of changing values, and on mind and intuition as the twin progenitors of truth introduced a new element that eventually dominated Toynbee's historiography. From this point on, his work became at least as much a great epic as a projected science of society. The *élan vital* was the spirit of God in man. An adversary—the devil—confronts man. These two mythical forces contended for the mastery and control of human destiny and became, in microcosm, rival forces within the human mind. In this struggle and drama, the final victory must be God's, but the challenge by an adversary sets in motion dynamic forces that His perfection alone would never have evoked. This is the cosmic drama that we may scrutinize, not in a laboratory, but in the minds of men and in their social relations.

The presence of this second element of legend and myth is not in itself proof that Toynbee has failed in his scientific venture. The ideal of the greatest historians has always been a reconstruction of the past that

---

8 Morris Cohen, *The Meaning of Human History* (La Salle, Ill.: Open Court Publishing Co., 1947), 171; Toynbee, *A Study of History*, I, 271.
9 Tangye Leon, "A Study of Toynbee," *Horizon*, XV (January, 1947), 24.

would be scientific in its method but imaginative in insight and formulation. Moreover, it is a truism that any observer begins, not with a
tabula rasa, but with a substantial fund of hypotheses and expectations.
The great British historian H. A. L. Fisher observed: "Mr. Toynbee
. . . does not wholly confine himself to facts. He is fertile in large
historical ideas and suggestive comparisons. . . . Mr. Toynbee keeps an
impartial mind." The English scholar G. M. Trevelyan writes: "Truth
is the criterion of historical study but its motive is poetic. Its poetry
consists in being true. There we find the synthesis of the scientific and
literary views of history." The scientific historian Jacob Burckhardt
placed the same elements of fact and spirit at the center of his outlook
on history: "The task of history as a whole is to show its twin aspects,
distinct yet identical, proceeding from the fact that, firstly, the spiritual, in whatever domain it is perceived, has a historical aspect under
which it appears as change, as the contingent, as a passing moment
which forms part of a vast whole beyond our power to divine, and that,
secondly, every event has a spiritual aspect by which it partakes of immortality."[10] Nonetheless, it is one thing to ascribe to spiritual and
moral factors their proper place in history; it is something else to allow
a concern for this dimension to blur and obscure the perception of material and corporeal factors. Some have condemned spiritual history in
general for refusing to confront the problems of that social and political
stratum in which men live out their common material lives.

Toynbee had a deep familiarity with classical literature, knew the
Bible at least as well as the theologians, and had so profoundly absorbed
the insights of St. John, Johann von Goethe, and William Blake that
he used them as his own. In addition, Oswald Spengler prepared the
way for the study of life histories of whole societies. Although Toynbee's
inquiry had already been launched, his reading of Spengler reassured
him positively of the validity of his plan and negatively of the importance of proceeding empirically. In two respects Spengler influenced
Toynbee's methodology. First, both men attempted to establish laws of
history that would apply to all societies. Where they differed was on the
nature of these laws. For Spengler such laws were irrevocable, but Toyn-

10 *Survey of International Affairs, 1924* (Oxford: Oxford University Press, 1926), v–vi; G. M. Trevelyan, "History and Literature," *History*, n.s., IX (1924), 91; Jacob Burckhardt, *Force and Freedom* (New York: Pantheon Books, 1943), 83.

bee was not so certain. Both conceded, however, that there was an element of inventiveness in man's conduct, which made absolute science impracticable. Spengler observed: "There is a vast difference between man and all other animals. . . . Technics in man's life is conscious, arbitrary, alterable, personal, *inventive*. It is learned and improved. Man becomes the *creator* of his tactics of living—that is his grandeur and his doom. And the inner form of this creativeness we call culture."[11]

Finally two less widely known scholars must be mentioned as probable contributors to Toynbee's system. His thesis of challenge and response was dimly foreshadowed in *The Martyrdom of Man* (1872) by Winwood Reade. What Toynbee called the "stimulus of hard countries" Reade described as "the struggle for bare life against hostile nature, first aroused the mental activity of the Egyptian priests, while the constant attacks of the desert tribes developed the martial energies of the military men." In the same way, the concept of an internal and external proletariat was implicit in the final chapter of *A History of the Ancient World* (1927) by the great Russian historian Michael I. Rostovtzeff. In a private interview, Toynbee confirmed his indebtedness to Rostovtzeff but added that he got the idea of challenge and response from the poet Robert Browning. He also noted that the ideas of Anne Robert Jacques Turgot as reflected in the writings of Frederich Teggart early caught his imagination.[12] Thus Toynbee was influenced by both social scientists and humanists. His method for dealing with history disclosed unmistakable evidence of these two mainsprings.

It is somewhat easier to identify the forerunners of Toynbee's historical approach than to analyze systematically his historical method. For one thing, his approach was different at three distinct periods in his life. These changes in emphasis and in frame of reference revealed his ability to formulate a theory, discover its flaws through trial and error, and exchange it for something he considered better. They also disclosed that his conception of history as a saga of civilizations and ultimately of religion is an idea that dawned on him only gradually.

Toynbee's first publications are clearly the child of his training. His

11 Oswald Spengler, *Man and Technics* (New York: Alfred A. Knopf, 1932), 28–31.
12 Winwood Reade, *The Martyrdom of Man* (London: Watts, 1925), 6; Michael Rostovtzeff, *A History of the Ancient World* (Oxford: Clarendon Press, 1927), II, 351–55; private interview with Arnold J. Toynbee, December 2, 1950.

education at Winchester and Balliol coincided roughly with the first decade of this century. The symbol of the times was the diamond jubilee of Queen Victoria; as a small boy, he had stood in the processions. Englishmen then shared the feeling of having reached the summit where history itself was being terminated. This philosophy could hardly have been very convincing to Toynbee, for his earliest writings reflect a concern for diverse peoples and nationalities in the spirit of President Woodrow Wilson's national self-determination. From 1914 to 1916, Toynbee's first essays and books were published: *The Balkans, Nationality and the War*, and *The New Europe*.[13] In them his methodology was reflected in the subjects he considered. Not civilizations but nations were the "intelligible units of history." He reserved for nations in general the same optimism that the Victorian era showed for Britain in particular. In that age "the national state is the most magnificent . . . social achievement in existence." National culture was sacred, and to oppose it was to defy God. Some of the same terms and metaphors that he later used to describe the role of religion were used to characterize the function of nation-states. For example, he found that "within the chrysalis" of absolute government a "common self-consciousness or Nationality" was born, and democratic nationalism was becoming a healthy and strapping youngster: "From the Ottoman Empire there would emerge . . . as from a chrysalis, a Turkish nation."[14] In the same way he later found that civilizations emerged from the chrysalis of great religions.

These examples of a rather naive belief in bourgeois progress through humanitarian nationalism were of course qualified in many ways. He early stated profound belief in some form of international authority. Eastern Europe had problems that required a Balkan Zollverein. Culture was not inherent in any one language but was the heritage of the race. However, these foreshadowings of later "universalism" were more the expressions of an idealistic philosophy of international relations than a denial of the primacy of nations as units of history. Indeed, he regarded

---

13 These and all books by Arnold J. Toynbee are listed chronologically, with full publication data, beginning on p. 248 herein.
14 Arnold J. Toynbee, *Nationality and the War* (London: J. M. Dent, 1915), 273, 481; Arnold J. Toynbee and Kenneth P. Kirkwood, *Turkey* (London: Ernest Benn, 1926), 4–5.

World War I as a kind of accident, which had but temporarily disturbed Europe's progress toward a warless internationalism—concrete evidence that at this stage in Toynbee's thinking idealism and nationalism were indissolubly wedded. The European national state was the norm of civilized society and had so far revealed a "faculty of indefinite organic growth."[15] A premonition that this perspective might change came in the last sentence of *Nationality and War* (1915). If nations continued cribbed and confined within parochial states in their struggles for existence and survival, their fate might prove to be no different than that of the Greek city-states. This was the type of history he wrote as a young man of twenty-five.

His early outlook was shattered by World War I. Any bourgeois illusions about human progress could scarcely have withstood so grim a parable of man's violence and brutality. For five years, Toynbee immersed himself in propaganda and intelligence work for the government. His assignment was to sift and rewrite reports of German atrocities. These lurid accounts flowed incongrously from the pen of the judicious historian. After the war he observed: "Atrocities seem to be outbreaks of bestiality normally 'suppressed' in human beings but almost automatically stimulated under certain conditions, and that so powerfully, if the conditions are sufficiently acute or protracted, that the most highly civilized people are carried away."[16] Moreover, he registered serious misgivings concerning the nation-state as the measure of things. No known civilization but his had grounded statehood on community of language. This formula had occasioned bloodshed and massacre in the Near and Middle East. It had climaxed in a totalitarian Moloch, in a demoniac effort after uniformity.

A second impression penetrated Toynbee's consciousness during this crisis. In the spring of 1918, as the German offensive under Erich Ludendorff exploded in one final thrust, a profound anxiety overcame Toynbee. In 1911–1912, immediately after earning his degree, he had made a nine-months walking trip through Greece and Crete. One impression engraved itself indelibly on his memory. In the faint shadows

15 Arnold J. Toynbee *et al.*, *The Balkans: A History of Bulgaria, Serbia, Greece, Rumania and Turkey* (London: Oxford University Press, 1915), 183.
16 Arnold J. Toynbee, *The Western Question in Greece and Turkey* (London: Constable, 1922), 266.

of the Minoan civilization in Crete, he came upon the deserted country house of a Venetian landowner. As he looked at the ruins of two and a half centuries, he imagined those of Britain heaped alongside them. In 1918 he recalled this *memento mori* of an extinct Venetian colony in Crete, which had lasted four and a half centuries longer than any British colony. The ominous prospect that the German drive might prove the "knock-out blow" for the West found Toynbee rereading Thucydides and Lucretius, including the latter's imperishable, if melancholy, counsel on how to face death. The somber accounts of Peloponnesian and Hannibalic doom, the fierce and brutal catastrophes that Toynbee himself was reading about and narrating, and his impending sense of the ephemeral nature of civilization became an obsession following his trip to the Balkans. These were the three elements destined to be blended in an alloy of fit temper and resiliency to provide Toynbee with a new vessel of history.

The second stage or period of Toynbee's historical method began in 1922, when at the age of thirty-three he drafted the main outlines of *A Study of History*. A work twice the size of Edward Gibbon's great classic, it required most of Toynbee's intellectual strength and vigor. During the war years, forces were carrying him toward a perspective that embraced and encircled the whole historical landscape. He made this clear in 1919 when he addressed the candidates for *literae humaniores* at Oxford following his first year of postwar teaching at the University of London. The thesis of the lecture was a concise paradigm of his new theory of history. Gone was the nation-state as the primary unit of study, for "the plot of civilization in a great exposition of it—like the Hellenic exposition or our own Western exposition—is surely the right goal of a humane education." Western society, he asserts somewhat later, is "a closer and more permanent unity than . . . the independent states that form and dissolve within its boundaries."[17] Having substituted civilizations for nations, Toynbee was ready with a second innovation. How were these great units to be analyzed and dissected? The answer Toynbee gave was the same as Spengler's, although the latter's writings were not yet known to Toynbee. The life histories of civilizations must be com-

17 Toynbee, *The Tragedy of Greece* (Oxford: Clarendon Press, 1921), 6; Toynbee, *The Western Question in Greece and Turkey*, 4.

piled, compared, and generalized in a "morphology" of history. Civilizations pass through determinate states of growth and decay. For the purpose of describing these stages, they could be considered as "biological organizms." In this limited sense, the life cycles of societies can be described as living creatures.

In the same way, Toynbee cast the life patterns of civilizations in the form of a second metaphor, that of a drama or tragedy: "The great civilizations . . . may all reveal the same plot, if we analyze them rightly." It was this plot and its three "acts"—growth and development; crisis, breakdown, and rally; and final dissolution—which the universal historian must gird himself to study. The Greco-Roman civilization was Toynbee's model, and he developed his own thesis to account for its decline. For him, the moment of moral failure and breakdown came in 431 B.C. with the Peleponnesian War.

A third and final technique must be mentioned. After choosing civilizations as his subject and breaking down their histories into the three parts or "acts" of a drama, Toynbee posed a third methodological problem concerning the relationships between these units or societies. There are issues in history that would be lost if one examined merely the uniqueness or, like Spengler, the "culture-soul" of each separate civilization. So for Toynbee the most absorbing problem in history involves encounters or contacts in which new civilizations are born.

The present encounter between Western civilization and the rest of the world is not something novel or unique. It is rather an outstanding instance of a recurrent historical phenomenon that can be examined in comparative terms. From the study of encounters between historic civilizations, "laws" can be deduced regarding cultural contacts. One of Toynbee's "laws" focused on the nature of relationships in the face of resistance by an assaulted society. When two civilizations collide, the culture of the more aggressive one is diffracted into its components, just as a light ray is diffracted into the spectrum by resistance from a prism. The more trivial components, which will not cause too immediate and violent a disturbance of the threatened society's traditional way of life, have the best chance of penetration. Illustrative were the two successive assaults of Western civilization upon China and Japan. In the sixteenth and seventeenth centuries, the Far East repulsed an attempt to introduce the Western way of life *en bloc*—including its religion—but in the nineteenth century it yielded to the more trivial force of technology. The Far East could accept technology while retaining the more basic qualities of its own way of life.

This diffraction of culture into its components leads to another recurrent feature of encounters between civilizations. An institution or social phenomenon that is an organic part of a total culture may, when separated from the whole in the form of a culture-ray, threaten or undermine the assaulted society. Thus the nation-state, when founded on common linguistic groups like Western Europe, has been less explosive. In Eastern Europe, Southwest Asia, India, and Malaya, where the linguistic map has not always provided a convenient or logical basis for the political map, the nation-state has been a disruptive force. From the Sudentanland to eastern Bengal, nations have been established through barbarism, because the historic and traditional local patterns of social life in the areas clashed with the imperatives of national self-determination. The original setting of modern nationalism, where linguistic groups were compact and homogeneous units, has frequently been missing in non-European societies, and the idea of nationalism therefore has become an unsettling, even volcanic, force.[18]

Toynbee's *modus operandi* in dealing with history has undergone radical transformations since 1914–1915. The most decisive change of all, however, took place in 1939 and ushered in the third period of his historical method. At the age of fifty, Toynbee shifted the pivot of his approach from civilizations to higher religions. Hitherto, religion had been a means to an end, an agent responsible for the reproduction and perpetuation of civilizations. In Volumes IV–VI of *A Study of History* an unexpected note was sounded.

> When we examine the universal churches we shall find ourselves led to raise the question whether churches can really be comprehended in their entirety in the framework of the histories of civilizations, within which they make their first historical appearance, or whether we have not to regard them as representatives of another species of society which is at least as distinct from the species 'civilizations' as the civilizations are distinct from the primitive societies. This may prove to be one of the most momentous questions that a study of history . . . can suggest to us.

18 Toynbee deals with these questions in the last four volumes of *A Study of History.*

The whole apparatus of disintegration in the later stages of all civilizations, with internal and external proletariats as well as religion, was a key element in Toynbee's conception of the pattern of history. In a curious but perceptible fashion, Toynbee had moved from nations to civilizations to higher religions, and these shifts in historical focus altered profoundly both his interpretation and the tools and techniques he employed. He summarized this change and its consequences thusly:

> Our present view of modern history focuses attention on the rise of our modern Western secular civilization as the latest great new event in the world. As we follow that rise, from the first premonition of it in the genius of Frederick II Hohenstaufen, through the Renaissance to the eruption of democracy and science and modern scientific technique, we think of all this as being the great new event in the world which demands our attention and commands our admiration. If we can bring ourselves to think of it, instead, as one of the vain repetitions of the Gentiles—an almost meaningless repetition of something that the Greeks and Romans did before us and did supremely well—then the greatest new event in the history of mankind will be seen to be a very different one. The greatest new event will then not be the monotonous rise of yet another secular civilization out of the bosom of the Christian Chruch in the course of these latter centuries; it will still be the Crucifixion and its spiritual consequences. [19]

Toynbee's approach to world order reflected a fervent belief in the unity of life and thought. He preferred, he said, to be a student of human affairs not of politics or culture, economics or religion. He protested the breakdown of human studies into "the so-called disciplines," when it was mankind as a whole that deserved study. In taking this stand, Toynbee saw himself as jumping from the eighteenth into the twenty-first century without becoming entangled in either the nineteenth or twentieth centuries. He believed that in this sense the past was the wave of the future. In 1964 he defined his vision of the future as he perceived it on his seventy-fifth birthday: "We are now moving into a chapter in human history in which our choice is going to be, not between a whole world and a shredded up world, but between one world and no world." Toynbee's vision of a universal world society was all-encompassing. He believed that over time sectarianism in religion could be subordinated to ecumenicalism and that specialization in the

---

[19] Toynbee, *A Study of History*, V, 23; Toynbee, *Civilization on Trial*, 237.

study of human affairs would be gradually subordinated to a more comprehensive view of the human condition. Despite the conflicts of the twentieth-century, he prophesied that world unity would emerge in the twenty-first century.

Toynbee rested his hope on the bedrock of his concepts about man and history. For him, spiritual rather than material forces controlled the unfolding of history, and individuals who were capable of both creative and destructive acts shaped its contours. (For this he was criticized in the Soviet Union and other Marxist countries, even though he had written of the need for coexistence between East and West.) History for Toynbee was also "God revealing himself," and the end of history was the Kingdom of God. (For this he was criticized by those who believed that God was dead.) He criticized Americans who refused to admit that the earthly paradise included tragedy and who thought that if America had tragedy it could not be the earthly paradise. (For this the self-appointed guardians of America's superior righteousness denounced and condemned him. The editors and publisher of *Time* praised his religious viewpoint but scorned his conciliatory attitude toward the Soviet Union, calling him an eminent historian when dealing with the distant past but a minor pundit when dealing with the present.)

It is of course possible to argue that Toynbee's vision of the future represented a romantic and utopian strain of thought, which periodically cropped up in his philosophy of history. In 1915 the panacea of Wilsonian national self-determination caught his fancy. In the 1920s, he believed that the impact of Westernization would arrest the trend toward the fragmentation of states and provide stable foundations for world unity. And after World War II, he believed that religions were progressing toward religious unity.

Although Toynbee's interpretations of history were sometimes endangered by false optimism, he was quite aware that Western civilization might deteriorate like the twenty-five other civilizations he had described. Until 1931 Western civilization had been living and growing continuously for some twelve or thirteen centuries with only temporary setbacks. With a worldwide economic depression and the rise of mighty states that threatened civilization, Toynbee pondered whether the West might be coming to the end of its history. He was reasonably specific about the four stages or distinct periods in Western history. First, from 675 to 1075, the West had experienced genesis and birth in the survivors of a shipwrecked Hellenic civilization. The decision of the papacy in 1075 to take up arms against the secular states may have signaled its first breakdown. The second period began in 1075 as the era of Republica Christianum and closed in 1475 as the Italian city-states reached the peak of their power. The third period from 1475 to 1875 was one of transition from the city-state to the kingdom-state with the birth of the institutions of democracy and industrialism. In the fourth period since 1875, these twin institutions were harnessed by nation-states, and the problems of rampant nationalism have been intensified by factors of war and class. Toynbee found warning symptoms in the history of other civilizations that were echoed in his own civilization. One of these was militarism. Assyria had destroyed itself by war despite its achievements in administration and science; in trying to conquer the world, the Assyrians finally provoked their neighbors into annihilating them. Toynbee found in Prussia another Assyria. The Greeks glorified the city-state, a remarkable instrument for political and cultural growth; but when no powerful Greek city-state was willing to sacrifice its sovereignty for a larger and stronger political unity or when unity came too late, Greece was overcome by the Romans. The parallel in our day, Toynbee wrote, is the transglorification of the nation-state, which has become the principal Western religion.

War and class are the major problems facing the world, according to Toynbee. War had brought about the demise of most earlier civilizations and currently threatens the whole human enterprise. Class, likewise, constitutes an unprecedented challenge because of the need for rapid readjustments in a society still geared to nineteenth-century requirements. The accelerated pace of contemporary technological progress has transformed war and class into enormities which may destroy all civilizations, not merely our own.

Faced with such a prospect, survival depends not solely on an ultimate religious solution foreshadowed in all of Toynbee's writings, but on an immediate and an ultimate political solution. The immediate political solution is a political settlement, and the ultimate political solution is world government. The intellectual foundations of the first are political realism and of the second, political idealism. The main purpose of a settlement is to buy time. World government is the most effective means of preserving world peace, but under present conditions it may be impossible. The best way to gain time for the ultimate enterprise is through a partition of the world into spheres of influence. Toynbee observed: "The possibility of a federation between Russia and America, which is the only form of world federal government that really matters—because only a federation between America and Russia would prevent another world war—is far away." A temporary division of the world "would be hard on the countries that happen to be on the borderline, but it would really be much better for everybody if it could be achieved, rather than to have another war with its quite uncertain aftermath." Because of technological advances, Toynbee warned that the Soviet Union and the United States had been brought into close proximity with each other. They were "people with extremely different pasts and traditions and religions and ideologies—without having time yet to learn how to live together in the same world by grinding off our rough edges against each other." He concluded:

> Russia and the West, Russia and the United States, have not had to live together intimately in the same world until recently. We do not know whether they can or cannot do it, but if it is going to be possible for them to do it, they need time to learn how to do it, time to get used to each other. It is very awkward for each of them to get used to the other, and they cannot do it unless they have time and patience.[20]

As a historian, Toynbee looked for precedents. Before the First World War, France and Great Britain were rivals in Africa, and Russia and Great Britain faced one another in Asia: "In 1904 France and Great Britain went into consultation, worked over the map of the world, and wherever there was friction between them they ironed it out and made a bargain on a fifty-fifty basis: 'You have this, we keep that; and we will forget about that old quarrel of ours.' In 1907 Great Britain and Russia did the same." Others pointed out that political settlements, such as the one arrived at through negotiations at the Congress of Berlin in 1878, mitigated conflicts that threatened war. Often political settlements have

20 Arnold J. Toynbee, *The Prospect of Western Civilization* (New York: Columbia University Press, 1947), 45–46, 47.

required a common enemy, such as the European rivalries at the turn of the century in Africa and Asia when the common enemy was Germany. Toynbee observed: "But, after all . . . America and Russia have a common enemy too, of whom I am sure they are likewise afraid, and that is atomic energy."[21]

Toynbee—no more than Winston Churchill, Walter Lippmann, Hans J. Morgenthau, or others who urged that Russia and America seek to negotiate a political settlement—did not offer a detailed blueprint of what might be expected. Boundaries and dividing lines, if they were possible at all, would be the product of hard bargaining and the traditional process of diplomacy. In the 1940s, the United States would have had the power to draw the demarcation line close to the Soviet political domain, gaining a large sphere representing "three-quarters of the world's area and four-fifths of its population."[22] Toynbee envisioned China, India, Indonesia, and Japan falling within the American sphere. The high price of "drifting too long" is evident in the shrinkage of a possible American sphere in any future negotiated settlement or in the boundaries of the Helsinki Accords, which represented the postwar territorial status quo. With all his humanism, Toynbee would almost certainly not link a territorial settlement directly with an accord on the explosive and divisive subject of human rights.

For Toynbee, the final purpose of a political settlement would be the creation of conditions essential for a voluntary world government. If the immediate task of diplomacy was to reduce international tensions and to provide for the mitigation and accommodation of political conflicts, its ultimate task was to help establish the foundations of world community. It was on this point that Toynbee's appeal for a political settlement hinged. If a provisional sphere-of-interest agreement "could be brought about—if things are not too far gone for that . . . [such an agreement] would give us time among other things, to try gradually to build these two spheres together and eventually to unite them in a cooperative world government."[23]

World government was the ultimate political solution, but how was

21 *Ibid.*, 44–45.
22 *Ibid.*, 50.
23 *Ibid.*, 46.

it to come about? Having asserted that it was a foregone conclusion that the world would be unified politically in the future and believing that world interdependence and the threat of nuclear annihilation were speeding that process, Toynbee searched for ways to achieve this. He found a stronger motive shared by more people to unite against the specter of war than had been true in the previous six thousand years. Toynbee found two alternative roads for the attainment of world government—by conquest and by voluntary federation. The profoundest difference between the two was the aftermath. As a historian of world civilizations, Toynbee saw world government as inevitable but warned that the means by which it was achieved would be all important. The alternatives were either the establishment of a universal state as the last desperate effort of a fading civilization (for which Toynbee found numerous precedents) or a new and creative enterprise at building a world state by voluntary agreement.

Toynbee discovered examples of world government by conquest in the imperial successes of Alexander of Macedon, the Ts'in Dynasty in China, and the Roman militarists. The secular trend has been toward an increase in the size of effective political units and a steady and consistent diminution in the number of powers. In 1860 and 1870, the model state in area and resources was France or Great Britain. In 1950 Toynbee reflected on the size of the two superpowers, the Soviet Union and the United States: "Everything below that is now too small to be really practicable or workable: and this not merely from the point of view of making war but also from the point of view of carrying on a peaceful life."[24] For Toynbee the logical result of this trend toward larger political units would be the emergence of a single great power as world conqueror or world state.

Toynbee found that the conditions for a universal state by world conquest were present in the three underlying revolutions of contemporary world politics. The first of these revolutions was the political revolution through which the two great powers had supplanted the eight major powers who dominated world politics in 1914, transforming the nature of the balance of power. He prophesied that the "dependence of other countries on either the United States or the Soviet Union

---

24 *Ibid.*, 30.

is going to increase and not decrease as time goes on." He saw in the promulgation of the Truman Doctrine, by which the United States committed itself to a defense of freedom around the world, "a move which might turn out, whatever the President's intention . . . to have given the whole course of international affairs an impulsion away from the new co-operative method of trying to achieve political world unity, and towards the old-fashioned method of fighting out the last round in the struggle of power politics and arriving at the political unification of the world by the main force of a 'knock out blow.'"[25]

Another factor favoring political unification by conquest was the world technological revolution. For the first time in history, a single state had the power not only to conquer but to control most or all of the world. The world revolution of technology was reinforced by the moral revolution in which the new political religion of "nationalistic universalism" had replaced universal religion (which had served historically as the major restraining and moderating influence limiting the effective ambitions of states). Moreover, psychologically, an attitude of war weariness had swept across the world with an accompanying pacifism and a "Vichy atmosphere," which prompted Toynbee to affirm: "It seems probable that the great majority of mankind is now ripe for being dominated." Political leaders bent on world domination, as was Hitler in World War II, might discover that "in a future world war the conqueror would have the whole world at his feet." The upsurge of worldwide pacifism had resulted from a deep and profound horror of war. The tendency was for extreme nationalism to turn into pacifism. A new mentality of the privileged class, especially in developing countries, predisposed them to be more interested in preserving their own favored positions than their countries' national independence. This attitude was foreshadowed in some of the concessions that business groups were willing to make to Hitler and during the Cold War: "The possessing classes . . . are still more afraid of communism, and . . . this fear would operate very powerfully in a third World War in inducing them to surrender their country's independence."[26]

Therefore, with the gradual decrease in the number of powers and

---

25 *Ibid.*, 37; Toynbee, *Civilization on Trial*, 135.
26 Toynbee, *The Prospects of Western Civilization*, 41, 43.

the growth of a defeatist sentiment throughout the world, "it looks, on the face of it, as it the 'knock-out-blow' were the obvious line of least resistance, the easiest way for the inevitable unification to come about." But the consequence of achieving political unity through conquest is that a conqueror only rarely has been able to abandon militarism to achieve his ends. Time works against the conqueror. Sword blades are foundations that never settle: "Exposed or buried, these blood-stained weapons still retain their sinister charge of *karma*."[27] Universal states have been the handiwork of a dominant minority who have found their last haven in conquest. Some have lasted longer than others, like the Egyptian civilization and the main body of Far East civilization in China, but all have ultimately fallen of their own weight. In general, the universal state has tended to become a mere shell of government and has dissipated its strength by requiring too much of its members in the military adventures it has pursued. The universal state brought about by conquest has seldom been a creative force and has therefore had to be repaired in order to survive. Nearly all universal states created by the sword have faced a day of reckoning and destruction brought about by the sword.

Thus Toynbee recommended that world unity be attained through world government by agreement. However, world government by agreement is a possible goal only insofar as it represents a final step for which the groundwork has already been laid. Toynbee, however, still found the main preconditions for world government lacking. For Quincy Wright and Philip Jessup, the United Nations provided the best path to world government. For Toynbee: "The United Nations cannot get nearer to world government than the United States can get to each other. The United Nations Constitution represents the nearest that two powers so unlike each other . . . can get together."[28] The fundamental weakness of the United Nations is that it is an extremely loose confederation. Its limits are political rather than constitutional. It lacks the bonds of community necessary for a more effective government. Before the United Nations can become a world government, it

27 *Ibid.*, 43.
28 *Ibid.*, 46–47.

must achieve political community through the accommodating and ameliorating process of diplomacy.

Toynbee saw a more practical route for achieving limited political unity, which might increase the chances for universal government in the future. This involves the establishment of regional federations illustrated by the possibility of a federation between the United States, the countries of Western Europe, Canada, New Zealand, Australia, and South Africa. A federation of this kind would have the advantage of restoring Europe to the status of a first-class power, if not the equivalent of the two great powers. Such an arrangement would transform the relations between the United States and Europe and would permit economic assistance on a mutually profitable basis. In the short run, it would provide the surest foundation for the security of Western Europe; in the long run, it would ensure the recognition of community in a limited area and would increase the possibility of its extension to a broader sphere. The practical problems raised, such as the relinquishment of sovereignty to a Western government, are admittedly difficult, but "at least this is a much more practical goal to work for in the immediate future than a worldwide federation would be."[29]

World government will never be a tidy system. At some point within the system there would be elements reflecting the ascendancy of a great power. Either the United States or the Soviet Union or, most likely, both would be dominant within the organization. The same would be true whether the government were created by agreement or by conquest, for no single power could govern the world directly. Local autonomy would still be necessary, and national governments would have to make crucial decisions on many issues. This local initiative would inevitably produce a demand for international cooperation and would increase the chances of world government by consent. World government, therefore, would represent a particular kind of mixed system, according to Toynbee. In the final analysis, he envisioned the building of world community through mitigating conflicts by diplomacy, extending economic ties through the specialized agencies of the United Nations, and forming stronger bonds of common interests

29 *Ibid.*, 49.

among spiritually and culturally similar peoples. The route to world government by consent would be a gradual and incremental process. Toynbee's design for world order must be taken on faith.

WORKS BY ARNOLD J. TOYNBEE

1914

Greek Policy Since 1882. London: Oxford University Press.

1915

Armenian Atrocities: The Murder of a Nation. London: Hodder & Stoughton.

Nationality and the War. London: J. M. Dent.

1916

The Destruction of Poland: A Study in German Efficiency. London: T. F. Unwin.

The New Europe: Some Essays in Reconstruction. New York: E. P. Dutton.

The Treatment of Armenians in the Ottoman Empire, 1915–16. London: H. M. Stationery Office, Sir J. Cranston & Sons.

1917

The Belgian Deportations. London: T. F. Unwin.

The German Terror in Belgium. London: Hodder & Stoughton.

The German Terror in France. London: Hodder & Stoughton.

The Murderous Tyranny of the Turks. London: Hodder & Stoughton.

Turkey: A Past and a Future. New York: G. H. Doran.

1920

The League in the East. London: League of Nations.

1920–1938

Survey of International Affairs, 1920–1937. London: Oxford University Press.

1921

The Tragedy of Greece. Oxford: Clarendon Press.

1922

The Western Question in Greece and Turkey: A Study in the Contacts of Civilization. London: Constable.

1925

The World After the Peace Conference. London: Oxford University Press.

1927

The Islamic World Since the Peace Settlement. London: Oxford University Press.

1928

The Conduct of British Empire Foreign Relations Since the Peace Settlement. London: Oxford University Press.

1931

A Journey to China. London: Constable.

1934–1961

A Study of History. Vols. I–III (1934); Vols. IV–VI (1939); Vols. VII–X (1954); Vol. XI (1959); and Vol. XII (1961). London: Oxford University Press.

1938

British Interests in the Far East. Nottingham: Nottingham Citizen Press.

ARNOLD J. TOYNBEE

1940

Christianity and Civilization. London: Student Christian Movement.

1947

The Prospects of Western Civilization. New York: Columbia University Press.

A Study of History. Abridgement of Vols. I–VI. New York: Oxford University Press.

1948

Civilization on Trial. New York: Oxford University Press.

1949

The Pattern of the Past: Can We Determine It? With Pieter Geyl and Pitirim A. Sorokin. Boston: Beacon Press.

1950

War and Civilization. Selections edited by Robert Vann Fowler. New York: Oxford University Press.

1953

The World and the West. New York: Oxford University Press.

1956

An Historian's Approach to Religion. New York: Oxford University Press.

1971

Surviving the Future. New York: Oxford University Press.